Outposts of Civilization

OUTPOSTS OF CIVILIZATION

Race, Religion, and the Formative Years
of American-Japanese Relations

Joseph M. Henning

NEW YORK UNIVERSITY PRESS
New York and London

New York University Press

New York and London

© 2000 by New York University

All rights reserved

Library of Congress Cataloging-in-Publication Data

Henning, Joseph M., 1962–

Outposts of civilization : race, religion, and the formative years of
American-Japanese relations / Joseph M. Henning.

p.   cm.

Includes bibliographical references and index.

ISBN 0-8147-3605-X (cloth : alk. paper)

1. United States—Relations—Japan.   2. Japan—Relations—
United States.   I. Title.

E183.8.J3 H46 2000

303.48'273052—dc21   00-008182

New York University Press books are printed on acid-free paper,
and their binding materials are chosen for strength and durability.

Manufactured in the United States of America

10 9 8 7 6 5 4 3 2 1

To Staci and Jake

CONTENTS

ILLUSTRATIONS

The illustrations appear as a group following page 120.

ACKNOWLEDGMENTS

Throughout the course of this project, I have been the fortunate recipient of generous support (more than I deserve, I fear) from mentors, colleagues, students, friends, and family.

I owe great debts to American University's Bob Beisner, Hyung Kook Kim, Peter Kuznick, and Anna Nelson, who were always available to answer questions, offer criticism, and calm my nerves. Their guidance greatly improved this study, and I thank them for their good company.

Kurk Dorsey, Amy Kaplan, and Lawrence Kessler read early drafts of chapters and asked provocative questions that helped me to sharpen the project's focus. Naoko Shibusawa and David Strauss generously shared with me their manuscripts and ideas on related topics.

At the Saint Vincent College Library, Margaret Friloux

rapidly tracked down even the most obscure of interlibrary loan requests, and Ruth J. Simmons at Rutgers University guided me through the William Elliot Griffis Collection, especially its numerous photographs. I thank also the staffs at the National Archives, the Special Collections Department of the University of Virginia Library, and the United Methodist Church Archives. And I commend the Library of Congress staff for their excellent work in difficult conditions.

The support of Niko Pfund at New York University Press has been invaluable. His first suggestions about the challenge of finding the book's audience changed my approach to writing.

American University, Saint Vincent College, and the Association of Asian Studies provided important financial support that made this project possible.

I also offer a special thanks to the Saint Vincent College community for its living model of Benedictine hospitality. And I am grateful to my students for sharing their first impressions of Japan and reminding me of my own.

In Washington, Angie Blake, Debbie Doyle, Ken Durr, Kurt Hanson, Ron Howe, and Chris Welch were always ready when I needed their merciless critiques and subversive humor. Our discussions encouraged me to explore not only what I wanted to say, but also how I wanted to say it.

Most importantly, my wife, Staci, is always beside me at each step, reminding me that there is more to the present than the past. And Jake, thank you for always requesting and singing along to *American Beauty*.

During the South Africa divestment protest at Columbia University in 1985, a demonstrator spoke to raise the spirits of the four hundred or so students camped on the steps of Hamilton Hall. "Look around you," she said. "Take a close look at each of your neighbors, and you'll see that this is a true coalition: everyone here looks different." Jake, that is the world I wish for you.

EDITORIAL NOTE

Japanese names are rendered surname first, given name second. In the case of Japanese authors writing in English, each author's preference is followed. Familiar Japanese place names (such as Tokyo and Hokkaido) appear without macrons.

Outposts of Civilization

INTRODUCTION

One hundred years ago, Japan offered a challenge to Americans. As the first Asian nation to become a modern power, it undermined beliefs that many Americans held dear. They had assumed that modern civilization and progress were white, Christian birthrights: no "Mongolian" or "heathen" people could hope to gain these blessings. Japan, however, now had a constitution and a parliament. It was a nation of railroads and gas lamps. It was Asian, yet modern; heathen, yet civilized. Alice Mabel Bacon, reflecting on one year of teaching in Tokyo, wrote in 1893 that "the word 'civilization' is so difficult to define and to understand, that I do not know what it means now as well as I did when I left home."[1] Many of her compatriots shared these new doubts.

Four decades earlier, white Americans had brimmed with confidence. They envisioned themselves atop a hierarchy of races.

On the lower rungs, beneath Caucasians, stood the allegedly un-civilized and semicivilized: Mongolians, Native Americans, and Africans. As white Americans reached westward across the con-tinent and the Pacific, they believed themselves ordained to ex-tend the influence of Christian civilization. When the gunboats of the Perry Expedition compelled the shogun's government in 1854 to abandon two hundred years of self-imposed isolation, Americans congratulated themselves on opening a stagnant country to the fresh air of Western influence. The United States and other Western powers soon pressured Japan to sign unequal treaties that enshrined its alleged backwardness. Japan lost in-definitely the sovereign authority to set its own tariffs and to ex-ercise legal jurisdiction over foreigners on Japanese soil. In American eyes, Japan's commercial and legal systems were infe-rior to those of the West.

The first Americans in Tokugawa Japan thought they knew exactly what "civilization" meant. The United States, which rep-resented its pinnacle, had cultivated a democratic society of Christian principles, commercial wealth, and technological inno-vation. Diplomats and missionaries expected to find few, if any, of these characteristics in Japan. Settling into the legation or their mission stations, they regarded themselves as "sentinels in the outposts of civilization."[2]

In the 1850–60s, these self-appointed sentinels indeed faced a precarious situation. The unequal treaties had sparked a fire. Longtime foes of the Tokugawa shogunate reacted violently to the national humiliation inflicted by the Western powers. De-nouncing the treaties and urging the expulsion of foreigners, they rallied around the emperor—a figurehead on whose behalf the shogun governed. Shogunate officials and foreigners fell under the swords of assassins. Attempting to extinguish the re-bellion, Japanese troops loyal to the shogun attacked and were defeated by troops loyal to the emperor. To many Westerners, these events confirmed the view that Japan was semicivilized at best, savage at worst.

The turmoil culminated in the Meiji Restoration of January 1868, when the emperor accepted the shogun's resignation and reassumed the responsibilities of government. Immediately, Meiji leaders began to enact a series of sweeping political and social reforms designed not only to strengthen the new regime, but also to enhance Japan's standing with the foreign powers. Rather than expelling the foreigners, Meiji leaders decided that Japan would persuade those powers to revise the unequal treaties and thus to restore its lost sovereignty. Japan set out to prove that it, too, was a civilized nation.

Until the Meiji Restoration, American visitors had seen little that challenged their assumptions about race and religion. They had not traveled across the Pacific to see a people resembling themselves. Instead, travelers sought out the exotic and depicted the Japanese as a diminutive, inferior people whom evolution had bypassed. Their accounts, with which this book begins, epitomized the belief that Asians had no capacity for progress. The Japanese were entertaining, but not to be taken seriously.

Reinforcing these accounts, missionaries described with dismay the practices of concubinage and public nudity. They criticized the status of Japanese women in Confucian and Buddhist doctrines and offered Christianity as the solution to the evils of heathen family life. Despite Japanese efforts to assimilate Western technological innovations and political practices, missionaries maintained that Christianity was the defining characteristic of modern civilization. To be civilized, a nation had to follow Christian principles. Missionaries urged the State Department to make this point in its talks with Japanese statesmen.

In turn, Japanese officials and scholars worked to influence American opinion and policy. The Japanese advanced their cause in a variety of forums, adopting the vocabulary of "civilization."

Their goal of restoring Japanese sovereignty spurred them to champion the adoption of Western institutions. Eventually, Japan became more like the foreign powers than Americans had believed possible. In the mid-1870s, the Japanese began to win supporters at the U.S. legation, and American diplomats became advocates of treaty revision. Arguing their case in diplomatic dispatches, American ministers and consuls reshaped official policy toward Japan.

Outside the realm of diplomatic relations, other Americans worked to influence opinion on the questions of race and religion. Missionaries, scholars, and artists made Japan a perennial and popular topic in Gilded-Age media. Like diplomats, they arrived in Japan convinced of white, Christian superiority. And also like diplomats, they began to acknowledge that Japan was not what they had expected it to be. Often they hoped to affect U.S. policy in favor of Japan, and often they succeeded.

Anthropologist Ruth Benedict wrote in her 1946 work *The Chrysanthemum and the Sword,* "It is hard to be conscious of the eyes through which one looks."[3] In the late nineteenth century, many Americans in Japan became conscious of their ideological lenses. They confronted and revised long-held beliefs. To the American public and its leaders, they argued that the Japanese, though "heathen," were a moral people who were gradually recognizing the value of religious freedom. Although Asian, the Japanese were proving to be adept at assimilating Western practices.

This book shows that Meiji Japan offered Americans an important opportunity. By challenging and discrediting the presumed linkage between white Christendom and modern civilization, Japan invited Americans to revise their assumptions. American observers of Japan had to acknowledge and address this challenge. A few accepted the invitation with pleasure and tried relentlessly to convince others to do likewise. Hence, Japan

served as a catalyst in the endeavor of some Americans to sub-
vert Gilded-Age hierarchies that separated Caucasian and Mongolian, Christian and heathen, civilized and barbarian.
Most, however, declined Japan's invitation. To the many who
refused to abandon entrenched beliefs about race and religion,
the real challenge was to reconcile this new, civilized Japan with
the *seemingly* indisputable fact that the Japanese remained
Mongolian and heathen. Prominent American experts on Japan
reinforced their racial and religious convictions by disputing this
fact. They devised new means of fitting the Japanese into the accepted hierarchies of race and culture and recategorized the
Japanese as white, Anglo-Saxon, and Christian. Reinventing the
"white race" and "Christendom," these Americans ultimately
helped to preserve the overall integrity of the hierarchies by
repositioning Japan within them.[4]

In the face of Japan's challenge, most Americans felt con-
strained to protect their privileged self-identity as civilized,
white Christians. Doing so required the construction of new
identities for the Japanese—identities that acknowledged their
progress but distinguished them from other Asians, who remained "heathen" and "uncivilized." From this perspective,
Japan was a remarkable exception among Asian nations. As an
exception, it disproved nothing about race or religion and served
to underscore the ostensible stagnation of its neighbors. To
Americans, Japan itself eventually became an outpost of civilization in backward East Asia.

As this book demonstrates, the formative years of American-
Japanese relations reveal much about the role of cultural interaction in international relations. They show how theories of race
and representations of difference provide an ideological under-
pinning for the exercise of power in relations between states.
Moreover, in this era, American domestic discourses not only
shaped but also were shaped by relations with Japan.

Although American diplomats, missionaries, scholars, and artists in Japan shared many of the same convictions, each group contributed its own distinctive interpretations of the Japanese. Throughout the late nineteenth and early twentieth centuries, these groups modified their views in response to Japan's industrialization and development into a modern power. Their evolving interpretations also reflected the influence of social and intellectual developments in the United States. These American responses to Japan constitute an important study in the construction, revision, and preservation of identities.

Like no country had before, Japan confounded American beliefs. When it pushed ideas about race and religion nearly to their breaking point, most Americans responded by reinforcing and reinvigorating these preconceptions. Their depictions of Japan and the Japanese reveal much about American assumptions, concerns, and fears in a dawning era of imperialism and cultural expansion. In order to fully appreciate the tenacity of the American faith in white, Christian superiority, we must understand American responses to the intellectual challenge offered by Meiji Japan.

Chapter 1

THROUGH A REVERSED OPERA GLASS

During the 1854 treaty negotiations, Commodore Matthew C. Perry sent ashore a detachment of twenty-four boats filled with gifts for the Japanese: rifles, pistols, clocks, agricultural tools, Irish potatoes, whiskey, and champagne. These were not merely tokens of friendship. All had been chosen to demonstrate the benefits of commerce, and some were meant also to exemplify the power of American innovation and civilization.[1]

Two items attracted special attention from the Japanese: a telegraph and a quarter-scale locomotive. After the Americans had unpacked and assembled the telegraph, its wires stretched from the treaty conference house to a building nearly one mile distant and carried messages in Japanese, English, and Dutch—all to the amazement of the Japanese. Another source of marvel was the steam locomotive, which came with a tender, a passenger car, and enough track to form a circle 350 feet in diameter. Because the locomotive was too small to enter, the engineer rode on the tender, feeding the fire with one hand and controlling the engine with the other. Although outfitted with sliding windows and upholstered seats, the car could accommodate passengers only on its roof. As the engine's steam whistle pierced the air, the train sped around the track at twenty miles per hour while Japanese dignitaries took turns perching on the car, a spectacle that the Americans described as "not a little ludicrous." As expected, these demonstrations of technological prowess duly impressed the Japanese, whose responses amused the Americans.[2]

Not to be outdone, the Japanese offered their own display of strength a few days later. Fifty sumo wrestlers, each weighing from two to four hundred pounds, filed out before the assembled Americans. Perry accepted an invitation to feel the immense arms and neck of one of these "stall-fed bulls" and was surprised to find solid muscle, which soon was put to use. Near the conference house, the Japanese had stacked two hundred bales of rice, weighing 135 pounds apiece, to present to the expedition. On signal, the wrestlers lifted and carried the bales past Perry and down to the beach three hundred feet away. Most bore at least two bales, whether above their heads, on their shoulders, or under each arm. Some managed four bales, while one wrestler even carried a bale suspended from his teeth. Next, the wrestlers engaged in sumo matches before the American sailors and officers. In the eyes of these guests, however, the bouts demonstrated little athletic skill. The Americans were truly fascinated by the wrestlers' size and strength but found their sport to be little more than a disgusting and barbaric curiosity that sharply contrasted with the American gifts. After the sumo exhibition, the Americans turned with pride to demonstrate yet again the telegraph and railroad. "In place of a show of brute animal force," noted the expedition's official report, "there was a triumphant revelation, to a partially enlightened people, of the success of science and enterprise."[3] The members of the expedition were confident that they had proved the superiority of their civilization. In their journals, they declared with both disdain and disappointment that the gifts of fabric and lacquerware presented by the Japanese were of little value compared to those presented by the United States. Reflecting on these displays, an interpreter for the expedition wrote in his journal:

> Indeed, there was a curious mélange to-day here, a junction of the east and west, . . . epaulettes and uniforms, shaven pates and night-gowns, soldiers with muskets and drilling in close array, soldiers with petticoats, sandals, two swords, and all in disorder, like a crowd—all these things, and many other things, exhibiting the difference between our civilization and usages and those of this secluded, pagan people.

From the perspective of the Perry Expedition, Japan's only impressive strength—its loincloth-clad wrestlers—was no match for the technological trappings of American power.[4]

Like their naval forerunners, Americans who visited Japan after the Meiji Restoration expected it to be a barbaric or semi-civilized land full of amusing curiosities. Most travelers were bound by these expectations and saw little to contradict them. Depicting the Japanese as despotic, diminutive, and inferior, Americans reported that evolution and progress had long ago ground to a halt in Asiatic and secluded Japan.

Before examining the accounts of American travelers, we should first inspect their baggage. From eighteenth- and nineteenth-century scientists and philosophers, Americans drew commonly held assumptions that influenced their interpretations of Japan. Japan eventually challenged many of these ideas, compelling American diplomats, missionaries, and scholars to reexamine and, in some cases, to revise their beliefs. In the case of the first American travelers to Japan, however, preconceptions tended to shape observations rather than vice versa. They considered the Japanese, as members of the "Mongolian" race, to be inferior to "Caucasian" Americans. A variety of racial and social theorists claimed to have demonstrated that this alleged inferiority was rooted in immutable biological traits and extended into social attributes.

Our understanding of the concept "race" has changed immensely during the last three centuries and continues to be the center of heated debate today. Anthropologists, physiologists, and geneticists currently are engaged in a discussion of the utility of race as an objective biological category. Many question whether race is a biological reality at all and explain it instead as a cultural construct, which physiologist Jared Diamond calls "another commonsense 'truth' destined to follow the flat Earth into oblivion." From genetic research we have learned that races are not comprised of neat, distinct sets of biological characteristics. Using physical characteristics such as skin and eye color as visual indicators of race, humans have created categories, such as "white" and "black," that do not hold up under closer scientific scrutiny. Genetic variation—blood type, for instance—does not cluster neatly within these categories; rather, it cuts sharply across them. In fact, variation between races is a minor component of human biological diversity; genetic variation is greater among individuals of the same race than between one race and another.[5]

Genetic data, of course, were not available to earlier scientists. In their efforts to explain human biological variation, these scholars too often were influenced—some unconsciously, some consciously—by social and cultural values. The result was biological determinism, in which social and cultural traits were ascribed to races as innate and permanent biological characteristics. Presumably, one's race determined one's character. Even the founder of the system of biological taxonomy, Carolus Linnaeus, included cultural characterizations in his descriptions of human subspecies. In 1758 he divided the species Homo sapiens into four geographic subspecies, and, though he did not organize them hierarchically, his characterizations reflected subjective value judgements: Americanus was "red, ill-tempered, subjugated"; Europaeus was "white, serious, strong"; Asiaticus was "yellow, melancholy, greedy"; and Afer was "black, impassive, lazy."[6]

A student of Linnaeus, Johann Friedrich Blumenbach, reconfigured this taxonomy into an ostensibly scientific hierarchy of races. Believing that Eurasia's Caucasus region was the likely birthplace of humanity, he coined the term "Caucasian" to refer to Europeans. He believed that Caucasians represented the ideal standard of physical beauty from which other races had gradually deviated. Also, by adding a fifth subspecies, the Malay, to Linnaeus's taxonomy, Blumenbach was able to propose a two-legged hierarchy capped by Caucasians. In one leg of the hierarchy, the Mongolian race deviated the most from the Caucasian ideal, while Americans appeared as an intermediary form. In the other leg, Ethiopians deviated the most, while the Malay race was intermediary. Blumenbach's hierarchical taxonomy became common fare in American science and culture.[7]

In the mid nineteenth century, the "American school" of anthropology, which embraced Blumenbach's classification system, attempted to explain racial diversity by championing the theory of polygenesis: the races had been created separately. Racial characteristics and capabilities were innate, permanent qualities coeval with each race's creation. Samuel George Morton, a Philadelphia physician with a skull collection described by contemporaries as "the American Golgotha," measured the average cranial capacities of the races and provided empirical evidence that seemed to support polygenesis. According to his findings as presented in *Crania Americana* (1839), Caucasians had the highest average capacity, followed by Mongolians, Malays, Americans, and Ethiopians. Morton argued that the Caucasian had "the highest intellectual endowments," while the Mongolian was "ingenious, imitative, and highly susceptible of cultivation." Ostensibly, these were permanent differences rooted in separate creations—they could not be explained by the effects of climate after a single divine act of creation. (Scientist Stephen Jay Gould has reanalyzed Morton's data and found a "patchwork of fudging and finagling," but no evidence of conscious fraud. Gould's inquiry revealed no significant differences among Morton's groups that could not be explained by differences in stature.)[8]

The American school's ideas were summarized at length and widely distributed in Josiah C. Nott and George R. Gliddon's *Types of Mankind* (1854), which they dedicated to the late Morton. The leading American text on race in the second half of the nineteenth century, *Types of Mankind* claimed to provide extensive evidence for the idea of a racial hierarchy capped by the Caucasian race. Illustrations purported to demonstrate similarities between the faces and skulls of Africans and those of chimpanzees. In the section Nott authored, he contended that the "Negro" had never raised or borrowed a single civilization, and the "Mongolian" had achieved only "prolonged semi-civilizations." In contrast, "Caucasian" history was replete with a series of distinct civilizations. Human progress, Nott wrote, had arisen primarily from racial competition and its stimulants of conquest and colonization.[9]

Lending additional support to the idea of racial hierarchy were Teutonic-germ theory and Anglo-Saxonism. Many Americans embraced the notion that England and the United States had inherited their capacities for free political institutions from

the Anglo-Saxon descendants of Teutonic tribes in the forests of
Germany. These tribes, who conquered Rome in the fifth century C.E., were believed to have established representative tribal
councils that exemplified their commitment to freedom and individual rights; they had enshrined legal principles of trial by
jury, private property, and the rule of law. Henry Adams and
John Fiske were among the prominent scholars who asserted
that the Anglo-Saxons, Germanic tribes who crossed the English
Channel, had planted this Teutonic germ of freedom and civilization in England. Although not identical to the ideas of Blumenbach and Morton, Anglo-Saxonism augmented their claims
for Caucasian superiority. Thus nineteenth-century Americans
could trace the westward migration of freedom and civilization,
beginning with the origins of the Caucasian race and continuing
through the Teutons, the Anglo-Saxons, and the English, finally
culminating in themselves.[10]

   This continuing advance was manifested in America's westward continental expansion, for which the telegraph and railroad
served as visual symbols in popular culture. The Currier and Ives
lithograph *Across the Continent, "Westward the Course of Empire Takes its Way"* (1868) depicts a passenger train steaming
through a settlement of log buildings, on the outskirts of which
some residents are clearing land. A telegraph line parallels the
railroad tracks. Across the tracks from the town, Indians on
horseback watch the train but are held back by a wall of smoke
from its locomotive. In *American Progress* (1872), John Gast
painted an allegorical female figure in a diaphanous gown float-
ing above a prairie landscape. Moving from right to left—east to
west—she carries a telegraph wire stretching back to poles behind her and is accompanied below by settlers in wagons and a
trio of railroads. Portrayed as tamers of the wilderness, the telegraph and railroad were engines of American civilization and
progress.[11]

Even Charles Darwin in *The Descent of Man* (1871) lent support to the common belief in the westward course of progress by suggesting that American success could be explained by the immigration of Europe's most "energetic, restless, and courageous men." Darwin's earlier work, however, had undermined theories of biological hierarchy and polygenesis. In *The Origin of Species* (1859), he argued that species had neither been created separately nor evolved along a hierarchy. Instead, different species had emerged through a process of natural selection in which random physical variations had facilitated survival and reproduction in certain environments. Individuals with such favorable variations were more likely to survive, reproduce, and thus pass on these traits to their offspring. Natural selection involved divergence, not linear progress. Species existed side by side in a taxonomy, not one above the other in a hierarchy.[12]

But natural selection was not the only influential nineteenth-century theory of evolution. While Darwin described a biological competition for survival that resulted in diverse species, Herbert Spencer addressed the evolution of both biological and social entities. Spencer, not Darwin, coined the phrase "survival of the fittest." Equating evolution and progress, his works sold more than half a million copies in the United States and were discussed in such journals as the *North American Review*, the *Nation*, and *Popular Science Monthly*. In his elaborate, multivolume "Synthetic Philosophy," Spencer adopted the pre-Darwinian evolution theory of Jean Baptiste Lamarck, who in the early nineteenth century had contended that physical traits can be acquired and transmitted to descendants. Giraffes, for example, had long necks because for generations their ancestors had stretched to reach food. Although Darwin had rejected Lamarckian theory, Spencer used it to argue that evolution produced progress, not merely diversity. Through the inheritance of acquired characteristics, species and races could gradually improve.

According to Spencer, this evolutionary process could be traced in social as well as biological organisms.[13]

On the level of individuals, Spencer applied recapitulation theory. The discovery that vertebrate embryos develop gill slits that later disappear led him to conclude that human individuals pass through developmental stages that parallel human evolution from savagery to civilization. Thus the minds of civilized children pass through a primitive stage. For Spencer, however, in savage races the childlike stage was permanent. The adults of primitive races, for instance, were emotionally impulsive, like the children of civilized races. "The intellectual traits of the uncivilized," Spencer proclaimed, "are traits recurring in the children of the civilized." To him, contemporary primitive societies were living representatives of earlier stages in evolution. By studying them, scholars could reconstruct the early evolution of human social organization. Furthermore, from Spencer's Lamarckian perspective, the nervous system of each individual was shaped by the experiences of preceding generations, and national and racial characteristics were inherited. Because the accumulation of historical experience in the course of civilization had produced higher forms of reasoning, civilized people inherited larger brains than the uncivilized.[14]

According to Spencer, both social and biological organisms evolved from simple homogeneity to complex heterogeneity. Societies evolved from the militant type, which restricted individual liberty, to the industrial type, which defended individuality. In his Synthetic Philosophy, the linkage of civilization and progress with the process of evolutionary natural selection buttressed the hierarchy first proposed by Blumenbach. Through biological competition, the human species had surpassed the rest of the animal kingdom; through social competition, Caucasians dominated primitive races. A theory of competitive social evolution now complemented the theory of biological selection and provided a "scientific" foundation for the development of Social Darwinism.[15]

Spencer's reputation today, of course, pales in comparison to that of Darwin. Yet it is an injustice to the latter—one of the nineteenth century's most brilliant thinkers—that the dubious creed of Social Darwinism bears his name rather than Spencer's, as its laissez-faire principles relied far more heavily on the philosophy of Spencer than on Darwin's science. And, adding further irony, Spencer himself was a Lamarckian, not a Darwinian.

In the second half of the nineteenth century, however, Spencer's star shined brightly. Darwin had designed an enduring theory of evolution, but it was limited to biological organisms. Spencer's ambition was more grandiose: he considered himself both a philosopher and a scientist. To him, evolution was a universal principle of nature. Consequently, he attempted to construct a general theory of evolution, a philosophy applicable to biological, social, and mental phenomena. In the judgement of William James, "Mr. Spencer's task, the unification of all knowledge into an articulate system, was more ambitious than anything attempted since St. Thomas or Descartes." Addressing a realm much larger than that of Darwin, his appeal likewise was much broader. Unlike Darwin's world of random variation and natural selection, Spencer's teleological philosophy promised a world that was ever improving. His works were a continual topic of discussion in the American press and directly influenced two generations. From the 1860s on, Spencer's followers were numerous and influential. In 1882, at the conclusion of his only visit to the United States, a farewell dinner in New York City attracted such luminaries as Lyman Abbott, Henry Ward Beecher, Albert Bierstadt, Andrew Carnegie, William M. Evarts, John Fiske, E. L. Godkin, Elihu Root, and William G. Sumner.[16]

Consequently, biological and social theorists in the Gilded Age pointed to Anglo-Saxon civilization as the consummation of historical processes. Racial hierarchy, Anglo-Saxonism, and Spencer's Synthetic Philosophy were each developed discretely, but they overlapped insofar as they all sustained confidence in American civilization and progress. Civilized societies cultivated individual freedoms. The ideas and innovations that naturally resulted were rationally applied to the ongoing improvement of society. Progress was the process of advance from primitive barbarism to civilization. If one believed in an immutable hierarchy of races, those on the lower tiers were innately incapable and would never know civilization. On the other hand, if one believed in Lamarckian or Spencerian visions of evolutionary progress, lower races had the capability of gradually improving, but higher races also would continue to progress and maintain their upper hand. Civilization and progress, then, were the social counterparts to the biological process of evolutionary natural selection. Whether seen from the perspective of biological or social theory, Caucasian Americans stood at the apex of a hierarchical taxonomy.

In both cases, destiny directed Americans westward across the Pacific, where they would continue the legacy of their forbears by implanting and cultivating civilization among the allegedly less evolved races of Asia. They saw the Perry Expedition as yet another great Anglo-Saxon endeavor. By bringing with him two symbols of progress, the telegraph and the railroad, he had ended Japan's seclusion and extended the reach of Western civilization.

Japan's relatively recent era of seclusion had an analogue in the mythical age of its gods. Amaterasu, the sun goddess and divine ancestress of the imperial family, had been grievously offended by the vulgar behavior of her younger brother, the storm god, and secluded herself in a cave, casting the world into darkness. In response, other gods gathered to lure her back out. Hearing their laughter, she peered out from her hiding place, whereupon another god took her hand and pulled her outside. Thus the sun's light was restored to the world. In the American imagination, the American role in ending Japan's Tokugawa-era seclusion seemed to mirror that of the god who had pulled Amaterasu out of the cave. Perry had "let in the flood of light," Americans believed, rousing Japan from centuries of slumber and opening it to the influences of civilization: "Japan sleeps no more."[17]

Japan and the Perry Expedition quickly became popular topics in the United States as Americans familiarized themselves with Japanese seclusion and the opening of American-Japanese relations. Accounts that captured public attention turned a sharp eye toward the defunct seclusion policy. Self-imposed isolation, they emphasized, was foolish and illegitimate. It was a juvenile stunt, akin to a child closing his eyes to the light all around him. For the benefit of all humanity, Providence had placed Japan as an oasis on the great highway of the Pacific; its seclusion deprived other nations of rightful commerce and cast Japanese civilization into stagnation. These accounts convinced Americans that civilization and progress had demanded the opening of Japan.[18]

After the Meiji Restoration, Americans found further evidence in the popular magazine essays on Japanese history written by the first foreigners hired as teachers by the Japanese government. William Elliot Griffis, for example, spent three and one-half years (1870–74) in Japan and, after returning to the United States, became the era's most prolific writer on that country. Griffis led American efforts to construct a historiography that focused on seclusion, Perry, and the Meiji Restoration. He and others who examined Japanese history believed that the United States had played an important, albeit indirect, part in the downfall of the shogunate (*bakufu*). These writers employed Japan's so-called dual system of government as a unifying theme in their narratives.

Before the restoration, American analysts wrote, two figures had seemed to wield authority simultaneously: the "spiritual emperor" and the "secular emperor." The spiritual emperor (often referred to by Westerners as the mikado) exercised authority in religious matters, while the secular emperor (the shogun) wielded civil and military power. The sovereignty of the spiritual emperor originated in his mythical descent from the sun goddess, while the shogun's authority originated in the military's usurpation of the spiritual emperor's rightful political power.[19]

But Americans who analyzed the dual system in more detail recognized that the shogun's nominal position rested on his appointment by the spiritual emperor. Although the emperor did not wield de facto political power, his absolute sovereignty had never ceased. In truth, Japan had only one emperor. The shogun was not Japan's secular emperor, but rather the military vassal of the one and only emperor, who had the authority to bestow the title of shogun. The shogun and the bakufu governed only in the name of the emperor. Griffis and other writers carefully marked the limits of the shogun's authority and thereby undermined the legitimacy of Japan's seclusion. By artificially isolating Japan from the rest of the world, the bakufu had solidified its control and achieved despotic supremacy in a rigid feudal system. According to this American historiography, seclusion had hindered Japan's natural development. Surrounded by "artificial barriers," Japan sank into lethargy and sleep. As one journalist proudly recounted, however, "A young people, just stretching its vanguard of civilization across the American Continent, was ready to knock vigorously on the gates of Japan."[20]

Throughout the treaty negotiations, conducted entirely with bakufu officials, Perry had referred to the shogun as the emperor and mistakenly assumed that he held complete sovereign authority. The bakufu had encouraged this belief by referring to the shogun as the emperor and *taikun*, or august sovereign (the origin of the word "tycoon"). In his historical analysis, Griffis harshly condemned the bakufu for taking this additional step in the usurpation of power, noting that the title of taikun had never been bestowed upon the shogun by the emperor: "The shōgun had no shadow of right to this bombastic figment of authority," which was, in short, "a diplomatic fraud." Misled by the shogunate, then, Perry had unwittingly signed a treaty with the true emperor's military underling.[21]

But like the frog who puffed himself up to impress the ox, Griffis wrote, the bakufu finally burst because of its arrogance. The treaties with the West added to the discontent that had accumulated under two centuries of Tokugawa rule. They offered the disaffected a weapon to wield against the shogun, who had proved himself incapable of performing the task required by his full title: *sei-i taishōgun*, or barbarian-subduing generalissimo. Within fourteen years of the signing of the Perry treaty, the Tokugawa shogunate had been deposed and the emperor restored to power.[22]

The dual system of government thus loomed large in American accounts of Japanese history. Having usurped power, the shogun had closed the country to outside contact. The bakufu served conveniently as the scapegoat for all that had gone wrong in recent Japanese history—or at least for what seemed wrong in the eyes of Americans. Japan's seclusion was proof enough that the dual system was a detriment. Depriving Japan and the West of contact, the shogun was an impostor who had also deprived the imperial court of its right to rule. With the arrival of Perry, the shogun had cloaked himself even more thoroughly in the guise of sovereign by assuming the title of taikun.

By carefully distinguishing the emperor from the shogun, this historiography lent additional legitimacy to the opening of Japan. The United States, Americans argued, had awakened a feudal nation and consequently played an indirect role in the restoration of the emperor. The new Japanese government had wisely concluded that it could protect its national sovereignty by learning from rather than rejecting the West. In sharp contrast to the shogun, who had barricaded Japan, the emperor was leading it into the modern world. Japan had exchanged a "dark, stormy past" for a "sunny present" with "bright hopes for the future." A Japan unified under its emperor recognized the necessity of reentering the world—an opportunity that reportedly had been prevented for so long by the shogun. Not only had the emperor been restored to power, but Japan also had been restored to the community of nations and was unveiled before Western eyes.[23]

"[I]n the difficult search for something new under the sun," American travelers stood on their steamship's deck after its passage across the Pacific. As they strained to catch their first glimpse of Japan in the morning light, the magnificent peak of Mount Fuji broke the horizon. Writing with awe of the landscape's fantastic appearance and pristine beauty, they described crystalline waters lapping the shores, leafy tapestries covering the hills, and craggy cliffs overlooking fertile valleys. Such spectacular panoramas demonstrated to them that the Japanese landscape was unsurpassed in its beauty.[24]

But soon thereafter, the scene changed in these travel accounts. A "grotesque group of navigators"—scantily clad "coppery" men—sailed up alongside the steamer. On shore, sweating coolies wearing only loincloths shouted as they hoisted their loads. Like beasts of burden, rickshaw men pulled passengers through the streets. Pagan herds churned together in a shocking concoction of noise and nudity. Travelers who ventured outside the treaty ports trod "soil virgin to alien feet" and deemed themselves "the first to penetrate into the midst of a new people." Through clouds of their own cigar smoke, sightseers scrutinized the local inhabitants and their customs at each new village. Just as these travelers had hoped, all was indeed novel and strange.[25]

Americans were not, of course, the first outsiders to write about Japan. That distinction goes to the Chinese, who in the third century C.E. called Japan the land of Wo, a term meaning "dwarf." To nineteenth-century American travelers as well, Japan appeared stunted. Their sense of its diminished scale produced a fictional, even fantastic, quality in their written accounts. The scenes through which they strode offered amusement, a diversion from reality. Wrote one visitor, "It seemed like a fairy park looked down upon from an eminence through a reversed opera-glass."[26]

From this perspective, travelers readily envisaged themselves as Gullivers and described the Japanese as Lilliputians. Indeed, no set of metaphors was more often used than that of American Gullivers strolling through a lilliputian Japanese fairyland. This focus on stature bolstered the idea that the Japanese were a childlike people, a youthful nation eager to learn from its elders. Unlike their full-grown Western visitors, the Japanese seemed to dwell in a fanciful world of playthings. Japanese houses and gardens, Americans wrote, were toylike and proportional to the short stature of their residents. In gardens, Americans found still more to excite their imaginations. The "dwarfed" shrubs, "pigmy" [sic] lawns, and "lilliputian streams" encouraged a sense of the fantastic. Failing to recognize these gardens as the physical embodiment of a traditional aesthetic that valued constraint, they assumed that the gardens were small because the Japanese were small.[27]

Roles were briefly reversed only when tourists went to see the thirteenth-century *Daibutsu* (Great Buddha) statue at Kamakura, a standard stop on most itineraries. Thirty-seven feet tall, the Daibutsu reduced foreigners to pygmies. Any sense of awe vanished, however, when they scrambled up the meditating

Buddha to sit in his lap. Some travelers who were more religiously inclined sang the Doxology from this position and explained to an inquisitive priest that the true God would soon conquer Buddhist idolatry. Entering the hollow statue, they observed with sarcasm and self-satisfaction that there was no brain inside its head. Even a sacred image, then, was a source of amusement rather than admiration. Although physically dwarfed by the statue, their assumption of spiritual superiority enabled them to continue belittling the Japanese and their beliefs.[28]

To some Americans, a more worldly amusement appeared in the seeming indifference of the Japanese toward public nudity and seminudity. They often noted with astonishment that grooms and rickshaw pullers, who were frequently hired by foreign travelers, habitually stripped down to their loincloths on warm days. In illustrations accompanying travel essays, many a groom "in full costume" sported tattoos that covered vastly more area than did his only article of apparel. American travel writers noted that Japanese women, too, shared this lax attitude toward nudity, sometimes letting their kimonos slip from the shoulder to the waist. Because Japanese houses were open to the streets, these Americans pointed out, a curious passerby could easily and often gaze on such sights.[29]

Even more intriguing to sightseers were Japanese bathing customs. They described men, women, and children happily socializing together each evening in public baths and in tubs next to the street. The Japanese seemed to have an unwritten code of propriety, noted these observers, one that allowed them to see but not to observe, or, worse, to admire, the nudity of their neighbors. An American artist learned this lesson when he attempted to sketch women who had stripped to the waist on a warm day. Noticing his attention, they quickly covered up. Such nudity for the sake of convenience, many Americans insisted, served a legitimate purpose and was not indecent. Japanese attitudes indicated an Edenic simplicity: "Eves, innocent of fig-leaves, tubb[ed] themselves together in the open street in broad daylight." One writer reminded his readers that cleanliness, after all, was next to godliness. The Japanese nonchalance regarding bodily exposure evoked for these travelers a primitive age of innocence.[30]

To other observers, however, nudity offered not amusement but offense. Samuel Wells Williams, a missionary to China who served as an interpreter on the Perry Expedition, wrote in his journal that modesty was unknown in Japan: "the women make no attempt to hide the bosom, and every step shows the leg above the knee; while the men generally go with the merest bit of rag, and that not always carefully put on." Other members of the expedition were appalled by their encounter with a public bath. They understood nudity to be a mark not of innocence, but of disgusting licentiousness and degradation. In the event that the American reader lacked imagination, the expedition's official narrative obliged by including a lithograph that featured, in straightforward detail, a crowd of nude men and women in a bathhouse.[31]

These encounters reinforced some of the descriptions that had filtered out of Japan via Dutch merchants (the only Europeans allowed contact with Japan during its seclusion). In these accounts, Japan was full of teahouses where, for a price, one could acquire a temporary female companion. The Dutch, it was reported, had taken full advantage of this custom. A secretary with the British treaty mission to Japan in 1858 saw fit to include in the appendix of his published report a separate section on prostitution, in which he recounted the systematization of vice in Japan: the government not only sanctioned the practice, but licensed and profited from it. According to a treaty-port adage, Japan was a land of flowers without perfume, birds without song, men without honor, and women without virtue. Some American visitors, when presented with the opportunity for firsthand observation, concluded that Japanese women utterly lacked the modesty innate to all others of their sex. Given to lewdness, they conceded liberties "that the most abandoned woman in the U.S. would not permit."[32]

Sharing these attitudes, missionaries and some secular writers in the 1870s agreed that public nudity in Japan was an affront to civilized eyes. Griffis claimed that American women, as a rule, nearly fainted at their first sight of scantily clad Japanese. Missionaries emphasized the contrast between Japan's extraordinary natural beauty and its naked, heathen inhabitants by paraphrasing lines from a hymn: "Every prospect pleases, and only man is vile." In the opinion of missionaries, indecency and shamelessness were readily visible and indicated an absence not only of modesty but also of morality. Public nudity was a lascivious display without legitimate purpose; they found nothing godly in "promiscuous bathing."[33]

In response to this missionary critique of Japanese customs, scientist Edward S. Morse and art scholar James Jackson Jarves emphasized that sensuality and nudity were not synonymous in Japan. In their view, the claim that Japanese bathing customs were evidence of immorality was a gross libel. Morse and Jarves told their readers that Japanese men and women bathed together with propriety: though naked, they were not indecent. In his personal journal, Morse noted that the only immodest behavior was that of foreigners who stared at unclothed Japanese. Publicly, Morse pointed out that some American attitudes toward gender relations appeared scandalous to the Japanese. He urged Americans to understand that a public dance, where women in décolletage mingled and cavorted with men, would seem like wild debauchery to the Japanese. And what, Morse wondered, would the Japanese think of young American men at seaside resorts ogling bare-legged young women in clinging wet wrappers? The underlying motive of such American social events, Jarves argued, was far more libidinous than that of a Japanese bathhouse.[34] Indeed, one missionary recalled his shock upon realizing that whenever he walked the streets of Kumamoto arm in arm with his wife, the Japanese stared with displeasure and regarded his behavior as that of a libertine under the influence of drink. On the other side of the Pacific, early Japanese visitors to the United States were dismayed by the sights they witnessed at public balls. To the Japanese, bare female shoulders in mixed company were a lascivious display without a utilitarian justification; to Americans, however, they had aesthetic value.[35]

These differing interpretations illustrate what anthropologist Clifford Geertz calls the "thick description" of culture: identical acts, when set in different cultural contexts, can have very different symbolic meanings.[36] In observing and describing the Japanese, many American travelers could not distance themselves from their own cultural context. To them, an act in Japan carried the same meaning as that of an identical act in the United States; public bathing in Japan was no different than the scenario—admittedly hypothetical—of an American family sharing a bathtub on a Boston sidewalk. Even those observers who were able to recognize a Japanese cultural context insisted on framing it within their own. For instance, they wrote that the practicality of public nudity in Japan was akin to the primitive simplicity of Adam and Eve. But to the Japanese, public nudity was neither lascivious nor primitive: it was utilitarian. One partially disrobed for the sake of comfort and fully disrobed for the sake of cleanliness. A notion of this attitude as primitive practicality represented the application of an American perspective on top of a Japanese perspective. Doubly thick, such descriptions were externally sympathetic but internally patronizing.

Of all the American writers on Japan in the nineteenth century, none developed a more elaborate and condescending framework for understanding Japanese culture than did Percival Lowell. The elder brother of the poet Amy Lowell, he distilled American thought on race, civilization, and progress into his observations, all the while echoing Spencer's Synthetic Philosophy. During his visits to Japan in the 1880s and 1890s, he epitomized the views of American Gullivers. In "The Soul of the Far East," an 1887 series of *Atlantic Monthly* essays that enjoyed ongoing popularity as a book, Lowell insisted that the Japanese seemed "never to have fully grown up." Predating history, the juvenile character of the Japanese and all other "Far Orientals" had persisted without change.[37]

Much like Spencer in his application of recapitulation theory, Lowell traced backward the ostensible westward migration of civilization to find that, as one moved from the West to the East, what he called the "sense of self" faded. Just as differentiation of species was the measure of organic evolution, individualization was the measure of mental and social evolution. As Spencer had demonstrated, societies evolved from homogeneity to heterogeneity; primitive societies stifled the individual freedom and thought cultivated by civilized societies. Without individualization, neither the mind nor society could mature. To Lowell, then, the West embodied the culmination of heterogeneity and individualization, while the "Far East" embodied the opposite.[38]

Designing his own format for thick description, Lowell mustered evidence from Japanese art, language, and religion in an attempt to demonstrate that the Japanese had not fully developed a self-conscious individuality. As a result, they retained childish minds into adulthood, constituting a case of arrested evolution, or "survival of the unfittest." Lowell believed that Japanese refinement and politeness were evidence of civilization, but he claimed that Japan's age-old tendency to imitate other cultures had allowed "unnatural selection" to prevail. Thus its evolution and progress had come to a halt.[39]

And the consequences? Civilization in Japan and the Far East had long since passed its zenith. Despite its beauty, it would never bear fruit. As surely as the sun passed from east to west, the races of the Far East were "destined to disappear before the advancing peoples of the West." Unchanged and isolated for centuries, the Japanese had now come into contact with individualistic, heterogeneous, and progressive societies. Ultimately, Lowell did not share Spencer's confidence in evolution as a universal principle. For Japan, time had run out. Stagnant societies that were too slow to make the leap from homogeneity to heterogeneity were subject to the more brutal laws of natural selection.[40]

But Americans were not Spencer's only devotees in Meiji Japan; his works were translated and widely read by the Japanese as well. They influenced the thought of Fukuzawa Yukichi in particular, a founder of the "civilization and enlightenment" (*bummei kaika*) movement whose works sold in the millions during his lifetime. Fukuzawa's influence on Meiji Japan was profound, and his face now adorns the ten-thousand-yen note. Fukuzawa agreed with Spencer's assertion that societies advanced because of the free exercise of reason and the exchange of ideas, that civilization resulted from independent thought. To Fukuzawa, Japan had mistakenly adopted Chinese civilization, with its overemphasis on ethical rather than empirical knowledge, and thus Japanese progress had been hindered. In *An Outline of a Theory of Civilization* (1875), Fukuzawa identified three stages in human development: primitive communal groups, literate semideveloped countries that lacked original ideas and critical thought, and civilized countries. Japan and China were in the second stage, while Europe and the United States were in the third. "Only the most ignorant thinks that Japan's learning, arts, commerce, or industry is on a par with that of the West," he wrote. "Who would compare a man-drawn cart with a steam engine, or a Japanese sword with a rifle? While we are expounding on *yin* and *yang* and the Five Elements, they are discovering the sixty-element atomic chart." According to Fukuzawa, the West had recognized the universal truths of rationality and empiricism before the rest of the world and therefore had advanced more quickly.[41]

The solution, he proposed, was not uncritical imitation—that would lead only to the adoption of Western vices as well as virtues. Instead, Japan could duplicate Western progress by quickly giving priority to scientific knowledge and independent thought. Steam power, the telegraph, printing, and the postal system, wrote Fukuzawa, "constitute the elements of modern civilization." He illustrated the title page of his immensely successful work *Conditions in the West* (1866) with a steamship, locomotive, and electrical wires. Scientific knowledge would empower Japan, while independent thought would enable it to separate the wheat from the chaff. Because advanced civilizations dominated backward countries, he argued, the stakes were high. Japan's independence was at stake, making it imperative that Japan rapidly catch up with the West.[42]

Like Lowell and many other Americans, Fukuzawa regarded Spencer's principles as valuable guideposts. Yet Fukuzawa and Lowell employed Spencer in different ways. From Fukuzawa's point of view, Spencer provided a map that would guide Japan onto the path of progress. Evolution was a universal law of history; the problem was clear, and a solution was readily available. From Lowell's point of view, however, Spencer provided a historical analysis explaining Japan's failure to progress. Used in this manner, Spencer helped Americans fit the Japanese into racial and social taxonomies. Fukuzawa sought a means by which to free Japan from its past, while Lowell defined Japan by its past.

Depicting the Japanese as juveniles and half-naked Lilliputians, Lowell and the travel writers who preceded him bolstered American assumptions about race and progress. As Japan became a playland for the traveler's imagination, contrasts in physical stature became concrete manifestations of hierarchy. Physically beneath and socially behind Westerners, the Japanese were juvenile innocents in a fairyland, not inhabitants of the modern world. Writers thus relegated Japan to a world of imaginative fiction. From box seats, operagoers observe a fiction staged below for their pleasure; in Japan, travelers beheld a mixture of the real and the fantastic. The scenes' diminished scale only increased their value as amusing diversions.

The eminence of American observers was a privileged perspective based on physical stature, racial hierarchy, and definitions of modern civilization. From the heights of a hierarchical taxonomy, sightseers felt able to observe, describe, and define Japan with little regard for the views of its inhabitants. The metaphor of Jeremy Bentham's panopticon encapsulates the relations of power inherent in these acts of observations. The panopticon, a prison complex proposed by Bentham in the late eighteenth century, was designed to encourage behavioral reform by allowing an individual to observe a multitude of prisoners without being observed. The panopticon's inmates, never knowing *when* they are under observation, come to act as though they are under constant observation. To twentieth-century philosopher Michel Foucault, the panopticon illustrated the operation of power and the internalization of discipline in modern society. One who is visible in a mechanism like the panopticon is "the object of information, never a subject in communication." The observer is active, and the observed is passive: the power of observation confers the power to define, and thus to control, the Other.[43]

The panopticon is useful in exploring American observations of Japan, but only to a point. In such a structure, the act of observation is unidirectional. But the foreigner in Japan who observed through a reversed opera glass frequently found Japanese eyes staring back, sometimes from behind their own opera glass. To some Americans, this was not merely a figurative truth.

In 1860, after learning that a daimyo (feudal lord) and his retinue were to pass through Kanagawa on the road to Edo, Francis Hall took his "Munich Glass" and climbed atop a cliff with a commanding view of the road. He met a trio of missionaries at the crest, and in a risky breach of protocol the four Americans looked down on the procession, several thousand strong, that accompanied the lord of Owari. Shouts rang out from below, commanding the impudent foreigners to bow down. They did not. For nearly an hour, they watched as swordsmen, pike bearers, archers, and musketeers passed. Crowds of Japanese, more mindful of the dangers inherent in not paying obeisance to such a lord, crouched on their knees along the roadside. When the lord himself reached the foot of the cliff, he called his retinue to a halt and slid open the window of his palanquin. Would he order his men to throw the foreigners headlong from the precipice? wondered Hall. Instead, the lord of Owari, "with an opera glass, a veritable opera glass, took a good long look at us." Hall tipped his hat and, perched precariously at the cliff's edge, bowed with as much grace as he could muster. After gazing at them for several minutes, the daimyo ordered the procession to continue, and the Americans returned safely home.[44]

Many Japanese who did not have the opportunity to see the treaty-port Westerners with their own eyes were able to see them through the eyes of Japanese artists. These artists depicted—and frequently caricatured—the foreigners in inexpensive woodblock prints. In the early 1860s, artists produced hundreds of prints featuring Western subjects. These attracted intense curiosity and sold well, providing Japanese with the opportunity to study indirectly—and probably to snicker at—these odd, hairy creatures.[45]

While foreigners could be the unwitting objects of caricature, they were quite conscious of other forms of observation as well. Many travelers were discomfited when Japanese villagers "swarmed" to stare at them from head to toe. And later in the nineteenth century, the foreign artists who came to sketch Japanese scenes discovered that they themselves were scenic attractions. One exasperated American, his nerves worn by being the target of continual stares, attempted to discourage his observers by turning to sketch them. His audience was unperturbed, and he succeeded only in getting a good drawing. In a temple garden, an American painter working at his easel began attracting more attention than the garden itself. Recognizing this, a Japanese guide included him as a regular stop on the sightseeing tour.[46]

At times, the panoptic process itself was reversed. Isabella L. Bird, an English traveler, described staying at a rural inn where the rooms were separated by shoji (rice-paper panels). Her room itself, she discovered, had been converted into a panopticon. "The *shôji* were full of holes, and often at each hole I saw a human eye. Privacy was a luxury not even to be recalled." Gulliver, too, was initially under constant scrutiny by the Lilliputians: before he had gained their trust, Gulliver was chained and, unbeknownst to him, viewed from a distant turret by the imperial court. Foreigners seeking curiosities in Japan shared this experience with Gulliver. They learned that they were walking curiosities on exhibit, viewed "as specimens of natural history." The traveler was both observer and observed, both a curiosity seeker and a curiosity sought.[47]

Just as the Japanese would not passively be observed at the pleasure of foreign tourists, they were also active agents in the landscapes that tourists so admired. Japan's rural vistas were stunning in part because of the fertile lands that stretched from the mountains down to the sea, and agricultural cultivation was an integral part of Japan's scenic beauty. Tourists described valleys checkered with terraced fields and dotted with farmhouses and hamlets. "[L]uxuriant rice-fields" not only filled the valleys, but covered the hills as well: terracing allowed Japanese farmers to cultivate every square foot of arable land. Americans saw "hills rising from the water's edge, cultivated in terraces to their summit." And in the terraced fields, farmers often were hard at work. Because of careful human labor, the fields that covered the valleys and hills were as picturesque as the jagged mountains that loomed above. The touch of the Japanese hand upon the landscape increased its appeal. And in shaping the scenery, the Japanese demonstrated to foreign observers that theirs was a country of "high cultivation," with some level of civilization.[48]

Observations of this connection between the Japanese landscape and its inhabitants separate these travel accounts from Western accounts of other lands and peoples. European Americans, for instance, frequently accused Native Americans of underutilizing the land. Appropriation of Indian lands thus gained validity as manifest destiny. And European travelers in Africa and South America sometimes excluded the native inhabitants from written descriptions of landscapes. Lands devoid of native title and presence appeared vacant, available for American and European conquest. Acting as discoverers of new worlds, Americans and Europeans staked claims to all that they saw.[49] But in American descriptions of Japan, the land did not stand empty and ready to be appropriated. Like the virtuous Jeffersonian yeoman, the Japanese had mastered the land: they used it intensively and efficiently.

Most visitors to Japan in the early Meiji period, while they acknowledged Japanese cultivation, retained their faith in their own racial and evolutionary superiority. They pictured themselves as the bearers of civilization and progress. As Edward Warren Clark observed, Japanese cultivation was no match for the material proofs of the West's supremacy. After Clark spent two years teaching science and English in Shizuoka (about 110 miles southwest of Tokyo), he took a new position at Kaisei Gakkō, a forerunner of Tokyo University.[50] Coming into Yokohama en route, he was amazed at the changes that had occurred since his arrival in Japan in 1871.

> We saw the locomotive and train coming as we turned down the hill towards the city, and the naked Japs who pulled our jinrikishas looked in astonishment at the smoking locomotive, wondering what kind of animal it could be!
>
> In journeying along the Tokaido, the newly constructed telegraph followed us the whole way from Shidz-u-o-ka, and the little wire seemed like a thread that bound me to civilization.[51]

To Clark and other Americans, the foreign society of treaty-port Yokohama—with its hotels, telegraph office, and railroad station—was civilization. They were confident that the United States, in the guise of Commodore Perry, had introduced progress to Japan and triggered old Japan's gradual transformation. The recognition that Japan exhibited some aspects of an indigenous civilization did little to shake the firmly held conviction of most travelers that civilization and progress were Western birthrights. As it had in 1854, a locomotive still held the power to amaze "the naked Japs." Rails and telegraph wires, which Perry had first brought to Japan, now stretched across the American continent and were beginning to reach into Japan. Here was tangible evidence of civilization's course westward.

This narrow perspective bears, of course, the telltale odors of racism and colonial discourse. Just as the unequal treaties limited

Japanese sovereignty, American travelers constructed images of Japan that belittled the Japanese and discounted the possibility of independent Japanese progress. Semicivilized and semiclothed, the Japanese existed to be described and dominated by their civilized superiors. From this angle, American images correspond with a Manichean colonial discourse: the hegemonic colonizer wields a power that displaces and destroys native culture. But, as literary theorist Homi Bhabha contends, there is an ambivalence in colonial discourse.[52] By spotlighting the written narratives of colonizing observers, we have overlooked depictions (such as woodblock caricatures) by the observed. By treating colonial discourse as monolithic and unidirectional, we are likely to omit those instances in which those under observation possessed and utilized their own powers of observation.

The case of Japan calls for a nuanced approach. While Americans categorized Japan within their frameworks of race and civilization, the Japanese were actively engaged in their own projects of definition. Yes, power inhered primarily in the Western perspective. After all, the United States and Europe had compelled Japan to sign unequal treaties that ended its seclusion and opened it to Western eyes. Over the next decades, on the basis of their observations, Westerners considered whether and when Japan would merit treatment as a sovereign equal. Yet the Japanese took both a deep interest and a central role in this process. Japan wielded its own powers of observation and assimilation to overturn these unequal relations, to revise the treaties, and to become itself a colonial power.

To these secular American views of race and civilization, missionaries in Japan added another perspective. Again, Clark offers a useful example. Although not a church-sponsored missionary, he took upon himself the duties of a Christian evangelist. After his arrival, he refused to sign his teaching contract because the Ministry of Foreign Affairs, which ratified the contracts of all foreign employees, had included a provision forbidding him to teach Christianity. It would be impossible, he argued, for him to live among pagans and be silent about his beliefs. The ministry agreed to delete the provision, and this self-appointed missionary began teaching the gospel independently on his first Sunday in Shizuoka, a practice he continued throughout his stay in Japan.[53] To Clark and his evangelical brothers and sisters, Christianity and civilization were inseparable. While secular American travelers were confident that civilization and progress were uniquely Western, their missionary compatriots believed fervently that Christianity was the source of these birthrights.

Chapter 2

CHRISTIAN LIGHT AND
HEATHEN DARKNESS

To evangelical men and women, the task was simple. Regions of
the world were dominated by either Christianity or "heathenism." If missionary cartographers were willing to draw
more complex distinctions, they labeled territories as Protestant,
Catholic, "Mohammedan," or heathen.[1] Believing themselves
divinely commissioned to relabel this map of the world, nineteenth-century mission boards dispatched missionaries to
China, Burma, India, Turkey, Africa, and Japan. A Christian
Prometheus, the missionary aspired to bring the Gospel's light
to dispel the heathen darkness.

Unlike sightseeing travelers, missionaries went to Japan with
sharpened purpose. They did not go to be entertained by Japanese curiosities; they went to transform them. Believing that they
had Japanese interests foremost in their hearts, they steeled

themselves to endure the hardships of living among heathen. They went to work for Christ.

To missionaries, the United States represented the apex of spiritual and material civilization, which the Japanese wisely were emulating. They considered religious, political, and technological reforms vital if Japan hoped to become a civilized, sovereign equal of the United States. Under American tutelage, the Japanese could overcome their past and become a civilized, Christian people. Missionaries' beliefs about religion and civilization shaped their attitudes toward Japan. And missionary depictions of Japan were widely disseminated in the United States and influenced American policy.

The American denominations most active in Japan energetically publicized their endeavors. Missionaries had large, active audiences composed of their supporters in the United States. To cultivate this support, the mission boards published magazines, books, and annual reports that featured accounts from missionaries in the field, fundraising achievements, and foreign-mission study programs. These media not only circulated missionary images of Japan, but they also served as recruiting tools to enlist evangelical Americans as participants in American-Japanese relations. Joining in the activities of the mission boards and their local auxiliaries, Americans at home sustained the efforts of their missionary brothers, sisters, sons, and daughters abroad. Although the typical mission society member never left the United States, he or she was enlisted in a foreign crusade.

In its first decades in Japan, the missionary endeavor proceeded along two parallel tracks. On one, missionary men attempted to influence American foreign policy to press for change in Japanese policy toward Christianity. On the other, missionary women strove to transform Japanese domestic life.

Working in tandem with American diplomats, male missionaries hoped to create enough external pressure to push Japan toward a policy of religious toleration. By treaty, Americans were allowed to worship freely in Japan, but the prohibition on the practice of Christianity by Japanese subjects still stood—and was reinforced—in 1868. Stationed at the open ports and working among the Japanese as secular teachers, missionary men served as a trip wire: they regularly reported to diplomats on incidents of religious persecution and urged their government to pressure Japan into repealing the prohibition. American statesmen took these reports seriously and acted where they could. With notable success, male missionaries created a role for themselves in the realm of American-Japanese diplomatic relations.

Excluded from this realm, female missionaries focused neither on influencing American diplomatic policy nor on reforming Japanese public policy. Instead, they applied internal pressure in the hope of transforming Japan from within. In so doing, they took part in a sphere of international relations distinct from the narrower field of diplomacy. As "mothers of civilization," they aimed to reform Japanese society by teaching Japanese girls and women how to create moral, Christian homes. Missionary women believed that regenerating the private sphere would ultimately regenerate the public sphere.

They attempted to mold Japanese society according to dominant American cultural values. To accomplish this work they constructed an organizational network that enlisted other American women in a massive and expensive foreign endeavor. Women's mission work abroad required the active support and participation of women at home. Missionary women were at the tip of a pyramid formed by hundreds of thousands of auxiliary women active in foreign studies and fundraising. This network amplified missionary reports on Japan and provided auxiliary women with an entry into foreign affairs. Excluded from the foreign policy realm, women nonetheless participated in international relations: they became diplomats of domesticity.

Thus, missionary men worked to reshape Japan from the outside in, while women worked to regenerate it from the inside out. Together, these missionaries were in the vanguard of American cultural expansion; they cultivated and motivated dynamic constituencies to join in their cause of civilizing Japan.

Christian salvation, missionaries believed, begat modern civilization. "Our civilization was consequent upon our Christianity, and not merely coincident with it," avowed Julius H. Seelye, an Amherst College philosophy professor and a Reformed Church minister who had visited Japan. In Seelye's view, no country without Christianity could be considered civilized, and only the gospel provided the power to lift people out of the degradation and depravities of heathenism. As one Baptist missionary to Burma put it, the only alternative to Christian missions was perpetual heathenism.[2] These beliefs gave purpose and power to the missionaries. They and they alone had been chosen; only they could convert and civilize the heathen. When the Japanese seemed reluctant to accept this guidance, the missionaries successfully encouraged the application of diplomatic pressure against heathenism.

The first Protestant American missionaries arrived in Japan in 1859, nine years before the Meiji Restoration. (Protestant missions in Japan were primarily an American endeavor, while Roman Catholic missions were primarily French.) Among the early arrivals were James and Clara Hepburn and Guido and Maria Verbeck. The Hepburns, who had served as Presbyterian medical missionaries to China in the 1840s, settled in Kanagawa, where James opened a dispensary and began developing a romanization system for the Japanese language—a system widely used today. The Verbecks, representing the Reformed Dutch Church, settled in Nagasaki. Using the New Testament and the U.S. Constitution, Guido began teaching English to students, including the future Meiji statesmen Ōkuma Shigenobu and Soejima Taneomi.[3] Later, Verbeck's reputation and connections would bring him several important government positions as an educator and advisor. Additional missionaries soon joined the work of these early couples, compiling dictionaries, translating the Bible into Japanese, and establishing schools.

American missionaries found that Japan readily adopted and assimilated many aspects of Western civilization, which made it anomalous among nineteenth-century mission fields. But this anomaly also constituted a knotty problem for missionaries: while opening its doors to Western arts and sciences, Japan retained its prohibition on Christianity. Here was a people who vainly believed that they could separate Christianity from civilization. But railroads and telegraphs did not make people virtuous, missionaries asserted. In constructing a new Japan, its "heathen builders" had rejected the cornerstone.[4]

The bakufu had banned Christianity in 1614 to eliminate the threat posed to feudal loyalties by Catholic missionaries and converts. In 1858, however, Article VIII of the Treaty of Amity and Commerce specifically allowed Americans in Japan the free exercise of religion.[5] (Treaties with the other powers contained similar provisions.) From Japan's legal perspective, then, the new missionaries were to serve as religious leaders in the foreign community, but only as secular teachers to the Japanese. They were allowed by treaty to build churches within the foreign settlements but, like other foreigners, were permitted to travel freely only within a radius of ten ri (about twenty-four miles) from the ports that Japan had been required to open. While the unequal treaties exempted foreigners from Japanese legal jurisdiction—placing them under the jurisdiction of their consulates—Japanese subjects, of course, were not shielded from Japanese law. Japanese who expressed too strong an interest or, worse, a belief in Christianity could be arrested. Hence the bakufu's prohibition on Christianity prevented conspicuous proselytizing. This did not please American evangelical leaders. In 1866 and 1867, leaders of the Episcopal, Presbyterian, Reformed Dutch, and Methodist Episcopal churches wrote to Secretary of State William H. Seward, asking that the U.S. government work to secure religious toleration in Japan. Seward agreed and instructed Minister Robert B. Van Valkenburgh to press for repeal of the prohibition.[6]

But the Meiji government came to power in 1868 with a different set of concerns. On 7 April it followed in the bakufu's footsteps by renewing the prohibition on Christianity. Posted on public notice-boards throughout the country, the proclamation described it as an "evil sect" and offered rewards to those turning in suspected believers. In the first years of the Meiji period, Christianity was not primarily a matter of foreign policy to Japanese leaders. Instead, most early Meiji leaders were far more concerned with Christianity's effects on internal security. In the immediate aftermath of the bakufu's collapse, they were eager to stabilize the volatile domestic conditions that had carried them to power. As a foreign religion with a history of triggering civil uprisings, Christianity seemed potentially dangerous. Until they were able to quell remaining bakufu forces and to consolidate their power, they considered it prudent to continue the prohibition on Christianity. Although diplomatic protests to the Foreign Ministry would gradually wear away at this prohibition, domestic stability was foremost for the new government's leaders.[7]

Van Valkenburgh learned of the April proclamation only after realizing that an item was missing from the gazettes presented to him by the Japanese government. After obtaining a copy of the prohibition, he urged the government to reconsider the edict, an action that Seward strongly approved. Under pressure from Great Britain as well, the government relented, but only slightly. In its revised notice, the first paragraph announced that the prohibition on the Christian sect was to be strictly observed.

The word "evil" appeared only in the second paragraph, which noted that evil sects were strictly prohibited.[8]

Just as the Meiji government maintained the ban, it also continued bakufu policy toward the numerous Japanese Christians in the village of Urakami, near Nagasaki. Nagasaki had been a center of Roman Catholic conversions in the sixteenth and seventeenth centuries, and the Urakami Christians were descendants of these converts. With mixed results, they had attempted over the years to hide their faith from government authorities. In 1865, shortly after the opening of a Catholic church in Nagasaki's French settlement, many began meeting secretly with the priests there. Two years later, the Urakami villagers made their faith public when they refused to use Buddhist priests for funeral services. In response, the bakufu arrested more than sixty of the villagers.[9]

By chance, Van Valkenburgh was in Nagasaki shortly after the arrests. In a letter and in interviews with bakufu officials, he expressed his concern. And together with the representatives of the other powers, he requested the release of the prisoners. In late 1867, the bakufu and the French Minister reached a compromise in which the prisoners were set free in exchange for a French promise that priests would no longer visit Urakami.[10]

After the Meiji Restoration in 1868, the new government announced a plan to send more than four thousand Japanese Christians into internal exile. Seward instructed Van Valkenburgh to moderately yet firmly impress upon the government that the plan would "excite profound apprehension and alarm among the friends of civilization and progress throughout the world." In January 1870, when the foreign representatives in Tokyo learned that the deportations had begun, they delivered a protest to the Council of State (the government's central executive body). In response, the Japanese maintained that the villagers had been exiled not because of their religious beliefs, but because they had been insubordinate, had harbored criminals, and had intimidated their neighbors. Vice Foreign Minister Terashima Munenori also complained that missionaries were conducting religious activities outside the Nagasaki foreign settlement. And Foreign Minister Sawa Nobuyoshi assured the foreign representatives that further deportations had been suspended. The next day, however, the representatives learned that nearly all of the remaining Urakami Christians had been deported.[11]

The plight of the villagers further fueled American missionary efforts to pressure Japan into adopting a more lenient policy toward Christianity. From a Nagasaki missionary, the U.S. legation in Tokyo received an eyewitness report on the deportations. As reports circulated in the American secular press, mission boards used their magazines as pulpits from which to denounce the persecution. In the Episcopal magazine *Spirit of Missions,* a dramatic firsthand account described Urakami families being brought before the Nagasaki governor and refusing to recant their Christian faith. Men, women, and children—their fate uncertain—were marched under guard to the wharf and loaded onto boats. Missionaries publicly praised their diplomatic representatives for protesting the deportations and exhorted them to continue these efforts.[12]

Some, however, were dissatisfied with the lack of results. Eight American and two British missionaries penned an open letter in May 1871 urging Western governments to demand the repeal of these "odious and cruel" laws. Because the powers had only protested feebly thus far, the Japanese government had ignored them with impunity. The missionaries did not specify the actions the powers should take to compel Japan to listen.[13]

The persecution of Japanese Christians hit the missionaries even closer to home during the night of 30 June 1871. Stationed in Kobe, Congregationalists Daniel Crosby Greene and Orramel H. Gulick learned that their Japanese-language teacher and his wife had been arrested and taken away. Although Ichikawa Einosuke had never professed to be a Christian, the missionaries wrote in the *Missionary Herald* that they thought of him as such and hoped that he would soon be Greene's "first convert from heathenism." He had in his possession two copies of Hepburn's translation of the Gospel of Mark, which were missing from his house after the arrests.[14]

Greene and Gulick quickly requested assistance from U.S. Minister Charles E. De Long, who was unable to learn the Ichikawas' whereabouts or the charges against them. The missionaries were convinced that their teacher's only misdeed had been his interest in Christianity. Rumors of Einosuke's death reached the missionaries, but they received no official word until December 1872, when the governor of Kobe informed Greene that Einosuke had died in prison on 25 November. Shortly thereafter, his wife was released and brought to the missionaries the only news they were to receive of Einosuke's imprisonment. Her husband, she told Greene, had professed himself a Christian during the preliminary questioning after their arrest and had held fast to his faith until his death.[15]

Writing shortly after the arrest of the Ichikawas, Gulick argued that, in one sense, its timing was providential: the case would intensify American attention to religious intolerance in time to affect treaty revision talks in 1872.[16] According to the terms of the 1858 treaty, it would be subject to revision after 4 July 1872. With this in mind, the Meiji government sent its first diplomatic mission to the United States and Europe in 1871–73. Led by Iwakura Tomomi, the embassy focused on exchanging views on treaty revision and studying the sources of Western power.

While the embassy was in the United States, missionaries continued to bring their cause before the American public and government. Jonathan Goble—once a marine in the Perry

Expedition, now a Baptist missionary in Yokohama—happened to return to the United States on the ship carrying the embassy and made use of this opportunity to talk with its members about Christianity. In a letter published in San Francisco and New York newspapers, Goble reported that Iwakura had assured him that the Japanese government would eventually remove restrictions on religious belief. Goble urged Americans to demonstrate to the embassy the benefits of freedom of conscience. The *Missionary Herald* continued to follow the Ichikawa case and reported on a memorial presented by Congregationalists to President Ulysses S. Grant urging him to push for religious freedom in Japan.[17]

The issue of religious toleration was already one of several items on the State Department's agenda. Like the missionaries, Secretary of State Hamilton Fish and De Long hoped that the Japanese embassy would see the advantages of the separation of church and state in the United States. In a series of meetings, Fish and the embassy discussed proposed revisions to the treaty. Fish asked the envoys to commit to the principle of freedom of religion, but the Japanese resisted. When Iwakura asserted that religious persecution did not exist in Japan, De Long cited the arrest of the Ichikawas.[18]

Although no revised treaties emerged from the embassy's conferences in Washington and Europe, two vice ambassadors were dispatched back to Japan in 1872 and carried a recommendation to the Japanese government that the prohibition on Christianity be removed from the public notice-boards. They explained that the ban led foreigners to regard the Japanese as barbarians who did not deserve equal sovereign rights.[19] Now that the Meiji government had consolidated its power and stabilized the domestic situation, Christianity fell within the realm of foreign relations.

In February 1873, Foreign Minister Soejima Taneomi (Verbeck's former student) notified De Long that the government had ordered the removal of the edict against Christianity from the public notice-boards. The missionaries initially were less than delighted; this was not the unequivocal declaration of religious liberty for which they had prayed and lobbied. The removal of the prohibition from the notice-boards did not signal its repeal. Yet the government made clear to foreign diplomats that this action signalled the tacit toleration of Christianity. The prohibition had not been repealed, but neither would it be enforced, and missionaries felt free to begin preaching publicly. In March, deported Japanese Christians were permitted to return home, though about 660 had died in exile. Diplomats and missionaries alike interpreted these government actions as important steps in Japan's progress toward freedom of religion. In a letter to Goble, De Long credited the foreign representatives, missionaries, and Christians abroad for spurring this advance: his gratitude did not extend beyond Westerners and Christians.[20]

The year 1873 marked the beginning of a period of great optimism among missionaries and their supporters at home. From 1859 to 1872, thirty-one Protestant missionaries had come to Japan. In 1873 alone, twenty-nine arrived, more than in any other year in the nineteenth century.[21] The new arrivals were encouraged by their belief that Japan had finally succeeded in freeing itself from the enslavement of isolation and intolerance. Japan's steady and rapid material progress, they purported, might now be matched by its spiritual progress.

For a time, this optimism seemed justified. In the 1880s, the missionaries had notable success in generating converts and establishing churches: membership doubled every three years. Many missionaries, recalling a verse from the Gospel of John, exclaimed that the fields in Japan were "white for the harvest." But just after that decade, church memberships grew at a significantly slower rate, taking twelve years to double again.[22]

Still, in the 1870s and 1880s, missionaries believed that they had succeeded via Christian example and diplomatic pressure in ending more than two centuries of darkness in Japan. "Perhaps never before has the Christian Church been called to the husbandry of a vineyard so promising," wrote a Presbyterian clergyman. Any hands the mission societies could send, he urged, would find work aplenty.[23]

Because the societies considered married men less vulnerable than bachelors to the alleged temptations of heathen societies, the typical missionary man was married and accompanied by his wife. Yet married women frequently found that the duties of raising their own children precluded their devoting sufficient time to their role as "assistant missionaries." Their names appear infrequently in the mission board reports and histories of missions. Maria Verbeck, for example, bore eight children and is scarcely visible in William Elliot Griffis's biography of her husband.[24]

Over time, though, the single women sent by women's mission societies grew increasingly important to the missionary endeavor. The recruiting and financial powers of these societies proved formidable. By 1889 the numbers of missionary men and single missionary women in Japan were nearly equal: 200 men and 171 women. A decade later, men were outnumbered by single women, 247 to 260.[25] These women came to husband the vineyard—without husbands.

The denominations most active in Japan had formed women's mission societies in the United States in the late 1860s and early 1870s. In fact, women's societies counted more members than any other mission-movement and were among the largest reform organizations of the nineteenth century. Great popularizers of foreign missions, these societies also provided their members with important new professional opportunities. In mission boards and auxiliaries, women drafted constitutions, elected officers, raised funds, and published magazines.

In their parody of Gilded Age society, Mark Twain and Charles Dudley Warner observed that the absence of useless Asian whatnots in the nooks of an American family's parlor might indicate a languidness toward foreign missions.[26] But much more than whatnots tied women to the missionary enterprise. Women's mission societies offered American women a vehicle by which they were able to enter the sphere of international relations. These societies included regional branches that at the grassroots level consisted of thousands of local auxiliaries and young women's circles and involved hundreds of thousands of women. The Methodist Episcopal Church alone counted 50,817 auxiliary members in 1878 and 123,488 in 1894.[27] In gauging the influence of women's missionary societies, however, numbers tell only part of the story. We must also keep in mind the ties that bound auxiliary women in the United States to the missionaries they supported. Hand in hand, mission society women at home and missionary women abroad worked to remold other peoples.

A typical auxiliary had forty members and met monthly to study foreign lands, read scripture, sing hymns, and pray. Mission magazines, with subscribers in the tens of thousands, served as source material and syllabi, featuring essays and lists of reference books. (Perennial favorites included Griffis's *The Mikado's Empire* and Alice Mabel Bacon's *Japanese Girls and Women.*) The syllabi also provided study questions on themes including missionary music, fundraising, and the mission work in specific countries. How, auxiliary women asked, did the religious heritage and social customs of a particular country affect mission prospects? In the Methodist *Heathen Woman's Friend*, a study guide on Shinto began with a reading of Psalm 72: "Yea, all kings shall fall down before him: all nations shall serve him." The guide continued with a list of questions and prompted auxiliary members to examine "the unsatisfactory character of this colorless, almost creedless, religion" by considering whether

Shinto worship was idolatry. Embedded in the program was an answer: Shinto worship revolved around the imperial regalia of the mirror, sword, and jewel.[28]

Missionary women not only acted as the hands of the auxiliaries in bringing Christianity to Japan; they also served as their eyes and ears. Those fresh to the field could expect to receive letters overflowing with questions. "How do you like Japan? What do you think of the people? . . . Is the language so very difficult?"[29] Appearing regularly in the magazines, missionaries' essays and letters gave their sisters at home detailed interpretations of the situation in Japan.

By intensifying the financial, spiritual, and personal links between auxiliary and missionary women, the magazines incorporated women into the business of foreign relations. To promote the fundraising necessary to support missionaries in the field, magazines regularly listed contributions received, itemized by church or auxiliary and often by individual. Hence, to give was also to receive—in the form of national recognition, albeit in only a line or two of print. The funds raised by women's boards and auxiliaries provided salaries, transportation and living expenses, language training, and teaching facilities. Some missionaries were supported by local auxiliaries, while others were supported by a regional branch or the society as a whole. By committing themselves to the sponsorship of a missionary, women simultaneously demonstrated and heightened their sense of personal obligation to those abroad. And because each board magazine devoted considerable space to publishing open letters from its missionaries, these women became familiar, sympathetic figures to auxiliary members at home.

The Congregational Church's *Life and Light for Woman* gently reminded members to "care for your missionary"—to send her frequent notes of kind greeting and tokens of remembrance, to follow her work with unfaltering interest, and to keep her in their hearts. Magazines tried to bridge the geographic separation by offering for sale, at nominal cost, photographs of individual missionaries. Auxiliaries sewed and sent quilts to their sisters abroad. Besides relying upon and appreciating these expressions of support, missionaries also asked those at home to pray for them.[30] Through these activities, societies and their magazines created a far-flung network of sisterly Christian ties that auxiliary members and missionaries carefully cultivated. Magazine readers, for instance, were engaged in a task that consumed their time and attention far beyond the minutes necessary to peruse a magazine article or two. The missionary magazine was a textual distillation of a larger endeavor. It reinforced auxiliary women's concerns about life in heathen lands and encouraged their efforts to support Christian evangelism spiritually and financially.

In pursuing Christian conversions, American evangelical women worked well within the constraints of their domestic sphere, "exporting femininity, not feminism."[31] In the nineteenth-century industrial revolution, economic production had shifted from households to factories, diminishing women's status. Catharine Beecher, the apostle of woman's sphere, responded by arguing convincingly that the household was the basic building block of a moral society and that only women were blessed with the talents necessary for nurturing a family. By emphasizing women's domestic role in shaping the family's moral character, Beecher attempted to elevate women's status as "mothers of civilization." Through work within the confines of the home, a mother and wife instilled virtues in her children and so gave the family and nation a moral center. The home was a sanctuary, and woman's work there was sacred.[32]

Evangelical women carried abroad this duty to nurture civilization and Christian morality among heathen peoples: they made "the world their household."[33] They aspired to mold other peoples and nations in a Protestant American image. Given American gender roles at that time, this was indeed a conservative venture. Yet from the perspective of the "heathen" who had been thus targeted, it demanded a fundamental social transformation linked to American cultural expansion and transmission.

Between hagiography and condemnation lies a path that both allows us to critically assess the condescension that suffuses missionary accounts of the "heathen" and compels us to recognize the individual missionary's altruism. Missionary women provide a helpful starting point. Despite the narrowness of their evangelical field of vision, its depths gave them personal courage and strength.

Arriving at the dock in Yokohama, the first missionary women could expect to be welcomed by the small community of veteran missionaries. After an introductory tour, newcomers soon settled into their work. They lived in or near the foreign concessions, but unlike their married compatriots, did not have the omnipresent comfort of a family. Many lived in their new mission schools. After establishing, administering, and teaching in these schools, they had little time for socializing.

The first missionary women faced difficulties unlike those that confronted later arrivals. Beginning in the late 1870s, newcomers were able to settle into an established community of missionary women, to live with and work alongside their sisters. But the first arrivals did not have this luxury. They grappled with the difficulties of geographic, linguistic, and spiritual isolation, which prompted them to pray for the arrival of coworkers and companions. In their letters and reports, missionary women frequently described their loneliness and personal hardships. Missionary men, on the other hand, bared few vulnerabilities. Their families provided them with companionship and left them free to focus exclusively in their letters on the expansion of Christ's kingdom. In contrast, single women directed a powerful personal appeal to the sympathies of their supporters at home. And in response, the branches and auxiliaries raised more money and appointed more missionaries.

While the names Griffis and Verbeck are familiar to students of early American-Japanese relations, few would recognize the name Dora E. Schoonmaker. Yet Schoonmaker was the first missionary to Japan appointed by the Methodist Woman's Foreign Missionary Society. Schoonmaker and other American women known in Japan for their pioneer efforts in Japanese women's education are virtually unknown in the United States.[34] In 1874, four years after graduating as a high-school valedictorian, Schoonmaker was appointed to Japan with an annual salary of $600. (The typical salary for a married male missionary was $1,200.) She resigned her position as principal of the Morris, Illinois, high school, and after her October arrival in Tokyo, she opened a mission school, a predecessor of Aoyama Gakuin University. After having difficulty finding a permanent location, she rented a building on the grounds of a temple the following summer and moved the school and her quarters into "the very den of paganism."[35]

Thousands of miles from her family and friends and a three-mile rickshaw ride from her nearest American and European neighbors, Schoonmaker fought homesickness. In order to take immediate advantage of a benefactor's donation, the Missionary Society had overridden its practice of sending women in pairs and sent Schoonmaker alone. She stipulated only that she be allowed to return after five years if her mother needed her care. In Japan, Schoonmaker's sense of isolation was compounded by her rudimentary grasp of the Japanese language. Like most of her missionary colleagues, she had begun her language training only after arriving at her post and so relied heavily on interpreters and language teachers paid for by the mission society. In Nagasaki, Elizabeth Russell and Jennie Gheer opened their mission school with one pupil: at first, she knew no English and they knew no Japanese. Another missionary confronted with language difficulties wondered wryly why the Pentecostal gift of tongues had been discontinued. Missionaries experienced feelings of frustration and insufficiency when confronted by the language barrier, and they worried about the amount of time they had to devote to their own studies rather than to teaching their pupils. Missionary life, they found, was filled with toil and disappointments rather than romance.[36]

In response, they prayed both for strength and reinforcements. Were there not members of the young ladies' mission circles who had been called to carry the Word? Would not the auxiliaries pray to the Lord to send a companion? After managing her school alone for more than one year, Schoonmaker wrote to her supporters: "Am I not lonely? Yes; so lonely that my most earnest efforts fail to keep me very *patient* in my waiting for the companion and helper whom I hear is soon to be sent me. For the work's sake, and for my own, I wish she were here *now*." Almost two years after Schoonmaker's arrival in Japan, her prayers were answered. Olive Whiting arrived after an eventful Pacific crossing during which a storm swept away her Bible and most of her wardrobe. (Three years later, Schoonmaker returned home to care for her mother but continued to write about Japan for *Heathen Woman's Friend*.)[37]

Once settled in Japan, missionary women took a special interest in the status of Japanese women. On this topic, they shared with Herbert Spencer some assumptions about civilization and women's position. According to Spencer, savage societies practiced polygamy and accorded low status to women, while civilized societies practiced monogamy and accorded high status. The elevation of women proceeded concurrently with social evolution.[38] Because missionaries regarded Christianity as a prerequisite of civilization, they considered the elevation of women to be a result of Christianization, which to them *was* social evolution. What savagery and civilization were to Spencer, heathenism and Christianity were to missionaries.

Heathen women, missionaries believed, lived under a curse. According to *Heathen Woman's Friend*, "In exact ratio with the degradations of paganism, is the vileness of the woman's slavery. In exact ratio with the light of Christianity, are the beauty and blessedness of her home life." Yet most missionary women began their observations by noting that Japanese women were more favored than those in other heathen countries; they were neither overworked nor kept secluded. But, continued these writers, their position was not enviable. Compared to the lives of Christian women, the lives of Japanese women were "aimless and hopeless."[39]

Missionary women described for their sisters at home those Buddhist and Confucian teachings that formed a canon of female degradation. Without Christianity to protect them, Japanese women were trained to feel insignificant. Buddhist doctrine denied women salvation until they were reborn as men. Confucian texts, such as the *Greater Learning for Women (Onna daigaku)*, taught that women were inferior to men and that their minds were afflicted with indocility, discontent, slander, jealousy, and silliness. Missionaries cataloged the vices that resulted from these beliefs.[40]

Marriage, for example, offered the Japanese woman little protection. In her popular work *Japanese Girls and Women*, Alice Mabel Bacon wrote that a wife was little more than her husband's servant. Bacon, not a missionary but a teacher in Japan, attended a Japanese Congregational church and was a favorite writer among evangelical women. She informed her many readers that the Japanese wife became her husband's maid, seamstress, and waitress. The husband was heaven, and the wife was the earth beneath his feet. Expected always to be obedient and compelled to walk behind her husband, the Japanese wife seemed to pass directly from girlhood to old age: "a woman of thirty seems old, care-worn, hopeless." And, noted Bacon, divorce was distressingly easy for a husband to attain.[41]

Missionaries also grappled with the practice of concubinage. Although the government in 1873 pronounced that in "cases of severe necessity" a wife could apply for divorce, in the same year it also issued an ordinance that placed the children of wives and concubines on equal legal footing. Too often, missionaries protested, men brought concubines into the household, bringing unhappiness along with them. The missionaries were disturbed, too, that the children of such a father might not be raised by their true mother.[42]

Prostitution was to missionaries the most distressing of all the problems confronting Japanese women. Before the arrival of female missionaries, American visitors had occasionally commented on its seeming prevalence, noting in particular the government-regulated brothel districts. While missionaries were appalled by the legality and openness of this practice, they rebutted the other visitors who described Japanese women as especially licentious, identifying Confucianism as the true culprit in disgracing Japanese women. Because it grotesquely exaggerated the principle of filial obedience, a daughter, in obedience to an impoverished father, would sacrifice herself to the brothel. Out of virtuous girls and women, Confucianism made slaves to be bought and sold.[43]

It is important to recognize that leading Japanese intellectuals, too, considered the status of women an important measure of civilization. Both Fukuzawa Yukichi and Mori Arinori, leaders of the civilization and enlightenment movement, were outspoken in their criticism of concubinage and other aspects of gender relations in Japan. Fukuzawa condemned the Confucian strictures of the *Greater Learning for Women* and contended that men who took concubines violated the laws of nature: "We should not hesitate to call such men beasts." Mori also was unequivocal. Writing in the movement's influential journal, *Meiroku zasshi*, he described the hatred and jealousy that erupted between wife and concubine. Marriage laws and practices in Japan, Fukuzawa and Mori argued, were unjust and encouraged immorality.[44]

In the eyes of missionaries, Japanese ethical thought and social practice negated the possibility that women could maintain moral households. What respect could a woman claim when divorce was so easy for her husband to obtain? In a household tainted by concubines, what moral authority did the principal wife and mother have? In a pagan society, the missionaries held, the family home was no sanctuary. As American children sang in a Congregational Church hymn:

I often think of heathen lands,
    Far, far away:
Oh! how I pity children there,
    Far, far away.
For there each heathen child is led,
To bow to idol gods its head,
While many muttering charms are said,
    Far, far away.

Certainly, missionaries believed, they had much work to do. They were determined to take Japanese girls as far as possible from the "shocking immorality" of idolatry and polygamy in their families.[45]

By offering girls an education in mission boarding schools, missionaries hoped to free them from these evil influences. And by instilling the conscious dignity of Christian womanhood in their young charges, missionaries expected to elevate Japanese womanhood and plant seeds that would eventually blossom into

Christian mothers and homes. Many of their pupils came from parts of the interior where missionaries could not reside, or from homes that missionaries could not easily enter. Through mission schools, these girls carried Christianity directly into their families. In Nagasaki, Russell and Gheer quickly expanded their boarding school to accommodate ninety pupils, who studied not only the Bible but also the domestic science of running a Christian household. Missionaries reasoned also that teaching sewing, cooking, and weaving was important because these skills provided Japanese women with a means of self-support, making them less likely to drift into disreputable employment.[46]

Armed with focused zeal, missionary women did make significant contributions to the development of women's education in Japan. From 1859 to 1905, Protestant missionaries established eighty-four schools, of which fifty-four were girls' schools. They helped spread Protestantism and provided a model for Japanese efforts in women's education as well.[47]

To teach Japanese women piety and purity, these missionaries took their American notion of the domestic sphere and attempted to transplant it in Japan as a civilizing instrument. While missionary men had public roles as ministers and policy advocates, women were to transform Japan via their special role in cultivating morality in the privacy of the household and schoolroom. As noted above, the missionary women attacked Japanese gender roles and worked to replace them with conventional American constructions.

Their work, however, implicitly altered these constructions. Single missionary women formed a Protestant priesthood in the domestic sphere. They did not take on the prescribed roles of wife and mother. Instead, wed only to their work, these single mothers of civilization established a new domestic vocation as they ventured into the world, convinced that they would regenerate heathen nations. While they did not explicitly challenge the boundaries of women's domestic sphere in American ideology, they did redraw them by internationalizing their "domestic sphere."

They were confident that Christianity alone could ensure women dignity, respect, and moral authority; to them it was woman's Magna Charta. As they saw it, Japanese girls were the future mothers of Japanese civilization, and only women could reach them. The fundamental goal of bringing civilization to Japan was to bring Christianity, but the first step was to bring Christianity to Japanese girls and women. In the view of American women, changes in the home would eventually effect changes in public life as well; pure women would build pure homes, which in turn would produce a pure people. This was woman's work in Japan.[48]

The missionary women's empathy with Japanese women was not merely an imperialist urge to dominate another society. Their opposition to concubinage and prostitution had at its heart a sincere altruism. Japanese intellectuals and reformers also were and would continue to be outspoken critics of these same institutions. Missionary women, however, did not venture beyond the bounds of their evangelical vision. Their diagnosis of these ills expressed their feelings of sisterhood with Japanese women, but these Americans prescribed Christianity as the only cure, a remedy that only they could dispense.

Missionary women thus expected to make Japanese women a central force in Japan's progress toward civilization. Further, missionary women assumed that they themselves were at the center of American efforts to transform the world. After all, they were engaged daily in the task of uplifting hearts and souls, whereas diplomats worked only on the edges of a foreign society, smoothing a rough spot here or there.

In at least one sense, they were correct. Missionary women were indeed vital players in American relations with Japan. These mothers of civilization made their domestic science a component of American foreign affairs. To them and their hundreds of thousands of auxiliary sisters, moral regeneration was integral to international relations. They insisted that gender roles be a measure by which Americans evaluated Japanese progress toward Christian civilization. As they toiled in the mission fields, their magazine articles and letters tilled the soil at home, spurring others to contribute and participate in the task of civilizing Japan. Few if any diplomats could claim so large and devoted a following.

Mission societies were mechanisms for the production, import, and circulation of images of other peoples. The magazines and auxiliary meetings enabled evangelical women to publicize these images widely and to implant them firmly within very receptive audiences. By strengthening the ties between the missionary and the women at home who supported her, missionary magazines cultivated an eager, active constituency with a personal interest in reports from "their" missionaries. Via mission activities, American women gained a direct stake in the course of Japanese progress and of American-Japanese relations.

This process went far beyond the export of femininity or evangelical beliefs; exporting domesticity had significant consequences at home as well as abroad. Excluded from ordination and the public, foreign-policy sphere, women took part in American cultural expansion by extending overseas their domestic sphere. They attempted to recast Japanese patriarchy to resemble American patriarchy, which they did not directly challenge. From an American social perspective, this was fundamentally a conservative venture. Yet the mission societies, their auxiliaries, and their publications offered American women entry into world affairs and provided them with spiritual incentive and financial means, and their endeavors ultimately blurred the boundaries of the domestic sphere. Although formulated as a conservative venture, mission societies ardently claimed new territory for woman's work: as diplomats of domesticity, women were to labor alongside their brothers in the realm of foreign relations. While women engaged in domestic diplomacy, missionary men continued using their public positions as ordained clergy to assess diplomatic relations and policy. In the early years of missions, they attempted to shape American foreign policy in order to reshape Japanese religious policy. In later years, after the Japanese government began to tolerate overt Christian activity, missionary men became prominent supporters of Japanese political reform and proponents of treaty revision. And they continued to use their magazines and secular journals to publicize their views, making them important interpreters of Japanese policy reform in the American public sphere.

The missionary voice would continue to resonate through the turn of the century in American debates on treaty revision, Japan's racial origins, Japanese and American strategic interests, and the nature of civilization. Try as they might, however, missionaries were unable to relabel their evangelical maps: Japan remained heathen.

Chapter 3

WISE MEN FROM THE WEST

Missionaries were among the first to conclude that Japan confounded American expectations about the intractibility of "heathen" nations. In the first decade of American missions, the Japanese had seemed similar to other benighted regions. In the 1870s and 1880s, however, missionaries came to think that Japan might be poised to adopt their framework for civilization. Many Japanese were converting to Christianity, and more were embracing Western education. Here was an Asian people who welcomed modern civilization.

As conversions increased at a rapid rate in the 1880s, missionaries should have been able to enjoy their successes. Yet they feared that material progress and secular thought were threatening to drown out the voice of Christ. Despite the growth of Japanese Christian churches, missionaries worried that too many Japanese were adopting the material fruit of Western civilization without reaching its spiritual root. This compelled a few missionaries to briefly reexamine their assumption that salvation preceded civilization. Was there a path to civilization that did not pass through Christendom? But most did not shed their evangelical assumptions. Undaunted, they continued to carry Christianity's civilizing light to a nation now crisscrossed by telegraph and railroad lines, a nation where gas and electricity also were dispelling darkness.

To the dismay of missionaries, secular Western scholars also claimed to bring enlightenment to Japan: their promised illumination was scientific, not spiritual. Missionaries were disconcerted by the growing number of American teachers who advocated the "scientific paganism" of Darwin and Spencer before attentive Japanese audiences. Missionaries feared that these "infidels" were undermining Christian evangelism in Japan and recognized that their own spiritual prescription for progress now had a vigorous secular rival. In the decade of their greatest success, they could not ignore the simultaneous victories of American scholars who brought a secular formula for progress to Japan. As a result, the target of their attack in Japan grew to include Western materialism and skepticism. These missionary anxieties were part of a broader American intellectual trend; in the United States, many Protestants identified evolutionary theory as a threat to religious belief.[1] In Japan, missionaries viewed their secular antagonists as a subversive fifth column intent on extinguishing a Christian light that was just beginning to burn brightly.

American scholars held quite different opinions on these issues. Their observations led them to conclude that the Japanese were a highly civilized people who were rapidly westernizing. The great majority of these Americans were supportive of Japanese reform efforts; fewer were sympathetic to the evangelical beliefs of missionaries. Secular teachers and journalists did not consider Christianity and civilization to be synonymous. Some, in fact, publicly challenged missionary images of Japan, satirized the missionaries in print, and mocked the very notion of Christian mission. Several who taught at Japanese schools were disciples not of Christ but of Darwin; they in turn were scorned by missionaries as atheists.

Just as the influence of Darwin and Spencer was an international phenomenon, the reaction against scientific skepticism reached across national borders and was an important part of the missionary contribution to American cultural expansion. Missionaries believed themselves divinely bound to resist and refute these doctrines in the United States as well as Japan. Churches, lecture halls, and the press in both nations served as the sites for their side of this contest. In the 1870s and 1880s, Japan was not only an arena for the conflict between American proponents of religious and secular views of civilization: Japan itself became an important topic in this debate.

At first, most Americans agreed that Japan had to remodel itself in the image of the Western (Christian) powers in order to be considered civilized. Some of its earlier secular visitors, however, began to argue that Japan, now revived and open to the world, was aspiring and already advancing toward the higher level of Western civilization without Christianity. They concluded that the Japanese deserved recognition and respect as a people striving to join the ranks of enlightened nations. Foreign intercourse, no longer restricted by Japanese isolationism, was helping to drive Japan forward. From this American perspective, the Japanese, unlike their still-indolent Asian neighbors, were demonstrating their capacity for progress by adopting Western technology. The Japanese were determined, commented one writer, to learn the lessons of history, which were replete with examples of less-advanced races facing degradation or extermination at the hands of European nations. Wisely, the Japanese were abandoning their antiquated systems and adopting "more advanced customs."[2]

Although Japan had not yet achieved a level of civilization equal to that of the West, many Americans marvelled at the eagerness and rapidity with which it was advancing. After shedding its dual system of government, Japan had established new schools and begun practicing religious toleration. The government was attempting to abolish "promiscuous bathing" (at least in the districts accessible to foreigners). Japanese steamships plied the coasts, while railroad and telegraph lines stretched farther across the land. The mighty forces of steam and electricity were propelling civilization on its continuing westward march. As the old Japan gave way to the new, the Japanese were taking their place among the civilized. Japan was becoming a "Star in the East."[3]

But Japan also began to undermine American preconceptions about Western superiority. In the early Meiji period, several American analysts noted that Japan had an ancient, refined, and dynamic civilization quite distinct from and in some respects superior to Western civilization: they found the Japanese an industrious, quick-witted, and noble people. Even though Japan was assimilating Western ideas, many Americans acknowledged that it had a civilization of its own from which the West might learn. In this view, because Japan was already civilized, its assimilation of Western ideas was not necessarily an unadulterated improvement. The Japanese were attempting to "'conform'—we will not say 'elevate themselves'—to the standards of Western civilization," insisted the *Nation*. To many Americans, Japanese traditions merited investigation and understanding. Western indifference, they charged, stood as the primary obstacle preventing Japan from receiving the respect it deserved.[4]

Two characteristics, politeness and cleanliness, frequently
caught the eyes of foreign observers and convinced them that
the Japanese had long been civilized. From customs officials to
the lower classes, the Japanese were more polite than any other
people these foreigners had encountered. Civility, Americans reported, was commonplace. The Japanese seemed to be born with
virtues that Americans had to be taught and were remarkably
courteous toward strangers, despite the arrogance and fraud
practiced by some foreign residents. Indeed, journalist Edward
H. House observed that to be the dinner guest in a Japanese
home was to enjoy an evening so hospitable and refined that one
might easily mistake the setting for that of a fashionable Man-
hattan salon.[5]

Cleanliness, another American hallmark of civilization, was
also a Japanese characteristic that captivated visitors. The
macadamized streets of Yokohama were swept daily; buildings
were "scrupulously" clean and bright. This trait, too, contrasted
with the vaunted "civilization" of Japan's visitors. While Americans littered their neighborhoods with broken glass and stray
cats, the Japanese cultivated landscape gardens. "If this is barbarism," declared one New Yorker, "save me from civilization."[6]

Noteworthy proponents of Japan in the 1870s and 1880s included three prolific writers: House, Edward S. Morse, and
William Elliot Griffis. And all three played prominent roles in
constructing American discourses on Japan. Writers on Japan
often divided into two camps: those who advocated secular and
scientific progress and those who championed Christianity as
the indispensable prerequisite for progress. House and Morse
represented the former position and frequently found themselves at odds with the missionary community. House staunchly
defended Japan against Western encroachment—diplomatic and
cultural—and was outspoken in his public criticism of missionary beliefs and activities. Morse aroused missionary ire because

he introduced Darwin's theory of evolution to Japan in numerous public lectures. Griffis, the most widely published and well-known American expert on Japan in the last quarter of the nineteenth century, was a firm believer in the primacy of Christianity, but also found much to respect in Japan and avoided the temptation to see it only as heathen. Although all three were employed as teachers in Japan, their greatest influence radiated from their work as teachers of the American public. Because their diverse writings encouraged Americans to recognize and appreciate Japan's achievements, the Japanese government decorated all three for their contributions.

Even among this trio of talented men, House's resume stands out as the most eclectic. Before going to Japan in 1869, House had worked as a musician, theatrical manager, and journalist. A former Civil War correspondent for the *New York Tribune*, he taught English and literature at Kaisei Gakkō but would make his most lasting mark as a writer and newspaper editor. After his first decade in Japan, he summarized his part in American-Japanese relations: "To lead my own countrymen to a just appreciation of this pleasant land, and of those who inhabit it, has been my self-assigned task for many years."[7]

House was among the first to decry American ignorance on Japanese topics. Criticizing the tendency to see Japan as quaint or grotesque, he asserted that its relations with the world were a matter for serious attention. Japan had abolished feudalism in a single stroke and was now claiming a respectable position alongside the civilized nations. House approached his task with wit as well as conviction. He delighted in lampooning the archetypal foreign resident who fancied himself a "pioneer of civilization" and whose "belt [was] an arsenal," despite the fact, House wryly noted, that no American or European city was as free from disorder and crime as Tokyo. Tourists also felt the sting of his pen; too many, he wrote, were convinced that only a few days were necessary to establish a full acquaintance with Japan. Each evening they retreated to the billiard tables and French restaurant of Yokohama, failing to understand that Japan's most interesting feature was its people. House complained that sightseers, after traveling thousands of miles, were impressed only by that which most resembled themselves.[8]

Those foreigners who made the effort, he asserted, could see daily proof of Japan's progress. As evidence, House introduced Dr. Matsumoto, a "talented and representative Japanese" who accepted only nominal payment from his patients. Matsumoto also recommended beer as a nutritional supplement—a step, House noted, that had boosted the good doctor's popularity both within and beyond the precincts of his hospital. While hosting a banquet that House attended, Matsumoto offered for the amusement of his guests a comic skit in which the characters Science and Truth conquer Neurosis, Paralysis, and Pyrosis by tricking the diseases into sampling the doctor's wholesome beer. The audience vigorously cheered the players, and House observed that it was a constant pleasure to applaud such enlightened activities. (Imagine the likely response of missionaries, who already disapproved of House's affinity for alcohol.)[9]

Less acerbic and droll than House, Griffis nonetheless was also an effective interpreter and advocate of Japan. He became familiar to American readers as a frequent contributor to the leading journals of the Gilded Age. The author of several books, he produced the era's most influential work on Japan, *The Mikado's Empire*, which was first published in 1876 and reached its twelfth edition in 1913. Always a popular writer among evangelical Americans as well, he published articles in their magazines and wrote missionary biographies.

Griffis's path to Japan began in New Brunswick, New Jersey. While studying at Rutgers College in 1865–69, he had befriended and taught Japanese students, among whom were two of Iwakura Tomomi's sons and a future interpreter for the Iwakura Embassy. Several of these students had been sent to study in New Brunswick by Guido Verbeck and Samuel Brown, Reformed Dutch Church missionaries. (Members of the church had founded Queen's College, a forerunner of Rutgers, in the eighteenth century.) In 1870, Verbeck and the Board of Foreign Missions of the Reformed Church, working at the request of the daimyo of Echizen, recruited Griffis to teach natural science at the domain's school in Fukui, Echizen's capital, near the Sea of Japan. The Rutgers connection to Japan continued when Griffis, at the request of an official from Shizuoka, recruited his classmate and friend Edward Warren Clark to teach there. Griffis taught in Fukui from March 1871 to January 1872 and then moved to Tokyo, where he joined Verbeck and House in teaching at Kaisei Gakkō until he left Japan in July 1874.[10]

Although not a missionary, Griffis was a devout Christian. He studied at Rutgers Theological Seminary for one year before going to Japan, and after returning to the United States he studied at Union Theological Seminary. After graduating in 1877, he went on to serve as pastor of Reformed and Congregational churches in upstate New York and Boston. While in Japan he shared the missionaries' confidence in the links between Christianity and civilization but was puzzled at first by the incongruities that he believed he had found there: indecency and immorality existed side by side with modesty and chastity.[11] Gradually he realized both that the Japanese were more like Americans than he had expected and that there was much more to admire in Japan than he had anticipated. While he championed Christianity, he also publicly praised Japan's capacity for secular reform.

His initial impressions, however, differed little from those of his tourist and missionary compatriots. In *The Mikado's Empire*, Griffis recorded his first glimpses of Japan after steaming into

Yokohama aboard the *Great Republic* in December 1870. After a handful of missionaries greeted him, the first curiosities to catch his notice were the cries of scantily clad laborers, whom he thought were being treated more like animals than men. Traveling on to Tokyo, Griffis stayed with the Verbecks, attended church, and went sightseeing in and around the city. When he signed his teaching contract with Echizen officials in Tokyo, he noted that it did not specifically mention religion but granted him freedom from duties on Sundays. Another clause, one that greatly amused him, prohibited him from getting drunk. He left Yokohama on 22 February 1871 and traveled for ten days by foot, boat, palanquin, and horseback to reach his teaching post in Fukui, about two hundred miles to the west. (As a foreign employee of the government, Griffis was permitted to travel to his post beyond the ten-*ri* limit imposed by the treaties.)[12]

Throughout the rest of his life, Griffis would make much of his months in Fukui, which he believed gave him unique insight into Japan. He regularly depicted himself as one of the few white men to have lived in a feudal capital, remote from Western influence—a nineteenth-century man living in a twelfth-century land without street cars or the "snorting locomotive." Riding his horse through the streets and catching his first glimpses of Fukui, however, Griffis felt his heart sink. It was a poor and muddy town, a tremendous disappointment compared to the magnificent "Oriental" city he had imagined. Disillusion soon turned to apprehension when he met his new students: "with their characteristic dress, swagger, fierce looks, bare skin exposed at the scalp, neck, arms, calves, and feet, with their murderous swords in their belts, they impressed upon my memory a picture of feudalism I shall never forget." Griffis wondered how long it would require to civilize them.[13]

Yet by the end of his months in Fukui, he came to believe that the Japanese, at heart, were just like Americans. His account of life in feudal Japan was sympathetic and balanced, rarely veering toward either condescension or romance. His every encounter with its people proved them to be friendly and generous. Those he had feared to be barbarians were, in fact, his peers. He described his students as eager and intelligent gentlemen who were able to teach much to him. To recognize the common humanity of Japanese and Americans, he concluded, was to understand a trite yet novel truth.[14]

When Griffis left Fukui to take a teaching position in Tokyo, he realized just how quickly Japan—and he—had changed. A few months before his departure, he had seen a momentous transformation that touched both the national and the provincial capitals. On 1 October 1871, he had attended the official ceremony marking the transfer of authority in Echizen from the local daimyo to the central government in Tokyo (formerly known as Edo). "Feudalism is dead," he wrote. "Progress is everywhere the watchword." Back in Tokyo, after an absence of just one year, he scarcely recognized the city. It was filled with carriages, colleges, and hospitals. The first railway was nearly finished. Less nudity and more clothes were visible. The city now was modern, Griffis reported. "An air of bustle, activity, and energy prevails. . . . Old Yedo has passed away forever. Tōkiō, the national capital, is a cosmopolis." In Yokohama, he discovered that he now saw foreigners through new eyes. Hairy, hideous, and overbearing, they appeared to him as they did to the Japanese. Life in Fukui, he wrote, had given him "the ken of a native."[15]

Sharing House's self-assigned task, Griffis summarized his agenda in the preface of *The Mikado's Empire*. He praised Japan as the first Asian nation to enter modern life. But despite this achievement, he protested, the West still considered Japan an enigma; in American eyes, Japan was a land of either licentiousness or purity, treachery or innocence. From his newly discovered perspective, Griffis urged his readers to cast aside these facile portraits: "It is time to drop the license of exaggeration, and, with the light of common day, yet with sympathy and without prejudice, seek to know what Dai Nippon is and has been."[16] Griffis and many other observers of Japan discovered that such a light revealed flaws in the conventional American hierarchies of race and challenged American assumptions about civilization and progress.

Like Griffis, Alice Mabel Bacon worked in Japan as a teacher and, after returning home, described her experiences in essays and books that attracted large audiences. Bacon candidly declared that living in Japan had changed her ideas. The word "civilization" had become much more difficult to define and understand: "I do not know what it means now as well as I did when I left home."[17] Seen from across the Pacific, the semicivilized Japanese fit comfortably into American beliefs; in Fukui or Tokyo, however, Americans were surprised to find a civilized people. When writers like House, Griffis, and Bacon concluded that the Japanese possessed a distinct, complex civilization, they called into question the assumption that Christian Anglo-Saxons had a monopoly on civilization.

Indeed, to these Americans, Japan was more civilized than the United States. They confessed themselves to be ill-bred in comparison with the Japanese, who by every right could call their visitors barbarians. The conventional categories of civilization and barbarism, of progress and stagnation did not hold true, finally leading some Western analysts to reverse the conventional labels. Nearly two decades before Frederick Jackson Turner described the meeting of "savagery and civilization" on the American frontier, Americans in Japan entertained the notion that they had come to the Pacific frontier as savages to meet the civilized Japanese. In the opening sentence of *The Mikado's Empire*, Griffis added another twist to this juxtaposition by reversing the standard use of compass directions to denote geographical regions. Japan, which had once been in "the far-off Orient, is now our nearest Western neighbor"; the Japanese were "the wise men from the West."[18] Most Americans, of course, persisted in the belief that modern Western civilization was dominant and that Japan had to adopt significant components of it to keep pace. But many others argued that the West should recognize the merits of Japanese civilization. If Japan was already civilized, they asserted, then its assimilation of Western ideas was not necessarily an advance. They developed a cultural relativism as they urged their readers to recognize that Japan, by transforming itself, might become richer but not happier.[19]

Griffis's three-and-a-half years among the Japanese convinced him that they were a gracious and civilized people, yet ultimately he fell back on his underlying faith in the primacy of Christianity. While modern science would enlighten the darkened minds of "pagan" Japanese peasants, this chemistry and physics teacher believed, Christianity was necessary to completely remove the superstitions that blocked the path of civilization. In his conclusion to *The Mikado's Empire*, Griffis expressed his hope that, with Christianity to guide it, Japan would gain equality with the world's leading nations. He prayed that the march of civilization would continue to follow the sun across the Pacific. But, he contended, Japan's mighty reform efforts would prove futile without a Christian foundation: "Can a nation appropriate the fruits of Christian civilization without its root? I believe not." If pagan Japan attempted to regenerate itself materially without a corresponding spiritual and social transformation, the Japanese would "fall like the doomed races of America." Two decades later, when asked by the editor of the *Missionary Review of the World* to contribute an article on the religions of Japan, Griffis was even more confident. In his eyes, failure was the feature common to Shinto, Buddhism, and Confucianism. The relationship between the morality of these religions and that of Christianity was akin to the relationship between the jellyfish and higher forms of life. All the "borrowed furniture of modern civilization" was not enough to make Japan an equal of the West. He ended by restating nearly verbatim the conclusion of *The Mikado's Empire*.[20]

It should come as no surprise that American missionaries and Griffis agreed on many points. Like him, they initially found much to admire in Japan's rapid assimilation of Western civilization but later came to lament its reluctance to convert to Christianity. As early as 1870, when the prohibition of Christianity remained in full effect, Verbeck and Hepburn had reported on Japan's "unmistakable, remarkable progress": a telegraph was operating and a railroad was being constructed between Tokyo and Yokohama; the army and navy were being reorganized; and many men of the upper classes were adopting Western attire. Both missionaries admiringly recounted the Japanese thirst for Western learning and science. They worried, though, that the Japanese remained suspicious of Christianity despite their attraction to things Western.[21]

As the Japanese plunged into "the rushing tide of modern life," missionaries emphasized the need for acceptance of Christian principles and refused to believe that Shinto and Buddhism would continue to satisfy minds opened by Western science. "[T]rue progress," insisted Clark, "depends more upon the development of sound principles within the heart of the nation, than it does upon costly importation of material appliances from without." America's "pagan neighbor" had not yet seen the light that it claimed to seek.[22]

Even worse, missionaries feared, Buddhism, which they called "a light that does not illumine," was keeping Japan in spiritual darkness. In a missionary poem, a dying Buddhist offers plaintive prayers to Buddha, who is depicted as an unhearing, pitiless idol offering no salvation to his followers.

> Is there no light? There's none! No help I see;
> None comes in answer to my bitter cry,—
> "A-mi-da-Buddha! save!" Alas for me!
> Alas! In darkness I am left to die.[23]

In the late 1870s and 1880s, missionaries grew increasingly concerned that Buddhism was stretching its shadows into the United States as well. In fact, American interest in Buddhism grew sharply in 1879, when the British writer Edwin Arnold published *The Light of Asia*. Favorably compared by Oliver Wendell Holmes to Shakespeare and the New Testament, this blank-verse account of Buddha's life sold at least half a million copies (many in unauthorized editions).[24] While missionaries toiled in heathen fields abroad, it seemed that their brothers and sisters at home were increasingly sympathetic to the very faith they were laboring to defeat. Missionary magazines responded quickly to this frightening phenomenon by recounting Buddhism's perceived weaknesses and failures.

They imagined Arnold's readers asking, If Buddhism truly is the light of Asia, then why do the Japanese need the light of Christ? In reply, missionary writers first attacked as a hideous joke the notion that Buddhism was enlightening. From Nagasaki, Elizabeth Russell reminded her readers that Buddha's followers basked not in light but in "ignorance and darkness and superstition." Most missionaries assumed that they had already familiarized their supporters at home with the specific characteristics of heathen societies; it was enough merely to remind Americans of heathen illiteracy, idolatry, and impurity.[25]

Missionaries charged, too, that Buddhism was atheism. Buddha was only a man, not a god, and his religion offered to its adherents no personal, divine creator. It thus could save no soul. According to its tenets, one did good not for the benefit of others, but as part of a perpetual, selfish scramble to achieve a vaguely defined Nirvana.[26]

And what of this Nirvana? Evangelical writers derided what they considered to be the ambiguous facade masking this concept and in its place substituted specific definitions. Nirvana, they proclaimed, was a renunciation of affection, a loss of consciousness, and eternal sleep. Those who passed into Nirvana were, like Buddha himself, "utterly unconcerned and stupidly apathetic." Christ, on the other hand, represented the quickening of affection, blissful consciousness, and eternal life. How could such a choice be difficult? missionaries asked. Spreading the light of Christianity continued to be vitally important despite Japan's progress, they averred, for behind the "veneer of material civilization," the Japanese were living and dying "without hope and without God."[27]

Arnold was not the only author who provoked American missionaries: House did so too with *Yone Santo*, a serial novel in the *Atlantic Monthly*. Its central characters include two missionary sisters, "curiously unintelligent and illiterate professors of a narrow and microscopic Christianity." Wolves disguised as lambs, they are incapable of recognizing anything good in Japan. The sisters unjustly condemn as wicked the title character, a young woman unhappily married to a coarse womanizer, simply because a young American globe-trotter attempted to romance her after her marriage. During a cholera epidemic, however, Yone nurses one of the sisters back to health. Ungrateful, the missionary recovers, but Yone herself is stricken and dies.[28]

Real-life missionaries reacted quickly, flooding the *Atlantic Monthly* with letters of protest and denouncing House in the religious press. Reassuring their supporters that the story was a grotesque caricature, "simply impossible" and "absurdly untrue," they accused House of stewing in prejudice toward missionaries and working to exclude from Japan all Western influence. Missionary women were nothing like those House had created; rather, they had done much for Japanese women and earned their trust. New York's *Independent*, a Congregational journal, wondered whether House himself was any more moral than those he attempted to discredit.[29]

Although they were loath to admit it, House and missionary women did share one view. All were sharp critics of the low status of Japanese women. In *Yone Santo* and the *Tokio Times*, which House had edited, he outspokenly condemned the blind obedience expected of Japanese women: foreigners wrongly pretended, he wrote, that Japanese women degraded themselves by eagerly surrendering to prostitution. House considered them victims rather than sinners. Indeed, he based *Yone Santo* loosely on incidents in his own life; he had adopted a former Japanese pupil as his daughter after learning that she was in a troubled marriage and on the verge of suicide. For their part, missionary women also attempted to disprove to American audiences the allegation that Japanese women were especially licentious. Like House, they identified repressive social mores as the culprit behind the debasement of Japanese women. These common sympathies, however, went unrecognized in the fray over *Yone Santo*.[30]

The criticism of House eventually took its toll. The *Atlantic's* publisher, Houghton, Mifflin and Company, had offered House a book contract for the story, but when the deluge of protest letters began, his editor pleaded with him to soften some of its harsher passages about missionaries. Taking great exception, House refused. Although the *Atlantic* continued the story to its end, Houghton Mifflin declined to publish it as a book. After other large publishers rejected the project, House turned to a smaller press.[31]

In a blistering postscript to the book, House described the campaign against *Yone Santo* and took a few last shots at the missionaries, who, he charged, were less intelligent than the average Japanese. He denounced the conviction that Japan had to adopt Christianity in order to be regarded as a sovereign equal of the Western powers. Besides, he wrote, even if Japan became a Christian nation of its own accord, the missionaries would not be appeased: "Perpetual paganism is preferable, in their estimation, to any form of Christianity not prescribed and regulated by their body."[32]

Arnold and House had challenged the missionaries on their own ground: the two approached the question of civilization and progress from the perspective of morality. The West, they claimed, had little if anything to teach the East about ethical behavior. But given House's own descriptions of Japanese gender relations and the steady stream of articles in the religious press on the same topic, Americans who were inclined to doubt the existence of heathen morality had at hand substantial evidence to support their suspicions.

Thus Arnold and House learned a hard lesson. Even though evangelical Americans acknowledged that Japan had demonstrated a capacity for material progress, they would not budge from their belief that such an advance was precarious without the corresponding moral progress of Christian conversion. This pair of writers, by contending that Buddhism offered ample light and that the missionaries themselves were benighted, had provoked a spirited defense of the claim that Christianity was the sine qua non of modern civilization. In all likelihood, then, the works of Arnold and House changed few minds and appealed only to those already sympathetic to the idea that morality was possible without Christianity.

A more difficult challenge to mission work came when "scientific paganism" reared its head. As discussed earlier, Spencer's work supported the idea of racial and social hierarchies. But Spencer and Darwin loomed as threatening figures to many religious Americans, who believed that theories of evolution attempted to banish all divine influence from the universe. As early as the 1870s, not long after the Japanese government began to tolerate Christian evangelism, missionaries discovered that Western teachers—ostensible representatives of Christendom—were planting seeds of skepticism among Japanese students and intellectuals. Worse, a frightening number of Japanese actively sought to separate Western religion from Western learning. The Japanese seemed to have a special aptitude, from the missionaries' perspective, for adopting the vices as well as the virtues of Western civilization. Missionaries, who considered Japan a mission field "white for the harvest," were dismayed to find foreign "skeptics and infidels" reaping a bounty among the Japanese.[33] Conflicts between American proponents of religious views of civilization and proponents of secular views erupted in Japan and spilled back into the United States.

Across the denominations, missionaries censured the "atheists" who were trying to convince the Japanese that religion and science were incompatible. Enlisting in the missionaries' cause was Joseph Cook, the celebrated preacher who delivered Tremont Temple's popular Boston Monday Lectures for nearly two decades. In these addresses, for which he claimed a published circulation of one million, Cook frequently explored the relationship between religion and science. In an 1882 visit to Japan, he did the same in lectures that he later repeated in Boston. Speaking before Japanese and foreign audiences from Tokyo to Nagasaki, he urged his listeners to reject agnosticism and to distinguish "between the cream of the Occident and its driftwood and scum." The latter were worldly men, ignorant and blind, who dismissed the Bible as a collection of fables that science had debunked. Missionaries had come to Japan girded to fight heathenism and now realized that they were fighting a battle against heathenism and Western scientific skepticism combined.[34]

Only in the rarest case did the missionaries identify and denounce agnostic instructors by name; instead, they targeted the works of Western authors whose popularity in Japan fueled indifference or hostility toward Christianity. Cook, missionary leaders, and prominent Japanese Christians listed these "atheistic" or "agnostic" works in the American religious press. The works of Darwin and Spencer regularly appeared, along with Henry Thomas Buckle's *History of Civilization in England* and John William Draper's *History of the Conflict between Religion and Science*.[35] Missionaries did not exaggerate the influence of these scholars. Buckle's work, for example, was first translated into Japanese in 1874, and influential journals such as *Meiroku zasshi* printed extracts. As a Japanese student at the school founded by Fukuzawa Yukichi recalled, "When Buckle's *Civilization in England* first appeared the whole atmosphere of Keiō Gijuku suddenly changed. People ceased altogether to study the Bible." And in the last quarter of the nineteenth century, Japanese publishers produced at least thirty-two translations of works by Spencer. A missionary who taught at Keiō complained that its students were unusually difficult to convert because Spencer's writings were used as textbooks. To readers of the *Missionary Herald*, another Japanese student provided what he considered a disturbing account of life at Tokyo University, where he was unable to find a single copy of the Bible in the library. Students instead read the texts of skeptics. The result? His colleagues learned to smoke, to drink, and to despise all moral principles.[36]

To the dismay of their evangelical critics, both Buckle and Draper praised the progressive features of scientific skepticism and discounted the achievements of religion. Buckle, who emphasized the influence of geography and climate on the development of civilizations, informed his readers that reason and skeptical inquiry had done more than faith to advance European civilization. Religion was the effect, not the cause, of mankind's improvement. As for Draper, the very title of his work incited the devout. Those who looked past the cover found that he wasted no time in stoking the fires. Faith was stationary, he asserted in his preface, and therefore incompatible with the progressive nature of science. Draper was primarily anti-Catholic (a bias shared by most Protestant missionaries), but the broad sweep of his presentation often failed to distinguish between denominations. Missionaries could hardly fail to be offended when Draper concluded, "Faith must render an account of herself to Reason. Mysteries must give place to facts."[37]

If Buckle and Draper were difficult for missionaries to stomach, Darwin made their blood boil. In Japan, his foremost Western disciple was Edward S. Morse, who relished the role in his many public presentations. No infidel was more prominent and threatening to missionaries. Morse had polished his oratorical skills in the United States, where he had traveled across the country to speak on the natural sciences. Morse even lectured on evolution to his fellow passengers on the steamer to Japan. After returning home, he added new subjects to his repertoire. At Boston's Lowell Institute in 1882, Morse presented a course of twelve standing-room-only lectures that had an especially significant effect. Among those in the crowd was Percival Lowell. His father, the institute's trustee, had commissioned Morse to deliver the talks, which persuaded the future author of The Soul of the Far East to visit Japan.[38]

On his Japanese audiences, Morse had a different effect: as a scientist, he introduced the theory of natural selection. Although he never finished high school, he had served a two-year apprenticeship under the renowned naturalist Louis Agassiz at Harvard's Museum of Comparative Zoology. Morse gradually rejected his mentor's creationism and in 1873 publicly endorsed evolution. Four years later, while visiting Japan to study brachiopods, he accepted an offer to serve as professor of zoology at the newly established Tokyo University. Morse soon came to regard both the entire nation and its foreign community as his classroom. During his residences there in 1877–79 and 1882–83, he spoke at universities, scholarly societies, and public lecture associations, where he introduced Darwinian evolution to large audiences that included university students, members of the imperial family, officials, and foreign residents. While Darwin's *The Descent of Man* (1871) had been published in Japanese in 1874, *The Origin of Species* (1859) was not translated until 1896. But a Japanese-language outline of Morse's lectures on Darwinism sold out quickly in 1878, and his lecture series was published in Japanese in 1883.[39]

An engaging and persuasive speaker, Morse used familiar zoological examples from Japan to illustrate his lectures. To that same end, he relied on his ambidexterity and his earlier career as a mechanical draftsman: he used both hands simultaneously to continually sketch figures on a blackboard, a feat that never failed to amaze his audiences. Equally impressed was Philadelphia's Wistar Institute of Anatomy. Hoping to discover an anatomical basis for ambidexterity, the institute asked Morse for permission to posthumously examine his brain. This man of science consented and promised to have it sent "when I am done with it." For the last twelve years of his life, Morse was in possession of a specimen jar on which was etched his name and birthdate.[40]

At his first appearances in Japan, Morse enjoyed full command of the stage and was delighted to find that his audiences were not warped by "theological prejudice." To *Popular Science Monthly* he reported that the Japanese were pleased to learn that some foreigners espoused beliefs different than those taught by the missionaries. And Morse's views were quite different indeed. He considered the missionary enterprise to be hypocritical and thought that the Yokohama foreign settlement, Christendom's representative, was the most "indecent and corrupt" city in Japan. If this was the best that Christians could do, he wondered, why attempt to propagate Christianity? He made little effort to conceal his jaundiced opinion of evangelism and religion in general, beginning the first lecture in his series on evolution with the motto: "To study the truth of things and not to follow the doctrines of religion." Morse served as an important expert on Darwinism and triggered great Japanese interest in evolutionary theory. Missionaries soon set their sights on this Darwinian heretic, whose public addresses had created for him a high profile.[41]

Fearing that Morse's untiring skepticism would destroy much of what they had built, missionaries adopted a dual strategy. At a monthly missionary conference in Tokyo, they decided to make him the special subject of their prayers. At the same time, declining to rely exclusively on divine intervention, they took to the lecture stage themselves to rebut Morse's views. This latter tactic proved necessary because Morse's energy showed no sign of flagging.[42]

Leading the public charge against him was Henry Faulds, a Scottish Presbyterian medical missionary. The founder of Tsukiji Hospital, Faulds believed that God had called him to be Morse's antagonist. At the hospital's weekly discussion series and in a tract published by the Congregational Church mission, he denounced Morse as an atheist. Pursuing his adversary with righteous zeal, he spoke against evolution at Morse's presentations, and in long letters to the *Japan Gazette* he ridiculed the Darwinist as a "blundering" and "blustering school-boy." Ironically, Faulds's own lasting contribution to science was made possible by Morse: Faulds was among the first scientists to hypothesize that fingerprints were unique to each individual, an idea inspired by his inspection of finger impressions on ancient Japanese pottery fragments excavated by Morse.[43]

Christian organizations, both foreign and Japanese, also took up the fight against Darwinism. The Tokyo Christian Association inaugurated its own lecture courses, including a series by Faulds, to demonstrate that evolutionary theory was insufficient without theism. The influential Christian magazine *Rikugō zasshi* argued that Japan's moral progress was lagging behind its material progress and repeatedly criticized Morse's lectures on evolution. Also joining the contest was the recently established Young Men's Christian Association of Tokyo, which sponsored symposia on Christianity and science that attracted audiences numbering in the thousands. These gatherings, however, did not always provide a home-field advantage to the missionaries and their converts. Instead, one Japanese Christian likened them to battlefields where the audiences were equally divided.[44]

The offensive against Morse reached to the United States as well. In the *New York Herald*, an anonymous correspondent condemned him as a dangerous eccentric who poisoned Japanese minds by ridiculing Christianity as a faith for the ignorant. Verbeck entered the field when he speculated in the *Independent* that students enjoyed listening to this skeptic's lectures but had no real respect for him. No doubt Morse had these episodes in mind when he later wished for a process of natural selection that would weed out the ill-mannered.[45]

Morse left Japan in early 1883, but theories of evolution did not. Hence, the missionaries continued their crusade. In the same year, Charles S. Eby, a Canadian Methodist missionary, organized a weekly lecture series on Christianity and civilization. Presented in English and Japanese at a large Tokyo auditorium, the series drew audiences of four to eight hundred and attracted the endorsement of Western diplomats: at the first two lectures, the American and British ministers presented introductory remarks. U.S. Minister John A. Bingham, a devout Presbyterian, paid tribute to evangelical belief by noting that Christianity was the mother of modern civilization.[46]

At the podium, Eby focused on Spencer, the high priest of scientific paganism himself. Although Spencer had shaped American views on racial capabilities and social evolution, most missionaries rejected his work, charging that it recognized no place for God: Spencer depicted science as knowledge and religion as the absence of knowledge and thus had written a manifesto against God's existence. They were partially correct. Spencer did indeed denounce religion as "irrational" but acknowledged that it addressed questions utterly beyond the bounds of scientific study and comprehension: religion's field of inquiry was "the unknowable." Scientists therefore had no business speculating on spiritual matters, and theologians had no business expounding on material phenomena, such as evolution. In Eby's critique, he noted that all healthy nations advance toward higher levels of civilization. There could be no true civilization, however, without morality, and no morality without religion. He urged his audiences to recognize that adopting Spencer's Synthetic Philosophy as a lodestar for modern progress would be a tragic mistake: it resembled Christian morality no more than an ape resembled a man. Only Christianity could withstand the testing of reason and science. It was, therefore, "the soul of all true progress."[47]

Eby's lectures did little to undermine Spencer's influence or to eliminate evangelical-secular tensions. Like Darwinian theory, the Synthetic Philosophy inspired moderation in neither its enemies nor its friends. Among Spencer's greatest admirers was Lafcadio Hearn, whose influence as a writer on Japan eventually equalled that of Griffis. Hearn refused to listen idly to attacks on Spencer and argued heatedly with missionaries in a barrage of letters to Yokohama's *Weekly Mail*, a volley so intense that it

caught the attention of the *New York Times*. Hearn, a British ex-
patriate who spent most of his life in the United States and Japan
working as a journalist, author, and teacher, accused the missionaries of evading the real antagonism between religion and
science.[48] Wishing in private that the missionaries could be taken
out to sea and scuttled, he publicly denounced them for using
evil as a means to achieve an imaginary good. Hearn made a
memorable debut as a literary interpreter of Japan: in the preface to his first essay collection, he claimed that the Japanese were
morally superior to Christians and had nothing to gain from
Christianity. The *Missionary Review of the World* responded by
labeling him "a malignant hater of Christ."[49]

Amidst the fervor of Morse, Faulds, Eby, and Hearn, some attempted to find a middle ground. Not all Christians took issue
with Darwinian or Spencerian theories of evolution. Missionary
and scientist John T. Gulick attempted to reconcile biological
evolution with Christianity during his 1878–79 lectures at
Dōshisha, a Congregational college in Kyoto. Noting that he
himself believed in evolution, Gulick cautioned that its laws and
causes were not yet clearly understood. The theory of natural selection did not address the question of the origin of life, he
stated, nor could it explain why variation so often moved along
the lines of progress. Like so many of his colleagues, Gulick was
concerned about the influence of such skeptics as Morse, but as a
scientist he tried to bridge the gap that separated religious and
secular views. Griffis—once a science teacher, now a clergyman—occupied a similar position. Referring to Spencer's theories as the "bastard philosophy of Christendom," he nonetheless
maintained that Spencer accepted the existence of God.[50]

Spencer thus continued to be subject to a variety of interpretations. In his Synthetic Philosophy he supported the notion
that societies existed on a spectrum from barbarism to civilization, but he also insisted that societies could progress whether or

not they were Christian. To Lowell in *The Soul of the Far East*, Spencer's philosophy provided a theoretical framework for characterizing Japan as an immature civilization. To skeptics like Hearn, however, Spencer offered a secular teleology that allowed them to discount or discredit Christian theology. They seized on Spencer's claim that organisms, both biological and social, evolved toward greater complexity. These progressive phenomena could be investigated and understood. Theological speculation about divine origins was insignificant and futile, these skeptics declared, when compared with the knowledge that could be gained by studying physical and social phenomena. But missionaries considered the evolutionary theories of Darwin and Spencer to be atheistic and believed their advocates to be a primary cause behind Japan's reluctance to accept Christianity. Nevertheless, Japan was an ill omen to those who assumed that Christianity and civilization were inseparable.

Japan thus became a test case in which a variety of Americans evaluated their assumptions about the relationships among civilization, religion, and science. Skeptics saw a sharp line separating religion from science and believed that civilization was not dependent on religion. Evangelical Americans maintained that religion and science were compatible, but would never concede the separation of the former from civilization. When men of religion and science like Gulick sought to straddle or dissolve the perceived border between religion and evolution, their views often were lost in the din of stridently righteous and skeptical voices. In the 1870s and 1880s, evangelical and secular observers of Japan were separated by seemingly irreconcilable differences.

Although Griffis and Morse disagreed on spiritual matters, they shared a common approach to interpreting Japan. The preface to each man's first book on Japan introduced readers to the goal of objectively examining another culture. Griffis had aspired to examine the Japanese "with sympathy and without prejudice" and hoped his audience would do likewise. In *Japanese Homes and Their Surroundings*, Morse recommended that if one could not shed all biases, "it were better that his spectacles should be rose-colored than grimed with the smoke of prejudice."[51] To a significant degree, other Americans in Japan agreed.

To those not engaged in missions, Japan demonstrated that modern civilization and progress were independent of Christianity. Writers like House and Morse steadfastly refused to doff their rose-colored spectacles and were outspoken in their criticism of missionaries, whose vision they considered to be clouded by prejudice, or, at best, narrowed by the blinders of evangelism. (One cannot doubt—despite their differences—that House, Morse, and the missionaries all had the courage of their respective convictions.) As secular writers attempted to understand and explain Japan, they became cultural relativists. Modern civilization, they believed, did not have to be founded upon Christianity. With a commitment to rational inquiry alone, progress was possible.

Even among devout American Christians, there were those like Griffis who acknowledged high levels of civilization and progress in Japan. Although evangelical at heart, he neither suffered from prejudice nor wore blinders. He and several missionaries willingly recognized admirable qualities in the Japanese and in many of their customs. But evangelical Americans' praise of Japan ended where religion began. Unlike secular analysts, they were not willing to grant legitimacy to the religious foundations of Japanese life. To missionaries, Japan raised sharp concerns. It was not discarding Buddhism, yet it was accomplishing deeds thought to be impossible for a heathen people. Might Japan disprove the causal relationship between Christianity and modern civilization? Evangelical Americans fought mightily against this notion.

The stakes were high. Missionaries and their supporters at home feared that the secular gospel of scientists directly contradicted Christian primacy. Darwin, Spencer, and their followers offered the Japanese a means of circumventing the missionaries in their self-appointed role as the reformers of heathen society. By providing alternative definitions of civilization and progress—definitions not dependent on religion—secular scholars threatened the self-identity of evangelical Americans. If scientific skepticism succeeded in Japan, the missionary enterprise itself might falter. Secular scholars might supplant missionaries and become pagan bearers of false enlightenment to Japan. Missionaries attacked scientific skepticism to protect their project of transforming the world. The competition between secular and evangelical Americans added an element of internal tension to American cultural expansion.

When missionaries disembarked at Yokohama, they had no doubt that a clear, divinely ordained line separated heathen from Christian. Yet their experiences in Japan encouraged some to accept points on a spectrum between the two: the heathen yet civilized Japanese occupied such a point. Moreover, Japan proved the validity of cultural relativism to secular observers, who used Japan as evidence in posing a challenge to conventional American religious beliefs. Japan had begun to undermine American assumptions about religion and civilization. The world no longer easily divided into the heathen and the Christian, the barbarian and the civilized.

Chapter 4

NIRVANA AND HELL

"How pleasant it would be to go off to Japan together and fill our sketch-books with drawings," suggested a character in Henry Adams's 1884 novel, *Esther*. Two years later, Adams took this advice. Still recovering from his wife's recent suicide, he invited artist John La Farge along as his companion on a three-month tour of Japan. Traveling across the United States by rail to depart from San Francisco, La Farge sketched landscapes while Adams read about Buddhism. In Omaha, the two were recognized by a young reporter who asked why they were going to Japan. When La Farge joked that they were in search of Nirvana, the reporter retorted that they were too late in the season.[1]

La Farge and other American artists who visited Japan in the late nineteenth century soon came to fear that this reporter was correct. In Japan, they hoped to experience first-hand what they presumed to be a civilization with unique spiritual qualities. Painters like La Farge shared this view with writers, art scholars, and collectors: accordingly, in this chapter the word "artist" refers to all of these groups. While missionaries condemned Japanese religious and philosophical traditions as morally bankrupt, artists admired Japanese spirituality—particularly Japanese attitudes toward nature—as a valuable artistic resource. They also expected to find picturesque scenes that they could take as subjects for their paintings, books, and essays. Although La Farge had spoken with tongue in cheek, Gilded Age artists did indeed seek out "Nirvana": they sought a Japan that was spiritual and traditional. Once in Japan, however, they lamented that this Japan was rapidly vanishing as its inhabitants tried to westernize.

Such visiting artists introduced a new issue into American-Japanese relations. Discussions of civilization and religion were facets of an American discourse that also included an antimodernist challenge to the definition of progress; artists disparaged the modern West as a defective model plagued by vulgarity, ugliness, and uniformity. In their works, Japan became a proving ground for American suspicions about progress and modernity.[2]

Foreign artists who spent time in Japan believed that Japanese artistic and cultural traditions were uniquely valuable. If preserved, they believed, these traditions could offset the harmful effects of industrialization and serve as a spiritual refuge from the materialism that they thought afflicted the modern West. Visiting artists familiarized Americans with the idea that Japan was in essence spiritual and traditional, and they declared that this essence possessed a value far surpassing that of Western materialism and progress. Missionaries had gone to Japan *to bring* spiritual regeneration, but artists went *to seek* it.

Hoping to preserve Japanese customs and arts against the forces of change, artists could not envision an authentic Japan that was anything more than the sum of its traditions. Japan, they feared, was on the verge of irreversibly sacrificing its most meaningful customs in a vain effort to gain something beyond its grasp. They doubted that Japan could ever fully succeed in becoming modern: though it was attempting to assimilate, it could do no more than imitate the modern West. Artists thereby played an important role in constructing the enduring stereotype of the Japanese as mimics.

By way of contrast, American statesmen expressed little doubt about Japan's choice of models. From their perspective, Japan had wisely set out to emulate the Western powers in order to merit treaty revision and sovereign equality; by elevating itself both materially and intellectually, Japan had proven a worthy aspirant. In the last quarter of the nineteenth century, ministers to Japan informed the State Department that Japan's new railways, telegraph lines, schools, and constitution had demonstrated "a most remarkable progress in civilization." The Japanese had "cut loose from the moorings of antiquity" and triumphed over their past. Japan had been obliged to prove that it sufficiently resembled the West and was capable of understanding, adopting, and administering Western technology and institutions. Read alone, the American diplomatic discourse on Japanese progress indicates little esteem for Japanese tradition. On the contrary, Japan's ancient customs were considered an impediment to its celebrated progress.[3]

A very different set of images flowed from the brushes and pens of artists. And when they asserted that the West should be learning from Japan, many Americans concurred. Those who took an interest in the unequal treaties were undoubtedly outnumbered by those who succumbed to the "Japanese craze" of the Gilded Age, when Japanese arts and crafts achieved widespread popularity. Inspired by exhibits at Philadelphia's Centennial Exposition (1876) and Chicago's Columbian Exposition (1893), countless Americans collected Japanese-style lacquerware, ceramics, and fans; they decorated their carpets, wallpaper, and doorknobs with Japanese motifs. Artists including James McNeill Whistler, Winslow Homer, and Mary Cassatt studied Japanese aesthetics and created the style of Japonisme, influencing Impressionism, Art Nouveau, and the Arts and Crafts movement.[4] Popular magazines prominently featured visual and verbal portraits of Japan. Enjoying circulations near two hundred thousand, journals like the *Century* and *Harper's Monthly* had lustrous reputations that rested in large part on their high-quality illustrations. As the fictitious manager of a magazine declared in a novel by William Dean Howells, in the twilight of the nineteenth century only a lunatic would publish a magazine without illustrations. In another instance of art imitating life, an editor of Howells's fictitious magazine decorated his studio with Japanese bric-a-brac.[5] In real life, editors recruited artists and writers to produce series on Japan to satisfy the contemporary American fascination with and appropriation of Japanese decorative arts. These images resonated within American society as an everyday, material presence implanted in homes by the Japanese craze.

As noted, American artists carried to Japan a Gilded Age debate over the meaning of progress, their faith having been shaken by the squalor that seemed to be the necessary consequence of industrialization. Progress and nature, which antebellum Americans had seen as compatible, had become antithetical to artists who sought a place where modernity had not yet overwhelmed picturesque tradition and natural beauty.[6] They sought a people who continued to treasure communion with nature.

Their quests also were part of the growing American interest in Buddhism. Arnold, who had sparked this trend with *The Light of Asia*, described Nirvana as a "nameless quiet, nameless joy" and a "change which never changes!" Adams, too, had grappled with Buddhism and the idea of Nirvana. In *Esther*, he had offered his own definition of Nirvana through the voice of an artist modelled after La Farge: Nirvana was paradise, which "consists in seeing God."[7] Discontented with the West's vaunted civilization, American artists were attracted to the supposed timelessness of Japan's artistic and spiritual traditions, in which they presumed Nirvana could be found.

When Adams and La Farge sought Nirvana in Japan, Adams saw only a childish "toy-world" full of fleas, fetid odors, and foul tastes, but his companion was enthralled. Due to a distaste for physical contact, La Farge habitually avoided shaking hands when greeting people by holding a brush in one hand and a handkerchief in the other: the Japanese custom of bowing must have seemed a godsend to him.[8] But more captivating to La Farge and other artists was Japan's beauty. Everything seemed to have been composed "for a painter's delight." Enchanted by Japanese scenery and customs, they likened themselves to lovers unable to intelligibly articulate their feelings. In their writings and illustrations, Japan became a charming and dreamlike land of human and natural beauties, its traditional essence embodied by Japanese women and expressed by the Japanese people's appreciation of nature.[9]

Kimono-clad Japanese women were foremost among the delights described by artists. Japan's "daughters" (*musume*) frequently appeared in text and illustrations as doll-like geisha catering to guests or as graceful "blossoms" in the cherry groves.[10] To artists, traditional Japan was young and feminine, a lovely human subject set before a beautiful natural background. Their accounts described Japanese women as innately traditional creatures who resisted Western innovations and provided a stabilizing influence at the center of Japanese life. Artists attached a feminine gender to Japan's essence by verbally and visually depicting women clothed in traditional attire and engaged in traditional activities.

No writer was more lavish or prominent in his praise of Japanese women than Arnold, whose essays on Japan helped him maintain his popularity in the United States. During his residence in Japan in the early 1890s, he continued to incite missionaries with his outspoken esteem for Buddhism. They confirmed their other suspicions about *The Light of Asia*'s author when the twice-widowed Arnold frequently associated with "native dancing girls" and drew on these experiences for his writings. (In Japan, Arnold married his third wife, Kurokawa Tama.) His *Scribner's* "Japonica" series, illustrated by Robert Blum, set the stage for his well-attended and profitable U.S. speaking tour in 1891–92. It featured sixty-five appearances from New York to Kansas City and attracted such guests as J. Pierpont Morgan, former Secretary of State William M. Evarts, and Columbia University president Seth Low.[11]

In his writings and lectures, Arnold depicted the Japanese *musume* as an angelic being, forever twittering with laughter or plucking a samisen. With "brown-velvet eyes," cheeks carved of "sun-burned ivory," and "small, faultless feet," she was "quick to pleasure, love, and song." Although this sensual idolization could never win the approval of the Christian devout, Arnold agreed with Alice Mabel Bacon and missionary women that social strictures oppressed Japanese women. But, he insisted, these conditions had also brought out the virtues of the *musume*. She belonged to a higher moral plane than the Japanese male. "Civilization and 'woman's rights,'" he feared, might forever spoil her charms, much as a clumsy human hand could destroy a butterfly's wing.[12]

To Arnold and other artists, the attire of Japanese women served as a visual signal that they remained relatively untouched by westernization. In kimono, women epitomized Japan. Nothing was more becoming to the complexion and figure of the Japanese lady, Arnold wrote, than the graceful kimono, and thus the Japanese butterfly should remain unsullied by ill-fitting Western fashion. For a time, however, artists grew troubled when it appeared that the kimono itself was passing out of season. In 1872 the emperor had begun wearing a Western-style military uniform for official ceremonies; the empress and her court adopted Western dress for public appearances in 1886. Griffis worried that Tokyo women might quickly follow her example by donning "the whole foreign toggery of bonnets, skirts, stockings, and shoes." Like other writers, he complained that European costumes on Japanese women robbed them of their native allure.[13]

Missionaries and reformers also took notice of this trend toward Western dress among Japanese women. Some missionary women initially welcomed the empress's change of wardrobe and the attention it brought to them: their female Japanese neighbors rushed to learn about every item of attire, "from our best bonnet to our last article of underwear." As a result, missionaries found a fresh opportunity to spread the gospel, using scissors and sewing machines as new tools in their crusade.[14]

Other American women, though they shared the evangelical hopes of their missionary sisters, doubted the wisdom of such a change in fashion. Led by H. Frances Parmelee, formerly a Congregational missionary in Japan, a group of eminent American women addressed an open letter to Japanese women in 1888. Urging them to reconsider their adoption of Western dress were such signatories as first lady Frances F. Cleveland, Lucretia R. Garfield (widow of former president James A. Garfield), and Frances E. Willard (president of the Woman's Christian Temperance Union). After granting that it was natural for Japanese women to wish to adopt the costume worn by "the women of nearly all civilized nations," the Americans declared that it was nevertheless inadvisable on the grounds of modesty, economy, and health. By closely fitting the upper body, Western dress made women immodestly "conspicuous," they warned; Japanese women were much more elegant and graceful in their familiar kimono. Furthermore, Western skirts and their trimmings were an extravagant waste of material in comparison with the Japanese costume; resources should be devoted toward bringing education and Christianity rather than petticoats to Japanese women. But the worst feature of Western dress, the Americans charged, was without doubt the corset. Dangerously unhealthy, it was more foolish and wicked than the Chinese custom of footbinding. Parmelee and her compatriots concluded the letter by expressing confidence that the women of Japan were too patriotic to endanger their health by abandoning their nation's beautiful costume.[15]

In defense of the new trend, Japanese women pointed out that they were adopting Western attire because it elevated them in the eyes of Japanese and foreign men. In kimono, a Japanese woman was likely to be treated as a servant or "tea-house girl," but in Western dress, she found that her husband allowed her to walk before him in public. "We dress, not for vanity, nor for healthiness," declared one woman, "but in order to get our rights as in civilized Christian countries." To Japanese women, then, their adoption of Western dress was emblematic of female participation in their nation's progress. They did so to demonstrate that women, as well as men, were able to assimilate Western civilization and hence deserved respect.[16]

With the best of intentions, Parmelee and her colleagues advised against this course by voicing a contemporary American concern that whalebone corsets and heavy petticoats had made invalids of too many women. Cautioning Japanese women about fashions that the letter's signatories themselves considered burdensome, they objected to such attire on both Japanese and Western women.[17] Yet in doing so, they reinforced the artists' conviction that the kimono was the only costume appropriate for the Japanese woman.

Those artists who had been dismayed when they began to see Japanese women in Western attire were much relieved when it became apparent in the early 1890s that most remained loyal to the kimono. The change into foreign toggery was merely a brief aberration, after which Western fashions usually were limited to accessories combined with kimono. In La Farge's eyes, the difference between the "ancient" and "modern" Japanese woman might be only the latter's shawl and Western-style umbrella.[18]

Through such concerns, American artists depicted Japanese tradition in gendered terms and positioned themselves as its preservationists. Ernest Fenollosa, a former Tokyo University philosophy professor and an imperial commissioner of arts, was instrumental in convincing the Japanese government to protect the nation's art treasures and in establishing the Tokyo School of Fine Arts. He also undertook this mission personally by assembling an outstanding collection of Japanese paintings, now housed at the Boston Museum of Fine Arts, where he served as head of the Oriental Department in 1890–96. According to Fenollosa, Eastern culture was refined and feminine, in contrast to the modern realism of the masculine West. Prophesying the impending marriage of these two halves of the world, he was optimistic that a new era of humanity was approaching.[19]

Considering themselves especially sensitive to the charms of Japan's women and the vulnerability of its traditional essence, artists believed that they were different than Japanese men, who allegedly neither appreciated nor deserved Japanese women. The West, in their estimation, was feminine Japan's proper suitor and protector. Artists deplored the haste with which Japanese men would "destroy everything, and . . . adopt anything" in order to imitate the West. Clad in wrinkled, ill-fitting suits and unnatural combinations of boots and derbies with Japanese silk trousers (*hakama*), they produced a "grotesque" and "doggedly disreputable" spectacle. In American eyes, westernization and progress were processes ineffectually conducted by the Japanese male, processes that smothered Japan's picturesque feminine charm. Artists linked Japanese tradition with the Japanese female, and imitation with the Japanese male.[20]

American artists were concerned but statesmen were pleased to see the Japanese adopt Western clothing styles. U.S. Minister Richard B. Hubbard, described by Adams as "the pompousest dodgasted [*sic*] old Texan jackass now living," praised this transformation in attire but noted that it was important to supplement this superficial change with corresponding intellectual changes. Addressing the second annual meeting of the Roman Alphabet Association, a Tokyo organization that favored substituting the alphabet for Japan's traditional writing system, Hubbard suggested that "a change in the dress and costume . . . in which you clothe your thoughts and put them on the enduring written and printed page" would bring Japan "into far closer union with all Western nations than the change of the raiment which embraces only the body and not the mind of a great people." In the eyes of this Texan, the closer the resemblance, the better.[21]

Nonetheless, Japanese in Western clothing offended artists' eyes and rarely appeared as subjects in illustrations. To them, too many Japanese men were persistently attempting to reshape, even jettison, elements of Japanese tradition. Artists contended that the Japanese could not fit comfortably into Western attire—material or intellectual. The Japanese might be able to change into the attire of the West or to adopt its institutions, but they could reconfigure neither their bodies nor their minds to match Western forms.

From this perspective, the Japanese were intelligent but shallow. They seemed to lack originality and were foolishly rushing to imitate, not to assimilate, superior Western institutions as well as fashions. According to Lowell, "The imitation pot-hat and accompanying aura of billycockism sit no less comically upon a *kimono* and cloven socks than does a modern Tōkyō court of justice upon an old-fashioned Japanese case." The entire nation, he declared, was in a hypnotic trance of blind imitation.[22]

To the artist, the ideal female subject wore a kimono, while the ideal male subject wore only a loincloth. While, as previously noted, early foreign witnesses differed over whether public nudity in Japan was evidence of innocence or depravity, artists saw in it an opportunity. The rippling muscles of the loincloth-clad laborer were a gift to artistic study.[23]

The greater exposure of the male body also came to signify an inferior status for Japanese men. Theodore Wores's painting *The Return from the Cherry Grove* drew high praise at a New York exhibition, where critics noted the juxtaposition of its female and male subjects: attractive Japanese women laden with blossoms were being pulled home by a swarthy native "steed." A male archetype for artists, the loincloth-clad beast of burden stood at the service of the foreigner and the Japanese woman. He was, as Griffis had first declared in *The Mikado's Empire*, more like a wheelbarrow than a man. Just as artists aspired to protect feminine tradition, then, they devalued the Japanese male. In their verbal and visual illustrations, artists suggested that Japanese men could not be authentically modern: they were either comical mimics or half-naked brutes.[24]

As a result, the Japanese project of modern progress appeared to artists as a case of flawed mimicry. The stereotype of the Japanese as imitators echoes in part the artists' belief that Japanese modernity could be no more than superficial. To American artists, the very act of mimicry underscored the persistence of differences between the mimic and the model. A mimic can only imitate: it can never become the model.[25]

But to most artists, as noted above, being non-Western was a Japanese asset. In *Japanese Homes and Their Surroundings*, Morse's popular book on traditional Japanese architecture, he wrote that refined aesthetic tastes seemed to permeate all social classes: even the keeper of a cheap, rural inn was likely to cultivate a fine, albeit small, landscape garden. Japanese aesthetic traditions, artists asserted, provided the foundation for a country characterized by beauty.[26]

Morse, the disciple of Darwin, became a devotee of Japanese art in 1878, when on his daily walk in Tokyo he happened across a ceramic saucer in the shape of a shell—the object of his zoological studies. His naturalist's predilection for collection and classification now had a new outlet. Although he had no previous aesthetic training, with the assistance of Japanese friends he learned to recognize rare ceramics and soon was "ransacking" old pottery shops, sometimes in the company of Fenollosa (whom he had recruited to teach at Tokyo University). In 1892, the Boston Museum of Fine Arts paid $76,000 for the large collection Morse had gone into debt to assemble and named him its curator.[27]

In *Japanese Homes and Their Surroundings*, he contrasted Japanese and American aesthetics by castigating the interior of the typical American home as a barbarous curio shop: "a maze of vases, pictures, plaques, bronzes, with shelves, brackets, cabinets, and tables loaded down with bric-à-brac." Instead of the materialism and vulgarity associated with American tastes, the Japanese favored simplicity in design and decoration, declining to clutter their homes with odds and ends. They cultivated a "civilized emptiness," La Farge observed admiringly.[28]

The refined aesthetic tastes of the Japanese were most apparent in their understanding and love of nature, a capacity that Hearn believed was embedded in the soul of their race. Americans described the Japanese as enthusiastic travelers, who undertook pilgrimages to see scenic vistas made famous by poets. Closer to home, newspapers announced the opening of the spring blossoms so that families could stroll under the flowering plum and cherry trees and compose verses extolling their beauty. To American artists, Japan became a haven where the mystery of nature continued to be appreciated and cultivated.[29]

Japanese landscapes—the lush vegetation, the hillsides bathed in azaleas, and the summit of Mount Fuji rising through soft clouds—thrilled painters. Unlike Americans, who decorated their city lots "with coal-ashes, tea-grounds, tin cans, and the garbage barrel," the Japanese enhanced their land's beauty, sculpting miniature landscape gardens and terracing the countryside into rice-fields. On a smaller scale, the simplicity of Japanese flower arrangements focused attention on solitary sprigs and facilitated communion with nature.[30]

Humanity and nature in Japan seemed to visiting artists to have achieved an organic, harmonious unity. The natural, the human-made, and the human blended into one another, revealing the mysterious links among them. La Farge's enchantment with the scenic landscape was so intense that he believed it led him to glimpse the meaning of Nirvana: "spirit and matter are one in absolute nature, which in its essence can neither be born nor be dissolved." After an uncomfortable day spent sketching under an umbrella in a steamy rain, trying to capture the light and heat of the mountains and clouds, he felt the spirituality of nature flow into the spirituality of humanity. The external and the internal passed into each other. "The wind whistling through the trees," he remembered, "the river breaking over its rocks, the movements of man and his voice,—or, indeed, his silence,—are the expression of the great mysteries of body, of word, and of thought." The artist had become a pilgrim paying homage to Japan's unspoiled beauty and the spiritual solace it offered. (Imagine La Farge's amusement when, after returning to New York and painting a mural in the Church of the Ascension, a friend complained that it included "pagan" clouds from La Farge's Japanese sketches.)[31]

Hearn, an admirer of Arnold's *Light of Asia*, also caught a glimpse of Nirvana. To him it was synonymous with ephemerality: the world was a mirage. Because change and impermanence characterized all things, the trees and stones of Japan's gardens all too soon would be replaced by factories and mills. He warned that efforts to preserve Japanese customs would only momentarily stave off the inevitable. Nirvana itself, in its Japanese incarnation, was doomed.[32]

To visiting artists, Japan seemed to be rapidly losing the qualities that made it appealing: it was becoming too much like the West. A noose of wires and rails threatened to strangle Japan's essence. The Japanese, American artists believed, should continue their tradition of maintaining harmony with nature. By attempting to control it—by laying railroad tracks and building steamships—the Japanese would reduce themselves to "one dull level of uniformity." Hearn feared that the cities of Japan would be plagued by "the tumult of hideous machinery,—a hell of eternal ugliness and joylessness" and that modern, mechanized Japan would be nothing more than a cheap imitation of the modern, monotonous West.[33]

Having traveled to Japan to escape temporarily from the West, artists soon concluded that they had to escape from urban Japan as well. As early as the 1870s, Griffis complained about the vulgar evidence that Western civilization was transforming "the Land of the Gods into a paradise of beef, bread, butter, milk and machinery." *A Handbook for Travellers in Japan* warned its readers that the cities and treaty ports of new Japan had been Europeanized. Tourists wanting to see old Japan were advised to come quickly and to travel into the districts not yet touched by railways. Such tourists were much reassured to find that rural Japan had not succumbed to Western vulgarity and was a refuge from the noise of the cities. In the mountain temples and shrines of the countryside, Nirvana still lingered.[34] Hence, artists' nostalgia for tradition had both temporal and spatial dimensions. After voyaging across the Pacific, they hoped to find the customs of centuries past thriving in the present. They wanted to experience and to depict a Japan that differed from the modern West in appearance and habits, a Japan that was, as much as possible, an Other. To their regret, they discovered that simply crossing the Pacific was no longer sufficient: they now had to venture into the Japanese hinterland.

Even more troubling, they found that Japanese art, the very element that had first attracted them to Japan, was deteriorating due to Western contact. In *A Glimpse at the Art of Japan*, acclaimed critic James Jackson Jarves denounced modern life as a "powerful solvent, pitilessly consuming all that which is most fascinating in the past without so far yielding in return any adequate artistic compensation." Perry's expedition to open Japan had been based largely on the conviction that foreign commerce was uplifting, but American artists unanimously described it as corrupting. The Western demand for Japanese artworks had encouraged divisions of labor, thus undermining artisanship and cheapening the final product. Where there had once been art, there now was interchangeable merchandise: inferior bric-a-brac churned out by the gross for foreign markets. Japan itself, visiting artists feared, would become interchangeable with other nations.[35]

For some Japanese, this was precisely the goal. Many Japanese intellectuals took Western civilization as a model. Recall

Fukuzawa's view that the West had been the first to discover rationality. Once Japan recognized that scientific laws governed history, he held, it could duplicate the progress made by Western civilization. Some Japanese scorned the preservationist activities of Fenollosa and were appalled by Arnold's likening of them to "birds and butterflies." They concluded that foreigners who urged Japan to preserve its cultural heritage were dispensing empty flattery and interested only in preserving Japan as a "playground" or "museum." So long as foreigners revelled in Japan as a quaint land of giggling damsels, the Japanese had to work alone for "the reform and progress that will make us a normal, civilized country."[36]

Still, other leading Japanese scholars rejected the overzealous adoption of Western institutions. Success, they asserted, did not depend on the extent to which Japan resembled the West, but on the extent to which it preserved its national essence (*kokusui*). In the early twentieth century, Japanese historians began to contend that their nation's progress was unlike that of the West because Japan possessed a spiritual core embodied in the imperial throne's divine, unbroken line from the sun goddess to the current emperor. Japan had separated itself from the stagnant "Orient" of Western thought by assimilating components of Western civilization, but it had done so without sacrificing this unique spiritual identity.[37]

Okakura Kakuzō brought these ideas directly to the American public. A leader in the effort to defend Japan's artistic heritage against widespread Western influences, Okakura had studied English with missionary James Hepburn and philosophy with Fenollosa, with whom his path continued to intertwine. Okakura sometimes interpreted for Fenollosa and Morse as they hunted for art treasures in shops and storehouses. In 1886, he and his former philosophy professor were appointed to an imperial commission charged with studying Western art institutions. This led

in 1890 to the founding of the Tokyo School of Fine Arts, which
Okakura directed. In the early twentieth century, he became an
adviser at the Boston Museum of Fine Arts, where Fenollosa had
worked earlier and Morse continued to serve.

Writing in English and publishing in the United States,
Okakura contrasted Eastern spirituality with Western materialism. "The West is for progress, but toward what?" he asked.
"The individuals who go to the making up of the great machine
of so-called modern civilization become the slaves of mechanical
habit and are ruthlessly dominated by the monster they have
created." In the West's unending competition for wealth, he
stated, happiness was extinguished. Vulgar and barren, the modern culture of the West was inimical to the variety and beauty of
Eastern ideals. Asia knew nothing of "the fierce joys of a time-
devouring locomotion, but she has still the far deeper travel-cul-
ture of the pilgrimage and the wandering monk." A Japanese
voice in America, Okakura complemented La Farge and Hearn.[38]

Okakura also argued that Japan's history of isolation and unbroken sovereignty had made it the repository of Asian culture.
Japan had always creatively accepted influences from Asia and
the West, he stated, without resorting to imitation. Her strength,
he told Americans, lay in remaining faithful to her ancient ideals
while selectively assimilating only those elements of Western
civilization she required to avoid becoming a victim of the vora-
cious West. Despite her modern garb, Japan remained traditional
at heart.[39] Thus, Japanese intellectuals as well as American artists
adopted essentialist views of Japanese culture. The contrasting
discourses of American diplomats and artists paralleled a Japanese debate on progress.

Before American audiences, Gilded Age artists in Japan added
their voices to the chorus of those who were concerned about the
consequences of mechanization and who questioned the benefits
of modernity. The railroad, initially perceived as an engine of

progress, had mutated into a destroyer of idyllic values and communities. In public addresses at home, Morse argued that communities, as they became civilized, suppressed unnecessary noises—only boys and uncivilized savages loved a clatter. The shrieking whistles, soot, and stenches of locomotives and factories were not simply a nuisance, they were a public hazard. The power of the machine, he warned, threatened to overwhelm the individual. To Japanese artists and writers as well, the railroad was an ambiguous symbol. To some, it represented civilization and enlightenment; to others, modern anonymity. In both the United States and Japan, technology and industry could be catalysts for progress or demons in the garden. Indeed, American artists may have imagined themselves as opponents of Mark Twain's 1889 Connecticut Yankee, who introduced the railroad, the telegraph, and dynamite to King Arthur's court, with murderous results. Modern progress, artists proclaimed, often wreaked social and physical destruction.[40]

The artistic movements influenced by Japonisme were, in part, responses to these concerns. Artists attempted to reincorporate nature's beauty and spirituality into an urban, industrial environment; they advocated making everyday, functional objects beautiful. Japanese aesthetics and customs were to be a refuge from industrialization. Craving a "oneness of mind and feeling," La Farge and his compatriots wished to shed their "modern armor."[41]

Yet this refuge was in danger of being overrun. Concerned about the acceleration of change in Japan, artists took their place alongside other American antimodernists who questioned the notion that untrammelled material progress was a universal blessing. Mechanization, they argued, carried a cost. In Japan that cost was the loss of a oneness of mind and feeling.

As a result, many of these artists continued their peripatetic pursuits of Nirvana beyond Japan. La Farge and Adams, for

instance, remained amiable travel companions, much to the surprise of their friend Henry James, who wondered how either
could have failed to murder the other; in 1890–91, the pair voy-
aged to Hawaii, the South Pacific, and Ceylon, where again they
found ancient, idyllic civilizations demoralized by contact with
the West. Adams, however, was less dyspeptic and distressed in
these locales than he had been on their Japan tour, which had followed his wife's suicide by a mere six months. In Ceylon, he attempted, albeit unsuccessfully, to attain the "total absorption
and silence" of Nirvana by sitting for half an hour under a bodhi
tree (the type of tree under which Buddha is said to have
achieved enlightenment).[42]

Although these tours fell within the two decades he omitted
in *The Education of Henry Adams*, his intellectual autobiogra-
phy, he did create a tangible legacy of his trip to Japan: upon his
return in 1886, he commissioned the sculptor Augustus Saint-
Gaudens to create for his wife's grave in Washington a bronze
memorial representing Kannon, the bodhisattva of mercy. Serving as intermediary, La Farge read stories of Kannon to Saint-
Gaudens. After the work was finished in 1892, Adams was an-
noyed by the cemetery's vacuous sightseers, to whom the sculp-
ture of a shrouded, seated figure was a mystery. Adams resisted
publicly naming and thus limiting the memorial, but privately
he called it "The Peace of God." The work, he believed, silently
posed a question, not an answer. Its meaning lay in its
anonymity and universality. Perhaps in Rock Creek Cemetery,
Adams at last found some of the illumination that had eluded
him in Asia.[43]

To painters, fame and profit were other important aspects of
these quests. After returning from Japan, they found an audience kindled by the Japanese craze and their published travel-
ogues. While La Farge had been well connected and well known
before visiting Japan (married to a grandniece of Commodore

Perry, he was already an important muralist and later added
stained-glass to his impressive repertoire), Theodore Wores and
Robert Blum are relatively minor figures in American art history who gained fame in their day because of their work in
Japan. They were, after all, among the first artists to bring color
to American visions of Japan. Previously, engravings in magazines and books had only hinted at the Japanese palette, but
painters made vivid use of color in their oils and watercolors of
Japanese kimono and foliage. Art critics revelled in these depictions of Japan's charm and urged collectors of Oriental bric-a-
brac to visit the exhibitions.[44]

At a series of shows across the United States and in London,
Wores sold almost all of his Japanese paintings. Many, such as
The Return from the Cherry Grove, disappeared into private collections and are known today only by photographs and magazine reproductions. A few years later, he returned to Japan to re-
plenish his stock of scenes to exhibit and sell.[45] Despite artists'
aspirations, then, the spiritual, antimodernist quest itself was
not entirely devoid of materialism.

Hearn, who never left Japan after his arrival in 1890, was
the most prolific writer among those highly appreciative of
Japan's arts, publishing nearly forty magazine essays and
books on his adopted home before his death in 1904. (His
translated works have long enjoyed popularity in Japan.) Born
a British subject, he spent most of his adult life in the United
States, writing for newspapers in Cincinnati and New Orleans.
After marrying a Japanese woman and fathering a son, he took
Japanese citizenship and adopted a Japanese name, Koizumi
Yakumo, to protect the boy's inheritance rights in Japan.
Deeply attracted to its customs, Hearn professed that "[t]o
escape out of Western civilization into Japanese life is like escaping from a pressure of ten atmospheres into a perfectly
normal medium."[46] He gradually came to believe that Japan's

construction of railroad and telegraph lines had not altered its fundamental character. As he traveled into the countryside as a pilgrim and preservationist, he recorded with awe his visits to religious sites that "no other foreigner has been privileged to see." The old Japan could still be found by those who knew where to look. Japan, he believed, had not imitated merely for imitation's sake, but only to protect itself while it grew stronger. The brief rage for Western dress, for example, had been in his view a matter of protective coloring or camouflage.[47]

But in the end, disenchantment overtook him. Unlike his earlier essay collections, his last work, *Japan: An Attempt at Interpretation*, was a sustained analysis and critique of Japanese religious and social institutions. A follower of Spencer, Hearn relied explicitly on the Synthetic Philosophy in arguing that the conservatism of Japanese society had prevented the development of individual freedom. Ancestor worship, which according to Spencer was a primitive stage that advancing societies pass through, continued to endure in Japan. This had produced a cult of obedience in which the individual was sacrificed to the family, an environment inhospitable to democracy. The race character of the Japanese, molded over centuries, could not be transformed in the space of a few decades, he argued. In the long run, Hearn predicted, such a society could not compete against the greater energies of the individualistic societies of the West. Although a decade earlier he had rejected Lowell's argument that the Japanese lacked individuality, in *An Attempt at Interpretation* he claimed that very point.[48]

Despite his Japanese name and citizenship, Hearn ultimately concluded that he could never truly understand the Japanese. Centuries of tradition posed insurmountable barriers. Bitterly he recognized that, as Koizumi Yakumo, he had been nothing more than a mimic. The Japanese could never become Western, and Hearn could never become Japanese. The "width of a world" would forever separate mimics and models.[49]

As Hearn's misgivings grew, many Americans at home also became increasingly apprehensive. Hearn's fears, however, were not theirs: they were concerned that Japan had become too powerful. Japan's victories over China (1894–95) and Russia (1904–5) had revealed it to be a potential military and commercial competitor. As a rival, Japan surpassed the impressionable-pupil image embraced by diplomats and broke through the spiritual frame imposed by artists. At first, the "appearance of Japanese in billycock hats must have seemed ludicrous," wrote a San Francisco editor, "but these [sic] who made fun of the tendency to imitate, did not see back of it the menace of meeting the Westerns [sic] on their own ground." With a shudder, Lowell also concluded that Japanese imitation was no longer so comical as he once had thought. He could not veil his revulsion upon seeing his Japanese "boy" clothed not only in copies of his clothes, but fitted out with exact reproductions of his mannerisms and gait as well. By becoming a military and commercial power, Japan subverted the differences that separated the progressive West from the traditional East: the mimic became a menace.[50]

On the eve of Japan's emergence as a competitor, American artists declared that its efforts to imitate the West were misguided because the Japanese were in essence a spiritual people, different from the materialistic West. Artists doubted the feasibility and desirability of melding this Japanese essence with the Western essence. In body and mind, they argued, the Japanese were unsuited for materialism and modernity. La Farge's "ancient" and "modern" female archetypes epitomized the yearning of artists, who hoped against hope that "modern" Japan would be no more than "ancient" Japan with a few cosmetic, Western accessories.

American artists fell into romances with a Japan that they believed was disappearing even as they arrived. In so doing, they shared intellectual kinship with earlier travelers who had portrayed Japan as a land of picturesque amusement and fantasy. To both groups, authentic Japan was the old, traditional Japan—a playland for the imagination. Now that Japan had become more like the West, its value as a fantasy world was quickly decreasing.

American artists' fascination with the fate of Japan's artistic traditions had a perverse result. In their devoted descriptions of Japanese customs, American artists devalued modern Japan as the misbegotten offspring of East and West. Most rejected the notion of the Japanese as racially inferior but hoped to preserve a Japan that was technologically inferior to the West: a Japan of artisans and rickshaw pullers, not one of factory workers and engineers.

Ascribing an essentialist character to Japan, artists preferred its model to that of the West. To them, Japanese customs exemplified an aesthetic and spiritual sensitivity that the "materialistic shams" of the West sorely lacked.[51] Artists wanted to keep Japan detached from Western influence and thus to preserve it as a spiritual culture, a distinct and different Other, peripheral to the West. Nevertheless, the material was overcoming the spiritual: the fulfilling work of the artisan was giving way to the uninspiring toil of the machine-laborer. Like the brief beauty of cherry blossoms, the evanescence of tradition heightened its value to artists.

Depicting what they believed to be vanishing traditions, they constructed a commentary on the Japanese past and rural present; in rural areas and among women, both of which artists believed were relatively untouched by foreign influence, the past continued to thrive in the present. This was the Japan that artists sought and admired. As they captured this

Japan on paper and canvas, they offered it to their readers and patrons as a source of solace in a grimy, modern West. Japan's surviving past became not only a temporary escape, but also a perspective from which Americans warily viewed progress and modernity.

Chapter 5

A DANCE OF DIPLOMACY

On the evening of 20 April 1887, four hundred ladies and gentlemen gathered at the official residence of Prime Minister Itō Hirobumi for Tokyo's first costume ball. The host and hostess, dressed as a medieval Venetian nobleman and a Spanish lady, greeted their foreign and Japanese guests, who included Foreign Minister Inoue Kaoru in the guise of a strolling musician. Under the electric lights of the ballroom, Britannia, Mother Hubbard, and Marie Antoinette danced with Benkei, Father Neptune, and Mephistopheles until four the next morning. Itō's government thereafter was dubbed "the dancing cabinet" by its critics.[1]

Itō and his ministers, however, were not merely engaging in grandiose amusements. His fancy dress ball was part of a broader strategy to prove to the treaty powers that Japan had successfully adopted Western customs. As one of his guests declared, the Japanese had "danced for the sake of the country."[2] Itō and Inoue were attempting to convince foreigners that Japan had earned revision of the unequal treaties and deserved to be admitted to the society of civilized powers as an equal.

Two years earlier, Fukuzawa Yukichi had issued a similar appeal but directed it toward his own compatriots. In his newspaper, he argued that Japan had to "escape from Asia." To the disadvantage of Japanese foreign policy, he pointed out, Westerners too often likened Japan to its neighbors China and Korea. Because these two nations were attempting to ward off the advance of Western civilization, their national independence was crumbling. Fukuzawa contended that Japan, which had already shaken off Asian "backwardness," could not afford to wait for its neighbors to do the same.

> Rather, we should escape from them and join the company of Western civilized nations. Although China and Korea are our neighbors, this fact should make no difference in our relations with them. We should deal with them as Westerners do. If we keep bad company, we cannot avoid a bad name. In my heart I favor breaking off with the bad company of East Asia.[3]

Over the course of Japan's treaty revision efforts from the 1870s to the conclusion of the first equal treaties in 1894, Japanese statesmen worked with mixed success to persuade the powers that Japan deserved to join their company. Japan's leaders attempted to ensure that the nation appeared and acted in ways familiar to its Western guests; Japan's orchestrated debut in the society of Western nations thus included costume balls as well as institutional reforms. To the consternation of Japanese opposition leaders—who attacked the government's repeated failures to regain full sovereignty—a succession of Japanese cabinets danced to the tunes of the Western powers. American diplomats and missionaries also had a deep interest in treaty revision. Unlike American artists, who described Japan's past as a treasure to be preserved, diplomats and missionaries depicted it as an obstacle to be overcome. While artists portrayed what they feared to be a disappearing "old Japan," these other Americans described an emerging "new Japan": a Japan that was dropping its "old errors and traditions" in order to make its "wonderful progress in civilization."[4] These observers noted approvingly that less than four decades after the Perry Expedition, Japan had a new constitution and parliament.

On the question of treaty revision, Japanese statesmen shared a vocabulary with American diplomats and missionaries. The Americans used the terms "civilization" and "progress" as criteria by which to measure whether Japan deserved to be treated as a sovereign equal. Beginning in the 1870s, many concluded that Japan had become a civilized power, and they attempted to convince Americans at home. The Japanese appropriated these terms in their efforts to demonstrate that Japan was more like the West than its Asian neighbors; Western powers were not prepared to accept Japan as an equal on its own terms.

The treaties that the Western powers had compelled Japan to sign in the 1850s sharply limited its sovereignty in foreign relations. They required Japan to open certain ports to foreign commerce and restricted Japanese judicial and tariff autonomy. To the Japanese, these restrictions were a constantly humiliating reminder that the Western powers viewed Japan and its institutions as inferior.

Under the treaty-established system of extraterritoriality, foreigners in Japan were immune from Japanese legal jurisdiction and subject only to their own nation's consular courts.[5] In agreements signed with Japan in 1857 and 1858, Townsend Harris, the first American diplomatic envoy to Japan, secured consular jurisdiction for American defendants. Because the powers had included most-favored-nation clauses in their earlier treaties opening relations with Japan, the rights gained by one power accrued to the others.[6]

Although Japan was compelled to open commercial ports and narrow its legal jurisdiction, it was empowered by treaty to limit foreign residence and trade to these ports and to restrict the travel of foreigners beyond them. Under foreign pressure to open the interior, Foreign Minister Terashima Munenori informed the powers in 1873 that Japan would permit interior travel and trade only upon the abolition of extraterritoriality. Terashima and the foreign representatives reached a compromise in the following year. They agreed to allow foreigners to travel into the interior under consular jurisdiction, but only for health and scientific purposes and on passports issued by the Japanese Foreign Ministry.[7] Foreigners reported no difficulty in obtaining such passports from the Japanese government and routinely escaped the summer heat of the ports by taking holidays in the mountains of the interior, using passports issued for health purposes.

The treaty powers limited Japanese jurisdiction because of their confidence in the superiority of their own legal codes and the inferiority of Japan's. Harris represented the views of Western diplomats when he described the Japanese as a "semi-civilized" people whose administration of justice could not equal that of civilized lands.[8] Foreign residents, the powers believed, deserved better justice than Japan could provide. Hence the treaties restricted Japanese sovereignty by allowing the sovereignty of the powers—in the form of consular jurisdiction—to reach into Japan itself.

To add injury to insult, the powers had also denied Japan the ability to set tariffs independently, depriving it of an important source of revenue. The U.S.-Japan Treaty of 1858, the first commercial treaty between Japan and a Western power, set duties ranging from 5 to 35 percent on imports to Japan; this served as the model for other powers. In 1866, the United States, Great Britain, France, and the Netherlands forced Japan to sign a convention that reduced duties to 5 percent on most items. Because the convention included no termination date, Japan's loss of tariff autonomy extended indefinitely.[9]

Throughout the first three decades of the Meiji period, the unequal treaties were a thorn in Japan's side. Treaty revision and the recovery of complete sovereignty continually loomed as Japan's primary foreign policy goals. Like Fukuzawa, Japanese statesmen believed that they could not allow their nation to be lumped together with its Asian neighbors, who were facing the threat of colonization. The denial of judicial and tariff autonomy allowed foreign merchants, beyond the reach of Japanese jurisdiction, to dominate Japan's foreign trade. Japanese leaders believed that treaty revision was vital if the nation was to recover and protect its independence, develop its wealth, and, ultimately, escape from Asia.[10]

When Japanese government officials considered various revision proposals, they realized that domestic opposition leaders and the public were watching carefully over their shoulders. A popular preoccupation, treaty revision inspired songs describing the "red-bearded louts" who brought "tears of indignation to pelt the cheeks of all red-blooded Japanese men who love their country."[11] Revision proposals provoked press leaks, political rallies, and even an assassination attempt. Opposition parties and significant sections of the public realized, sometimes more clearly than the government, that Japan's future was closely tied to the outcome. In fact, public opposition had a direct effect on the revision process: it helped to ensure that Japan gained complete, rather than partial, abolition of extraterritoriality.

In the first years after the Meiji Restoration, the government began the long process of revision by dispatching the Iwakura Embassy of 1871–73 for an exchange of views with the powers. Ambassador Iwakura Tomomi set the tone for Japan's revision efforts in his opening statement to Secretary of State Hamilton Fish at the 1872 talks in Washington. Japan's new railroad, telegraph lines, and steamships were just the beginning of the "national progress which is our ultimate aim."[12] In this overview of Japan's achievements since the treaties of 1858, Iwakura emphasized Japan's technological advances and equated progress with westernization. Japan, he pointed out, had resolutely embarked on a path of reform and was busily recruiting foreign advisors. These were not idle boasts: Verbeck, House, and Griffis were all teaching at Tokyo's Kaisei Gakkō in 1872.

The embassy, however, found the powers unready to eliminate the restrictions on Japanese sovereignty. To them, technological improvements were necessary but not sufficient indicators of civilization and progress; Japan also would have to reform its legal and political institutions. The perceived inferiority of these institutions, after all, was the proximate cause of the treaty restrictions. Only when Japan's legal and political institutions resembled those of the West might the powers accept Japan as a fully sovereign representative of civilization. After the Iwakura Embassy's return, Foreign Minister Terashima concluded that a full restoration of sovereignty was beyond Japan's immediate reach. Japan, he decided, should not address extraterritoriality until the government had revised its legal codes to the satisfaction of the powers. Terashima therefore concentrated his efforts on recovering tariff autonomy.[13]

During the first Meiji decade, Japanese exports increased, but imports increased at a higher rate, causing trade deficits. Without tariff autonomy, the government did not have the ability to raise import duties to protective levels and had to rely on the land tax as its primary revenue source. (The tax provided 86 percent of total national revenue in 1875.) This placed a significant burden on the agricultural sector and would prove to be an important, recurring factor in the debate on treaty revision.[14]

Recognizing the financial difficulties imposed by the treaty tariffs, Terashima was concerned that antiforeign sentiment could develop if the Japanese public connected its tax burden to the unequal treaties. Tariff autonomy, he argued in 1876, was essential in order to "satisfy public sentiment, maintain law and order, and expand foreign trade."[15] During U.S-Japan treaty negotiations, Terashima highlighted the economic losses that Japan was suffering.

At the American legation, he found a sympathizer. Minister John A. Bingham was a strong proponent of American-Japanese friendship and saw early treaty revision as a natural component of this relationship. Bingham did not believe that Japan was ready to assume legal jurisdiction over foreigners. Tariff autonomy, however, was a different matter, denial of which, he reported to Fish, was a "manifest injustice." Bingham considered the land tax oppressive and attributed it and Japan's trade deficit to the 1866 tariff convention. He harshly criticized Great Britain's opposition to tariff autonomy and insisted that the guiding rule of British policy was the desire for empire.[16] Although Bingham's Anglophobia prevented him from admitting it, the British would have much more at stake if Japan regained tariff autonomy: British exports to Japan dwarfed those of the United States by more than a seven-to-one ratio.[17]

Bingham attempted unsuccessfully to persuade Fish that the United States alone should restore tariff autonomy in exchange for the rights to interior travel and trade under consular jurisdiction. By doing so, he argued, the United States would secure "the perpetual friendship of this Empire," advancing its own interests by giving Japan the justice it deserved but could not obtain from the other powers.[18]

Delivering of the American Presents at Yokuhama [sic]. The Perry Expedition displays its tokens of American civilization, including a quarter-scale locomotive and a telegraph (note the poles and wire stretching into the distance). Courtesy Library of Congress.

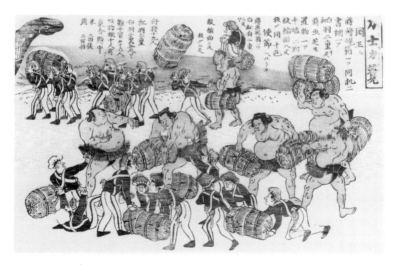

Sumo Wrestlers Carrying Rice Bales at Yokohama. The bakufu's exhibition of strength in response to Perry's gifts. Courtesy The Mariners' Museum, Newport News, Virginia.

Fanny Palmer, *Across the Continent, "Westward the Course of Empire Takes Its Way."* A popular portrayal of continental expansion by European Americans: the westward migration of civilization, led by the railroad and telegraph, through the (nearly) vacant wilderness. This print was published one year before the completion of the transcontinental railway. Currier and Ives lithograph, 1868. Courtesy Library of Congress.

A Street Scene in Japan. The first shock described by recently embarked sightseers: seminude and swarthy heathen men sweating through the noisy streets. In W. H. Hallock, "Jaunts in Japan," *Scribner's Monthly* 2 (July 1871): 241. Courtesy Library of Congress.

THE decree was written on wooden tablets about three feet long and posted all over the country. Although these tablets were taken down some years ago when the decree was revoked, many of them are still preserved. The ancient edict referred to below as "heretofore decreed" was as follows: "So long as the sun shall warm the earth, let no Christian be so bold as to come to Japan; and let all know that the King of Spain himself, or the Christian's God, or the great God of all, if he violate this command, shall pay for it with his head."

THE DECREE OF THE JAPANESE GOVERNMENT AGAINST CHRISTIANITY IN 1865

TRANSLATION

"The prohibition of the Christian religion is to be enforced as heretofore decreed. The worship of the 'depraved religion' is positively forbidden.   By order of the Government.   3rd month, 4th year of Keio [1865].

"The above regulations are to be strictly enforced.   By order of the Inugami Prefecture."

Above: The Decree of the Japanese Government against Christianity in 1865. A bakufu notice-board preserved by the American Baptist Missionary Union. Other Protestant missions also collected and preserved specimens of bakufu and early Meiji notice-boards. *Baptist Missionary Magazine* 79 (October 1899): frontispiece. Courtesy Library of Congress.

Opposite: A Quintette of Veterans. The Congregational Church's first missionaries to Japan, who together served more than a hundred and fifty years. In James H. Pettee, comp., *A Chapter of Mission History in Modern Japan* (Okayama: Seishibunsha, [1895]): between 6 and 7. Courtesy Library of Congress.

ARTO-TYPE TOKYO SEISHI-BUNSHA

A QUINTETTE OF VETERANS.   EARLIEST FIVE MEN OF THE MISSION.

Elizabeth Russell (standing) and Jennie Gheer, Methodist missionaries who established a Nagasaki girls' school in 1879. At first, their single pupil knew no English, and they knew no Japanese. Within three years, they had built a boarding school for ninety students. Courtesy United Methodist Church Archives, Madison, New Jersey.

Alice Mabel Bacon and Bruce, who accompanied her to Japan. Author of the popular *Japanese Girls and Women* and a Hampton Institute teacher, Bacon helped found Tsuda College and taught at the Peeresses' School and Tokyo Women's Higher Normal School. Courtesy Hampton University Archives.

William Elliot Griffis and His First Science Class, Tokyo, 1872. The late nineteenth century's most prominent American interpreter of Japan with his Kaisei Gakkō students. In the second row, fourth from the left, sits Komura Jutarō, who later served as minister to the United States and as foreign minister during both the Russo-Japanese War and the 1911 negotiations that restored tariff autonomy to Japan. Courtesy Rutgers University Special Collections and Archives.

Edward S. Morse introduced Darwin's theory of evolution to Japan. This scientist became a devotee of Japanese art and architecture, assembling a large ceramics collection later purchased by the Boston Museum of Fine Arts. Courtesy Peabody Essex Museum, Salem, Massachusetts.

Lafcadio Hearn. Despite his affection for Japan, expressed in his many popular works, he lamented that foreigners could never understand the Japanese. Courtesy Special Collections, University of Virginia Library.

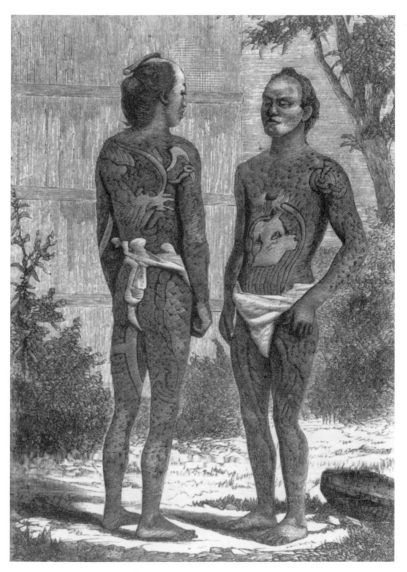

Bettos, or Grooms, in Full Costume. Japanese men as artists preferred to see them: loincloth-clad laborers offering ideal models for studies of the human body. In Lyman Abbott, "Pictures of the Japanese," *Harper's Monthly* 39 (August 1869): 308. Courtesy Library of Congress.

Left: John La Farge, *Ancient.* The archetypal Japanese woman bore no trace of Western influence. *Right:* La Farge, *Modern.* Artists hoped that Japanese women would continue wearing the kimono while adopting no more than "modern" accessories, such as Western-style umbrellas and cloaks. In La Farge, "An Artist's Letters from Japan," *Century* 39 (February 1890): 490–91. Courtesy Library of Congress.

Theodore Wores, *The Return from the Cherry Grove*. During Wores's exhibition tours, this canvas frequently attracted praise from critics. In London, he sold it to a private collector. In Wores, "An American Artist in Japan," *Century* 38 (September 1889): 675. Courtesy Library of Congress.

Left: Ōkuma Shigenobu. An outspoken advocate of constitutional government, Ōkuma established Waseda University and served as foreign minister and prime minister. In 1889, he survived an assassination attempt by a nationalist opposed to his treaty revision proposals. Courtesy Rutgers University Special Collections and Archives. *Right:* Mutsu Munemitsu. As foreign minister, Mutsu successfully revised the unequal treaties in 1894, restoring judicial autonomy to Japan. Courtesy Rutgers University Special Collections and Archives.

Ainu Man. In Paul Carus, "The Ainus," *Open Court* 19 (March 1905): 167. Courtesy Library of Congress. In this photograph and the one on the next page, the fairness of Ainu skin and the full beards of Ainu men were claimed to indicate their racial affinities with Russians.

A Typical Russian Peasant. In Carus, "The Ainus," 166. Courtesy Library of Congress.

In Washington, Fish remained skeptical. Despite Bingham's numerous dispatches, Fish supported working in cooperation with the other powers because American "interests in the East are so closely identified with the interests of all other civilized nations." In Washington in 1876–77, Fish exchanged views on revision with Minister Yoshida Kiyonari but would not allow the United States alone to agree to the possibility of higher tariffs.[19] Revision attempts failed until a change in presidential administrations brought William M. Evarts into the State Department as Fish's successor. Bingham's lobbying finally paid off in 1877, when Evarts supported his call for revision.[20]

One year earlier, Terashima had instructed Yoshida to emphasize to the Americans the economic losses that Japan was suffering without tariff autonomy. By relying on internal taxes, Japan was exhausting "the fountains of national prosperity at their sources." He authorized Yoshida to offer the opening of one or more additional ports and the abolition of export duties in exchange for American recognition of Japanese tariff autonomy. In July 1878, Evarts and Yoshida signed a convention restoring to Japan the right to set its own tariffs, but Article X stipulated that the convention would not take effect until all the other powers had signed similar conventions. The other powers did not.[21] The victory for Terashima and Bingham thus rang hollow. Disappointed to learn of Article X, Bingham recommended in vain that it be stricken from the convention. Great Britain, he predicted accurately, would not relinquish control of Japanese tariffs.[22]

Journalist Edward H. House later attempted to stir American opposition to the unequal treaties by publicly denouncing the 1878 convention as "monstrous" and "idiotic." Article X, he told the New York World, was like telling a dying man that a cure was readily available but was in the possession of his deadliest enemy. Bingham sent Evarts copies of House's pronouncements.[23] With these opening salvos, House began a personal campaign in the American press to sink the unequal treaties. In the *Atlantic Monthly* and the *New Princeton Review*, he attacked the unequal-treaty "incubus" in a series of articles describing "the martyrdom of an empire." The United States, House wrote, had the luxury of relying entirely on tariffs for government revenue. Japan, however, was destitute because the treaty tariffs were barely enough to cover the costs of customs administration. As a result, Japanese farmers were bearing an unjustly heavy tax burden. Japan was not merely a land of amusing fancies, he asserted; instead, it deserved the serious attention of Americans. The United States bore a special responsibility for these developments, House reminded his readers, because it had ended Japan's seclusion.[24]

Missionaries also began to assume a more active and public role in advocating the cause of treaty revision. Instead of concentrating on tariff autonomy, they focused on the abolition of extraterritoriality, a cause in which they had a professional interest. The agreement that foreigners could travel into the interior only for health and scientific purposes was an irksome obstacle to missionaries: a strict interpretation of this regulation would prevent evangelical activity in the interior. At their general conference in Osaka in 1883, missionaries debated this issue. Some reported that they proselytized in the interior using passports issued for reasons of health, pointing out that the treaties guaranteed them the free exercise of religion. Others considered this a "pious fraud" and limited their evangelical work to the treaty ports. They recounted the charges of dishonesty and hypocrisy that some Japanese levelled at missionaries using health passports to work in the interior.[25]

One solution to this dilemma lay in exchanging the opening of the interior for the abolition of consular jurisdiction. In 1884, the American and British missionaries stationed in Kobe and Osaka unanimously adopted a resolution supporting this course of action. They agreed with the Japanese view that extraterritoriality was an unjust infringement on Japan's sovereign rights. The time had come, the missionaries declared, to agree to any reasonable demands made by the Japanese government. Reprinting the resolution in the United States, the *Missionary Herald* expressed its hope that "the Christian nations [would] act in a Christian way."[26]

Terashima's successor as foreign minister, Inoue Kaoru, resolved to learn from his predecessor's experience and shifted the focus of Japan's revision efforts. Instead of postponing negotiations on consular jurisdiction, he attempted to partially restore Japan's judicial autonomy. Rather than eliminating tariff limits, Inoue attempted to increase their rates.[27] His tenure as foreign minister (1879–87) has earned the title "Rokumeikan era." A symbol of westernization, the Rokumeikan was an Italian-Renaissance building designed by a British architect and opened by the Japanese government in 1883. The Japanese elite came in Western attire to this brick, two-story hall to dine, dance, and play billiards with foreigners. Indeed, Inoue, who helped to supervise the Rokumeikan's design, intended it to be a venue for displaying Japan's adoption of Western civilization.[28] Although Prime Minister Itō's costume ball of 1887 did not take place under the Rokumeikan's roof, it embodied the spirit of the Rokumeikan era.

To critics of the government, however, the Rokumeikan and the dancing cabinet represented not civilization and enlightenment, but frivolity and betrayal. Opposition activists regarded both the Rokumeikan and Inoue's plans for partial restoration of Japanese sovereignty as evidence of government complicity in the powers' humiliation of Japan. Many of these critics had roots in the People's Rights movement (*jiyū minken undō*), a coalition of farmers, intellectuals, and former samurai who opposed the government oligarchy and called for popular participation in politics. The movement flourished in the 1870s, when it petitioned the government for the creation of a national assembly and constitution. In 1881, the government responded by announcing that the emperor would do both by 1890.

The land tax also emerged as an important issue for the opposition, as Terashima had warned. Deflationary policies carried out by the government in the early 1880s had helped to reverse the trade imbalance, producing an export surplus. The effect in rural areas, however, was not so favorable. The land tax was a fixed tax payable in cash. Thus, when the price of rice fell, the rural tax burden rose. And the price of rice plummeted, losing more than two-thirds of its value from 1881 to 1884. While the deflation was a success from a purely fiscal perspective, it triggered a collapse in the rural economy. Bankruptcies soared.[29]

Against this backdrop, Inoue negotiated with the powers in a series of multinational conferences in 1882 and 1886–87. In April 1887, they completed draft conventions on commerce and consular jurisdiction. The commercial convention did not restore tariff autonomy but raised tariffs by an average of 1 percent and attached a twelve-year limit to the new rates. Under the terms of the jurisdictional convention, Japan would open the entire country to foreign travel, trade, and residence within two years. Consular jurisdiction would be limited to the treaty ports and would remain in effect for three more years after the opening of the country. Further, Japan agreed to revise its legal codes "in accordance with Western Principles" and to submit English translations to the powers. Finally, the convention provided for a system of mixed courts: cases involving foreigners would be heard by tribunals on which a majority of the judges would be foreigners. The convention was to remain in force for seventeen years after the exchange of ratifications. In this convention draft, Inoue was able to set an end to consular jurisdiction but in exchange had to accept mixed courts.[30]

Before the drafts became public, Inoue ran into opposition within the government itself. Gustave Emile Boissonade de Fontarabie, a French adviser to the Japanese government, had played a leading role in drafting new legal codes. He had refused to attend Itō's costume ball, held just two days before the conference adopted the jurisdictional convention, claiming privately that he could not enjoy such extravagance when the powers were toying with Japanese sovereignty. Boissonade regarded the jurisdictional draft as dangerous. He warned that the requirement to translate the new codes would be interpreted by the powers as their right to intervene in drafting Japan's laws. He also objected to the mixed-court system, which he predicted would be disadvantageous to Japanese plaintiffs and defendants. "The new draft is far worse than the old treaty," Boissonade charged, because it would spread the evils of the old system to the entire country.[31]

Boissonade soon found an ally in Tani Kanjō, Japan's agriculture and commerce minister. A nation's laws, Tani argued in a memorandum to Prime Minister Itō, had to be framed in harmony with its history and customs. Japan would sacrifice even more of its independence if it revised its laws only to satisfy foreigners. Like Boissonade, Tani objected to the requirement that Japan provide translations of the new codes. He advocated postponing treaty revision until 1890, when the Diet would be established and Japan could use the force of public opinion to influence negotiations.[32]

Inoue, his revision program under attack, did not retreat from his commitment to outfitting Japan in Western attire. To Tani's memorial he responded that Japan had to "build up a European civilization here on a par with that of European civilized states." In the course of treaty revision, he argued, it was necessary for the Japanese to make concessions because "our present level of civilization is lower."[33]

With Itō continuing to support Inoue, Tani resigned his post on 26 July. Three days later, the multinational conference adjourned after having been informed by Inoue that Japan wished to postpone revision until after it had finished drafting new legal codes. Tani's opposition had cost him his cabinet seat, yet it had also forestalled a revision plan based on only a partial restoration of sovereignty.

The controversy, however, was far from over. The revision plan and Tani's memorandum leaked to the press and were widely circulated, whereupon the People's Rights movement quickly claimed him as a hero. Two thousand activists from all over Japan came to the capital to accuse the government of being more accommodating to foreigners than to its own people. The debate over Inoue's revision plan revived the People's Rights movement by enabling it to fuse a trio of issues: at large rallies and in petitions and memorials, opposition leaders called for an end to the unequal treaties, a reduction of the land tax, and freedom of speech and assembly. Tani's opposition eventually cost Inoue his cabinet post as well when he resigned on 17 September.[34]

Before the end of the year, Itō and his cabinet had had enough. On 26 December, the government issued the Peace Preservation Law, under which anyone within three *ri* (about seven miles) of the imperial palace who was plotting or inciting a disturbance could be expelled. The police rounded up about six hundred People's Rights activists and banished them from Tokyo.[35]

Having recognized his error in underestimating the stamina of the People's Rights movement and the power of treaty revision as one of its weapons, Itō adopted a new tactic. He attempted to split the opposition by bringing Ōkuma Shigenobu into the cabinet as foreign minister in February 1888. Ōkuma had been expelled from the government seven years earlier, after publicly calling for a constitution and parliament. He had then helped found and lead the Constitutional Reform Party. As foreign minister, though, he devoted himself to treaty revision, attending only the first of the newly created Privy Council's meetings on the Constitution. (In April 1888, Itō resigned as prime minister and became chairman of the Privy Council, which had been charged with revising the final draft of the Constitution.) Ōkuma, instead of employing Inoue's conference tactic, chose to negotiate with the powers separately in the expectation that a revised treaty with one would prompt the others to follow suit, though Terashima had already tried this tactic and failed. Ōkuma's experience would prove to be similar, but at a much greater personal cost.[36]

Also like Terashima, Ōkuma found the State Department sympathetic. In 1888, Ōkuma began secret negotiations with the powers. In February 1889, Ōkuma and Minister Richard B. Hubbard, Bingham's successor, signed a treaty that was not conditional on the signing of treaties by the other powers, as the U.S.-Japan Convention of 1878 had been. Great Britain balked at Ōkuma's proposals, but Germany and Russia signed treaties modelled on the Ōkuma-Hubbard text.

The Ōkuma treaties did not immediately restore either tariff or judicial autonomy but were an improvement on Inoue's 1887 drafts. On the question of tariffs, the treaties did not differ from Inoue's version. The treaties also repeated many of the 1887 provisions on judicial autonomy. Ōkuma agreed to open the interior and to continue consular jurisdiction at the treaty ports for a period of five years, to be followed by the restoration of Japanese jurisdiction. The Ōkuma treaties also established a system of mixed courts, but reduced their life span from seventeen years (as agreed to by Inoue) to twelve years. Unlike the Inoue proposals, however, the Ōkuma treaties neither required Japan to revise its legal codes according to Western principles nor to submit them to the powers. The Ōkuma treaties thus promised to eliminate the possibility that the powers would claim the right to reject the codes; they also promised to bring the full restoration of judicial autonomy five years closer.[37]

In April, word of Ōkuma's secret negotiations leaked in the London *Times*. When the news reached Japan, an avalanche of public criticism quickly followed and lasted into the autumn. Ōkuma's allies in the press were greatly outnumbered by his enemies, who attacked the mixed-court system as an unconstitutional and humiliating restriction on national sovereignty. Hundreds of petitions bearing tens of thousands of signatures poured into Tokyo.[38]

The Japanese press and public also debated the wisdom of opening the interior to foreign residence (referred to as *naichi zakkyo*, mixed residence). The influential and popular journal *Kokumin no tomo* cautioned the Japanese people to be prepared for commercial competition with foreigners but argued that mixed residence was no cause for alarm. In response, critics of the Ōkuma treaties warned of dire consequences that would follow the opening of Japan's interior. In a widely read critique of mixed residence, scholar Inoue Tetsujirō drew on the lessons of Darwin and Spencer, whom he had studied under Fenollosa at Tokyo University. If superior races conquered the inferior, Inoue reminded his readers, the Japanese would suffer in a struggle for survival against foreigners. The inferior Japanese would be overpowered: foreigners would occupy the best land, foreign capital would dominate, and Japan's unique customs would disappear. (When Inoue returned to Japan after studying in Germany, another scholar sardonically congratulated him on having safely survived his own mixed residence.)[39]

Beset by public opposition, Ōkuma fared no better within the government, where factional politics worked against him. His predecessor at the Foreign Ministry, Inoue Kaoru (now minister of agriculture and commerce), feared that Ōkuma's party would dominate the first Diet if he succeeded and schemed to isolate him. On 11 October, Itō resigned as Privy Council chair in a public signal that he, too, regarded the mixed-court system as unconstitutional. Six days later, Inoue Kaoru resigned. On 18 October, Ōkuma was returning to his office after an imperial conference when he was wounded by a bomb thrown into his carriage by a right-wing nationalist. Ōkuma survived, but doctors amputated his right leg. The cabinet fell the following week.[40]

By the time the Japanese government had informed Washington of its desire to hold the Ōkuma-Hubbard treaty in abeyance, Secretary of State James G. Blaine had already suspended action on it. He did so primarily in response to American opposition. The new U.S. minister, John F. Swift, helped to temporarily reverse American policy on treaty revision. A California Republican and an opponent of Chinese immigration to the United States, Swift now shifted his focus to a newly perceived threat. With dispatches notable for their physical length if not their intellectual depth, he blanketed Blaine's desk with reasons to oppose the treaty. Because the Japanese were accustomed to draconian punishments, he asserted, the adoption of a humane, Western-style legal code would unleash a crime wave. The powers should not abolish extraterritoriality "as an inducement to savages to abandon uncivilized customs."[41] On 18 October, Swift was at the Rokumeikan when he received word of the attempt on Ōkuma's life. He regarded the act as proof that Japanese social progress and evolution were still in their infancy. The Japanese, he held, had engaged in a mad rush to adopt foreign institutions without any real understanding of their operation. Swift took it upon himself to correct what he believed to be Americans' gross misperceptions about Japan.[42]

He arrived at his post encumbered with racial assumptions that prevented him from serving as a useful observer of

Japanese affairs. For this reason, he stands out as an exception among American diplomats in Japan in the last quarter of the nineteenth century. His predecessors Bingham and Hubbard and his successors Frank L. Coombs and Edwin Dun evaluated Japanese readiness for treaty revision by the criteria of civilization and progress. According to their measurements, Japan had surmounted the inferiorities of its past and had become a sovereign equal of the United States. According to Swift, however, these inferiorities were innate and continued to loom as an immovable obstacle to the restoration of Japanese autonomy.

Despite his intellectual myopia, Swift did report to Washington on the unanimous support among leading American missionaries for the unconditional abolition of extraterritoriality. When queried by Swift and earlier by Hubbard, missionaries emphasized that there was no danger in immediately placing American citizens under Japanese law. Furthermore, they saw no evidence that the Japanese government was interfering with religious liberty.[43]

To most Americans in Japan, the promulgation of the Constitution in 1889 and the opening of the Diet in 1890 were unmistakable signs that Japan had fully joined the community of modern, civilized powers. Receiving close press coverage in the United States, the Constitution and Diet confirmed the belief that Japan deserved equal treaties recognizing its full sovereignty. Emperor Meiji bestowed the Constitution upon the nation in a palace ceremony on 11 February—the date on which, according to myth, Japan's first emperor had ascended the throne in 660 B.C.E. The eleventh was a gala day in snowy Tokyo. Electric lights and red and white lanterns hung from arches spanning the streets, which were lined with forests of flags. After the promulgation ceremony, a 101-gun salute boomed, while telegraph wires carried the news to the rest of the country. Sunshine dispelled the clouds just as the imperial party began its slow pro-

cession through the Tokyo crowds that had turned out in cele-
bration. Later, fireworks lit the winter night.[44]

The eleventh had additional significance to missionary
women. They were pleased that the empress had sat beside the
emperor in an open carriage after leaving the promulgation ceremony: this marked the first time in history that the two had
ridden publicly side by side. Missionary women saw in this act
their own handiwork. It was, they believed, "a result of the dif-
fusion of Christian principles."[45]

With the exception of Swift, American appraisals of the new
constitution were overwhelmingly positive. Prominent missionaries provided public votes of confidence. They noted that it
guaranteed religious freedom, albeit "within limits not prejudi-
cial to peace and order." Despite this restriction, long-time residents and analysts of Japan were more than satisfied. Daniel
Crosby Greene, who had arrived in Japan twenty years earlier as
the Congregationalists' first missionary, praised the foresight of
Japan's leaders and the fitness of its people for self-government.
Griffis added from his Boston pastorate that the constitution
verified that Japan was "the most progressive of Asiatic nations."
In 1890, the first Diet elections and its opening attracted similarly favorable reviews. To both evangelical and secular Americans, Japan had passed an important test of civilization and
progress.[46]

American business journals, which devoted little attention to
Japan and treaty revision, offered no significant opposition to
these views. When they did look at Japan, business journals
praised its reforms and technological advances: they acknowledged that Japan was joining the ranks of the "civilized" and
"modern." American merchants in Japan tended to prefer extraterritoriality but accepted revision as inevitable because they
thought that the old treaties no longer fit the changed conditions in Japan. Some even welcomed revision in the hope that

commercial opportunities would increase after Japan's interior was opened to foreign trade.[47]

When soliciting the opinions of businessmen, American diplomats concentrated on discovering the reason for the relatively low level of American exports to Japan, especially when compared with British exports. In their responses, American merchants blamed neither Japan nor Great Britain for the situation. Instead, they noted that American products were poorly adapted for the Japanese market. Protected by tariffs, American manufacturers could rely solely on their domestic market. American trading companies in Japan wanted to ensure that treaty revision would not bring higher import duties in Japan, but they also advocated reducing duties in the United States to compel American manufacturers to focus more on foreign markets.[48]

On the question of treaty revision, American businessmen in Japan assumed a role secondary to that of missionaries. Despite their preference for the protection of consular jurisdiction, businessmen did little to sway American public opinion and did nothing to block revision efforts. Like the missionaries, they recognized the authenticity of Japanese reforms.

Diplomats, missionaries, and other Americans in Japan worked to call American attention to Japanese political reform in the hope of spurring a final and successful campaign for treaty revision. Whatever foundation there had once been for extraterritoriality had now vanished, they argued. Japan had gradually yet finally discarded "Oriental absolutism," a pronouncement that Fukuzawa would have applauded. These American witnesses concluded that only one thing was needed to guarantee continued progress: revision of the unequal treaties. Such efforts would soon bear fruit.[49]

Swift, the principal American opponent of revision, died at his post on 10 March 1891. In the same year, Great Britain's dilatory approach to revision suddenly gained speed when Russia began constructing the Trans-Siberian Railway. The Franco-Russian agreement of August 1891 and the Franco-Russian military alliance of January 1894 also induced a more conciliatory British attitude.[50]

As foreign minister in the second Itō cabinet, Mutsu Munemitsu was finally able to achieve what had eluded his predecessors. To the powers, Mutsu proposed the abolition of extraterritoriality. He calculated accurately that this approach would prevent the political problems at home that had been stirred by the Inoue and Ōkuma proposals. Like his predecessors, however, he was compelled to argue to the powers that Japan was unlike its Asian neighbors. As he explained to the Diet, successful treaty revision required Japan to "show the foreign countries actual proof for the fact that our progress, our civilization is truly a special case in all of Asia, and that we are a strong, civilized country."[51]

Nevertheless, Japan's opposition parties were hardly docile. The Diet was a double-edged sword. On the one hand, it served as a symbol to the powers that political reforms were effectively making Japan a sovereign equal. On the other, it provided a prestigious platform for the opposition parties, who criticized the cabinet's revision efforts as weak. They saw the issue of treaty revision as a popular cause to use in embarrassing the cabinet. Itō twice used imperial rescripts, in December 1893 and June 1894, to dissolve the Diet temporarily so that it could not disrupt treaty negotiations with Great Britain.[52]

To remove the most persistent obstacle to revision, Mutsu decided to focus first on Great Britain. Negotiations began in December 1893 and were successfully concluded with the signing of a treaty in July 1894. Japan committed itself to opening the entire country to foreign travel, trade, and residence in exchange for Great Britain's agreement to abolish consular jurisdiction after five years. The treaty did not establish a mixed-court system.[53]

When Mutsu turned his attention to the United States, he found a long-time friend of Japan in the American legation. Minister Edwin Dun had lived in Japan for twenty years. He had been decorated by the emperor for his work with the Hokkaidō Colonization Commission in 1873–83 and had begun working at the American legation as second secretary in 1884. As minister, Dun advised Secretary of State Walter Q. Gresham that the time had come to give Japan jurisdiction over foreigners. Gresham concurred. In November 1894, the United States and Japan signed a treaty that was modelled on the Great Britain-Japan text. Russia, Germany, and France also fell into line.[54]

The end of extraterritoriality was in sight, but Japan would wait until 1911 for treaties that restored tariff autonomy. Mutsu would witness neither. After a long battle with tuberculosis, he died in 1897.

More than forty years after extraterritoriality had been imposed on Japan, the new treaties took effect without incident on 17 July 1899. In Washington, Minister Komura Jutarō, one of Griffis's former students, observed that this was the first time the Western powers had recognized the full sovereignty of an "Oriental state." American newspapers carried Komura's statement and concurred that Japan was now a "civilized" equal among the world's powers.[55]

Missionaries gathered on the seventeenth to pray for the treaties' success, taking pleasure in their conviction that decades of mission work had helped to bring civilization to Japan. This was the first time in history, they reminded their supporters at home, that "white-skinned, occidental, Christian peoples have put themselves and their belongings under the rule of a yellow-skinned, oriental, non-Christian people." Why had they done so? M. L. Gordon, a missionary in Japan since 1872, answered that Japan, though Oriental by geography, was now Occidental in government and law.[56] In order to regain its lost sovereignty, Japan had indeed found it necessary to escape from Asia. Only after its political institutions resembled those of the West did the powers see fit to relinquish consular jurisdiction. In American discourse, Japan was now politically Occidental.

The failures of Inoue and Ōkuma to regain Japanese judicial autonomy had been a blessing in disguise; the treaties signed in 1894 were much more favorable to Japan than the 1887 and 1889 proposals. Opposition protests blocked piecemeal revision and, in so doing, helped ensure that Japan regained full judicial sovereignty before the end of the nineteenth century. Boissonade and Tani had served as the leading edge of the opposition to the earlier proposals, while People's Rights activists and party leaders provided its bulk. Adversaries of Inoue and Ōkuma, both inside and outside the government, prevented Japan from prematurely accepting a partial abolition of extraterritoriality.

The opposition to partial revision was part of the mid-Meiji shift toward conservatism and away from westernization. This emerging nationalism elevated Japanese tradition and the imperial throne and rejected the blind assimilation of things Western. The intransigence of the powers on treaty revision catalyzed antiforeign sentiment in Japan and fueled the assertion of national confidence. These trends were the political and social counterparts of the cultural philosophy of art critic Okakura Kakuzō, who had criticized Western materialism. From these conservative and nationalist quarters came the "dancing cabinet" epithet.

Even as conservatives and the opposition parties castigated government leaders for pandering to foreign powers, the government adopted an effective strategy for promoting treaty revision. It had to persuade the powers that Japan had escaped from

Asia before they would consider Japan progressive and civilized enough to merit revision. The Constitution and Diet were significant factors in convincing Americans that Japan had discarded Oriental backwardness and permanently triumphed over its past. The growing strategic influence of Russia tipped the scales for revision by Great Britain, but the Constitution and Diet provided other necessary weight. Thus we can see that, over the long run, foreign ministers and their opponents were not working at cross-purposes on the problem of treaty revision. Inoue, Ōkuma, and Mutsu worked to convince the powers that Japan deserved revision; at the same time, widespread opposition to partial revision served as evidence to those powers that the Japanese would not tolerate the unequal treaties indefinitely.

To abolish extraterritoriality, Japanese leaders were compelled to adopt the institutions of civilization and progress championed by the powers. Political equality, however, was not full equality. Treaty revision, when finally accomplished, represented the statutory acceptance of Japan as a sovereign and political equal of the Western powers. Acceptance as a religious and racial equal, however, was another matter entirely.

Chapter 6

"THE MOST UN-MONGOLIAN
PEOPLE IN ASIA"

By American criteria, the Japanese at the turn of the century successfully acquired and wielded the instruments of modern power: they developed a constitutional government that fought and won wars, defeating China in 1895 and Russia in 1905. Japan's success, however, undermined the widespread American preconception that modern civilization and progress were inseparable from Christianity and Anglo-Saxon ancestry. Japan had assimilated Western secular institutions without a national religious conversion. Its military and commercial prowess seemed to contradict the American belief in Asian inferiority. As the first "heathen" and Asian nation to become a power, Japan presented several challenges to Americans.

Many Americans responded by beginning to regard Japan as a competitor. As both nations took colonies in the Pacific,

Americans grew increasingly concerned about both Japanese territorial and commercial ambitions and Japanese immigration to the United States. Japan, they worried, posed a racial and strategic challenge. Some, motivated by racism, warned of an impending "yellow peril" and launched a campaign to exclude Japanese immigrants. Others warned that Japan's alleged imitativeness and cheap labor posed an imminent commercial threat to American industry. But American statesmen such as Theodore Roosevelt and Alfred Thayer Mahan, driven primarily by strategic considerations, tried to harmonize American and Japanese interests. These statesmen hoped that Japan would serve as a proxy for American interests by holding open the door for commerce in East Asia.

In this environment, Japanese statesmen worked deliberately to shape American opinion. Japanese diplomats had finally succeeded in convincing their American and European counterparts that Japan deserved revision of the unequal treaties because of its political and legal reforms. At the turn of the century, a more public campaign followed these diplomatic maneuvers. In the American press, Japanese officials and intellectuals attempted to demonstrate that Japan, as a result of its reforms, had become much like the United States. They refuted claims that Japan was a peril and tried to persuade Americans that Japan and the United States had many interests in common. Alone among Asian nations, they declared, Japan had become a standard-bearer for Western civilization.

Just as American and Japanese statesmen tried to reduce strategic friction between their nations, American missionaries and scholars worked on a similar project: they attempted to equate the racial traits and religious aims of the two nations. After all, many Americans saw Japan as an intellectual and a strategic challenge. How could they reconcile Japan's allegedly inferior racial and religious characteristics with its emergence as a modern power? Missionaries and scholars worked diligently to calm American fears.

The yellow peril thesis itself thus had a vigorous competitor as these experts on Japan contended that it was the Asian proxy of Christian nations and that racially the Japanese had much in common with Americans. When confronted by the perceived anomaly of a modern yet "heathen" Asian people, missionaries and scholars responded by emphasizing similarity rather than difference. They sought evidence that the Japanese somehow were Christian and white.

As Japan was demonstrating its new military prowess against China (1894–95) and Russia (1904–5), many Americans grew concerned that it was also directing its commercial prowess against the United States. The Japanese, some Americans believed, were better imitators than assimilators and were conquering American markets by taking advantage of comparatively low labor costs.[1] These voices of alarm did not go uncontested; voices of calm also received much attention, insisting that a wealthy Japan would offer a better market for American goods than an impoverished one. What was the "plain truth about Asiatic labor"? The U.S. consul in Osaka reported in the *New York Herald* that the inventive American worker was more than three times as productive as his imitative Japanese counterpart.[2]

The Japanese themselves also attempted to allay American concern. In influential American journals, Japanese statesmen published a wave of essays affirming the importance of American-Japanese friendship. "We may not be a Christian nation in the strict sense of the expression," Minister Hoshi Tōru noted in *Harper's Monthly* in 1897, "but we have omitted no effort to assimilate to our use the substance of Christian civilization." (Hoshi had been among the People's Rights leaders expelled from Tokyo under the Peace Preservation Law a decade earlier.) The Japanese assured American readers that there was absolutely no basis for fears of a Japanese commercial, military, or immigration onslaught. Japan was eager to import American manufactures, they stated, and would not adopt protective trade policies if it regained tariff autonomy; furthermore, they pointed out, the Japanese government was working to restrict the emigration of laborers.[3]

These efforts to soothe American concerns had a firm foundation in American consciousness on which to build. During the Sino-Japanese War, a battle for hegemony in Korea, Japanese officials and intellectuals had begun to court American popular support by depicting Japan as America's "Yankee brother" in the Orient. Minister Kurino Shin'ichirō, Hoshi's predecessor, pointed out that while both China and Japan had an interest in preventing Korea from falling to Russia, China was bound to tradition and permeated by corruption. It was too weak to protect itself, much less Korea. In contrast, Japan was the only Asian nation to have recognized the merits of Western civilization. This was not a war of conquest, Kurino informed his American readers, but a struggle between modern progress and stagnation: Japan itself was fighting to establish outposts of civilization on the Asian continent.[4]

Kurino and his compatriots enjoyed considerable success in persuading Americans that Japan was engaged not only in a fight for self-defense, but also in a larger battle to reform East Asia. In their campaign to win over public opinion, they found allies among Americans regarded as authorities on Japan. Griffis, whose *Mikado's Empire* went into its fifth edition in 1894, identified Korea's rejection of Western civilization and its consequent corruption and weakness as the real menace to peace. Kurino's reasoning and Japan's military victories also greatly impressed Joseph Cook, Boston's celebrated lecturer who had toured Japan in 1882. In an address to an overflow crowd at Park Street Church in February 1895, Cook praised Japan's "Occidental" reforms and its efforts to bring them to continental Asia.[5]

Although Kurino, Griffis, and their colleagues had built a solid base of support for Japan, public opinion was not entirely favorable. The sharpest blow against Japan in the American press fell in the last weeks of 1894 and was, for the most part, self-inflicted. On 21 November, Japanese forces attacked Port Arthur, a town at the tip of China's Liaodong Peninsula. Accompanying them were war correspondents Frederic Villiers of the London *Standard* and James Creelman of the *New York World*. In their dispatches home, Villiers and Creelman reported that the defending Chinese forces had fled, leaving only civilians in the town. Encountering little resistance, the Japanese advanced and found the mutilated heads of several Japanese prisoners hanging from trees near the first bridge into Port Arthur. Enraged and unopposed, the soldiers "commenced shooting every living thing they met." Creelman reported that an "unrestrained reign of murder" continued for three days until the streets were "choked up with mutilated corpses." He estimated that the Japanese had killed at least two thousand unarmed men, women, and children. Other American newspapers and magazines quickly repeated these front-page reports.[6]

Japanese statesmen moved rapidly to minimize collateral damage in the United States. Kurino warned Foreign Minister Mutsu Munemitsu that the revised U.S.-Japan treaty, signed in Washington on 22 November, might be in danger. U.S. Minister Edwin Dun, after speaking with Creelman following his return to Japan, met with Mutsu, who attacked Creelman's account as grossly exaggerated. Mutsu acknowledged that there had been more bloodshed than necessary but insisted that Japanese soldiers had been provoked by the sight of their mutilated comrades. Moreover, he claimed, many of those killed had been soldiers clothed as civilians. In statements to the American press, Japanese diplomats repeated this explanation.[7]

Dun received another firsthand report from Lieutenant Michael J. O'Brien, the military attaché to the U.S. legation in

Japan. O'Brien, who had also accompanied Japanese troops at Port Arthur, confirmed to Dun that on 21 November, unarmed Chinese prisoners had been killed and their corpses mutilated. But, he reported, he had seen no atrocities on the following two days. He had witnessed only principled behavior by the Japanese army prior to Port Arthur and considered the events there to have been an aberration. Giving more credence to Mutsu and O'Brien than to Creelman, Dun informed the State Department that a "slaughter of Chinese soldiers" had occurred on the twenty-first, but that Creelman's report was "sensational in the extreme and a gross exaggeration."[8]

The Port Arthur massacre, despite its inflammatory potential, did not ruin Japan's reputation in the United States. In an exchange of acidic letters between Villiers and Alice Mabel Bacon in the *New York Times*, Bacon tried to undermine his credibility by accusing him of malicious ignorance in misrepresenting Japan's leaders as bloodthirsty zealots. (She was a close friend of the wife of General Ōyama Iwao, commander of the Second Army at Port Arthur.) Yet Villiers, in trying to set the massacre in context, had earlier conceded that Japanese troops were known by the Chinese for their humane conduct before Port Arthur. And even in the midst of the *New York World*'s reports from Creelman, the paper editorialized that Japan represented "progressive as opposed to retrograde civilization, intelligence as against stupid conservatism, enlightenment as against barbarism." Although Japanese troops had committed a massacre, most Americans believed that it was uncharacteristic of Japanese military behavior.[9]

The conviction that Japan was more civilized than China endured despite Port Arthur. Japan had won many American friends, who affirmed that it had displayed the utmost regard for the modern rules of warfare. To them, Port Arthur was a lone exception: it indicated not that the Japanese were barbarous but that war itself was. Japan's fortunes suffered little in Washington, where the massacre had no effect on the treaty. In January 1895, the Senate rejected an amendment to allow the exclusion of Japanese immigrant laborers. The following month, it unanimously approved the treaty, which President Grover Cleveland then ratified.

A decade later, Japan again was at war. In the Russo-Japanese War, the nation representing Christendom emerged victorious: Japan defeated Russia. To many Americans, Japan, not Russia, better embodied the principles of Western Christendom as well as those of modern civilization. Their advocacy of Japan came to include arguments based on both religious and racial characteristics.

A few days before the first shots were fired in that war, the Japanese government sent former cabinet minister Kaneko Kentarō to the United States with instructions to encourage support for Japan unofficially.[10] Kaneko, an 1878 graduate of Harvard Law School who had helped to draft the 1889 constitution, followed in Kurino's footsteps by vigorously taking on the task of public relations. He repeatedly underscored similarities between Japanese and American interests in East Asia and warned of the differences between these and Russian interests.

In the United States, Kaneko worked closely with Minister Takahira Kogorō in presenting Japan's case to the American public and its leaders. In speeches and essays, they repeated points from one decade earlier: Japan was fighting for peace and stability in East Asia. They argued that Japan, along with the United States, advocated the open door for trade, as enshrined in Secretary of State John Hay's 1899–1900 "open door" notes to the powers. The United States and Japan were working side by side to open the wealth of China to a fair commercial contest, they claimed, while Russia aimed to absorb Manchuria and to close the door to its trade. If Saint Petersburg controlled Manchuria, they warned, China would collapse and the open door would slam shut, depriving the United States and Japan of their rightful share of commerce and preventing the further spread of Western civilization.[11]

Much like Kurino during the Sino-Japanese War, Kaneko urged Americans to recognize the contrast between the enemy's conservatism and absolutism and Japan's steady efforts to introduce Western institutions to East Asia. Japan had devoted itself to opening Korea and China to the influences that it had already assimilated. According to Kaneko, Japan, "though Oriental, stands for modern western civilization, and its success will mean . . . the occidentalizing of the East. The other, though European, stands for an absolutism that is Oriental, and its success will mean the perpetuation of ignorance and the reign of force."[12]

As Kaneko and Takahira tried—with notable success—to extend their influence widely in the American press, they also managed to reach the White House. President Theodore Roosevelt, they found, was a sympathetic listener and an eager student of Japan. Kaneko was already acquainted with fellow Harvard alumnus Roosevelt and met with him frequently during the Russo-Japanese War. On one occasion, Roosevelt gave Kaneko a bearskin—whose former inhabitant the president had recently shot—to present to the emperor as a symbol of defeated Russia. At Kaneko and Takahira's recommendation, Roosevelt read Nitobe Inazō's *Bushido: The Soul of Japan,* a book that purported to offer a simple explanation of the uniqueness and merits of Japanese civilization: *bushido,* a military code of moral principles, had shaped and guided both "Old Japan" and "New Japan." (Griffis contributed the introduction to some of its several editions.) Roosevelt, who was taking judo lessons three times a week, was much impressed and ordered copies for his friends and children.[13]

Even though in his private letters Roosevelt repeatedly referred to the Japanese as "non-Christian" and "non-Aryan," it mattered little to him, he wrote, that the Russians were white and the Japanese were not. He claimed to be unswayed by the argument that Americans had more in common with Russians as members of the same race. Furthermore, he scoffed at the notion that the Japanese and Chinese were of the same race. To Roosevelt and his contemporaries, "race" was a pliant term based not only on skin color, but also on language, ethnicity, and nationality. In Roosevelt's opinion, the Japanese were a "highly civilized people" who deserved great respect for their industrial skill and martial valor. Ever the pragmatist, Roosevelt believed that Western statesmen would have to monitor this new power closely, but he was confident that Japan made an important addition to the great nations. "The Japs have played our game," he wrote Hay, "because they have played the game of civilized mankind." He was convinced that the twentieth-century descendants of the Mongol Empire's yellow peril were fighting under the flag of Russia, not Japan.[14]

American journals were inclined to agree with their president and Kaneko. They attacked Russia for breaking its prewar promise to withdraw troops from Manchuria and concluded that Japanese diplomacy was "two centuries more Christian" than that of Russia. Japan had shed its Asiatic features to become a nation more Western than its enemy.[15] America's protégé for nearly half a century, Japan now would teach its neighbors Korea and China to follow in its footsteps. As a sentinel in these new outposts of civilization, it would defend against the peril of Russian absolutism.

These images of Japan, Russia, and East Asia grew primarily from strategic and political calculations. As the pronouncements of statesmen and journalists, they had significant influence. But most of these strategic scenarios were based on cultural declarations: Japan was said to be "more civilized" and "more Western" than Russia. On these questions, missionaries and scholars might serve as higher authorities. Indeed, both groups set out to explore the validity of these claims.

In 1903, missionary Sidney L. Gulick described the intellectual challenge that Japan posed. "This 'little nation of little people,' which we have been so ready to condemn as 'heathen' and 'uncivilized,'" had in a single generation made itself into a world power. "Are our theories wrong?" Gulick asked. "Is Japan an exception?"[16] Other American missionaries also turned to examine whether Japan's success undermined their faith in Christian superiority.

Nevertheless, during both the Sino-Japanese and the Russo-Japanese wars, missionaries reported that a great good was emerging from the horror of bloodshed: war brought new opportunities to spread the gospel. In their articles and letters to missionary magazines, they wrote that Japan's victory in convincing the powers to revise the unequal treaties had undercut Japanese nativism. Just as important, the patriotic conduct of Japanese Christians in the army and navy had weakened anti-Christian prejudice. Such sentiments had been stirred in 1892 by Imperial University professor Inoue Tetsujirō, formerly an outspoken opponent of mixed residence, who had declared in a series of essays that Christianity was incompatible with Japanese nationalism. Consequently, missionaries were pleased to find that the Japanese government allowed them wide access to minister to soldiers and sailors at the front, at home, and in hospitals.[17]

Everywhere they looked, then, missionaries found new means of spreading the gospel. Missionary women rolled bandages and assembled comfort-bags—containing pencil, paper, needle, and thread—for the troops. In hospitals, they led hymn services and brought flowers to the wounded. "Just a spray of cherry blossoms," Elizabeth P. Milliken wrote from Tokyo, "and I am friends with some big soldier I never saw before." Military authorities allowed missionaries and Young Men's Christian Association (Y.M.C.A.) workers to travel with the army; they also permitted Japanese Christians to serve as chaplains at the front. In 1905, Emperor Meiji himself contributed ten thousand yen to the Y.M.C.A. in recognition of its work during wartime. On the home front in both wars, missionaries and Japanese Christians were free to preach in the barracks and to distribute Bibles and tracts among the soldiers and sailors.

Thus, the curse of war, missionaries told their brothers and sisters at home, contained blessings. It provided a nationally significant cause and context for mission charity work. It brought the missionaries into contact with more Japanese than ever before. And it ensured that many in these new audiences were in great need of the solace missionaries professed to offer. "The Church has never had fairer prospects," concluded one Presbyterian.[18]

The work of American women during the Russo-Japanese War made a significant impression, not only on Japanese soldiers, but on the American public as well. Dr. Anita Newcomb McGee, who had served as acting assistant surgeon in charge of the U.S. Army Nurse Corps during the Spanish-American War, described in two *Century* essays the observations of a group of nine American nurses, also war veterans. Together the ten women volunteered and traveled to Hiroshima to work in the army's main hospital.[19] Such efforts struck a chord at home. Frances Little's *The Lady of the Decoration*, an American best-seller in 1907–8, consists of the letters sent home by a fictional teacher in a Hiroshima mission school. (Frances Little was the pen name of Fannie Caldwell Macaulay, who worked as a kindergarten teacher in Hiroshima in 1902–7.) During the war, the novel's heroine and her colleagues volunteer at military hospitals. While its plot traces a long-distance romance, the setting interweaves Russian brutality, mission work, and the narrator's growing attachment to the Japanese. The novel's great popularity in the United States indicated a substantial interest in missionary labors—an interest reaching well beyond the membership of mission societies. Even those who read the novel primarily for its romantic plot received a large dose of information about the Russo-Japanese War and American missionaries. While war had opened barracks and hospital doors to the gospel in Japan, it also opened a new door to Japan for American readers.[20]

These open doors were important, but Japan's victories had even broader significance to missionaries: they believed that their successes in Japan would now ensure an open field for Christian evangelism in Korea and Manchuria. Missionaries in Korea and China agreed with this assessment. Together they warned that Russia could not be trusted to maintain an open door of any kind; commerce, civilization, *and* Christianity would not be safe in Russian hands. Baptist missionary Ernest W. Clement, in his successful *Handbook of Modern Japan*, assured Americans that Japan, in contrast, would preserve "the open door, not of material civilization only, but also of the gospel of Jesus Christ."[21]

Japanese clergymen and officials recognized the importance of missionaries in cultivating American goodwill. At a Tokyo conference of religious organizations in May 1904, one thousand Japanese and foreign clergy approved unanimously a resolution declaring that the Russo-Japanese War had nothing to do with differences of race or religion. To the assembly, an American Presbyterian missionary recalled his recent interview with Prime Minister Katsura Tarō, when Katsura had urged Americans to remember that Japan's constitution guaranteed religious freedom. Therefore, Katsura stated, one could not say that Russia stood for Christianity and Japan for Buddhism. On the contrary, Japan's leaders emphasized, it stood for the same religious and political freedoms that were dear to Americans.[22] Japan and the missionaries found another ally in war correspondent George Kennan.[23] A confidant of Roosevelt and a well-known critic of Russia, he accused its Orthodox Church of "ecclesiastical semi-barbarism" because it persecuted followers of other faiths. (Fresh in American minds was the 1903 anti-Semitic pogrom in Kishinev, which the American press had widely condemned.) "So-called Christian Russia," missionaries added, did not practice the religion taught by Christ. Of the two nations at war, only Japan was civilized, Kennan and the missionaries agreed. Japan also was morally superior to its adversary because its leaders advocated the ideal most necessary to Christian civilization: freedom of thought. In fact, Kennan informed Roosevelt, Japan was America's equal in both civilization and Christian virtues.[24]

Yet missionaries did not jettison their faith in the primacy of Christianity. They did, however, find a means of reconciling their recent observations with their long-held beliefs. They continued to regard religious freedom as a uniquely Christian ideal; therefore, if a nation espoused it, that nation was Christian at heart. Because the Japanese constitution granted religious freedom, Japan was more Christian than Russia and was holding open the door for Christ as well as for commerce. Once missionaries had concluded that Japan's domestic policies and strategic interests roughly coincided with their own, they began to minimize the differences that they previously had emphasized. Japan, which two generations of missionaries had depicted as heathen, now was Christianity's proxy in Northeast Asia.

On the question of Japan's racial categorization, American scholars also highlighted similarities rather than differences. While identifying racial differences between the Japanese and other Asians, scholars claimed simultaneously to have discovered racial similarities between the Japanese and Westerners. The racial classification of the Ainu—Japan's aboriginal people—became pivotal in this discussion.

In the Meiji period, the racial backgrounds of the Japanese and the Ainu attracted intense scholarly attention. Many leading Western experts on Japan took great interest in identifying its racial origins, which they believed enabled them and their readers to locate Japan's proper position in the hierarchy of races. This task often proved difficult because the Japanese and the Ainu seemed to exhibit characteristics that contradicted the commonly ascribed qualities of their respective racial categories.

The question of Ainu racial categorization and its relationship to the Japanese centered on three observations. First, the Ainu seemed to be uncivilized, perhaps even savage. Second, the Ainu's historical relationship with the Japanese seemed analogous to that of American Indians with European Americans. Finally, and most puzzling, the Ainu looked Caucasian. As for the Japanese, it was clear to most American observers that physically they were an "Asiatic" people. Unlike their racial brethren, however, the Japanese proved remarkably capable of assimilating Western civilization.

At the turn of the century, American analysts made Japan's racial classification a perennial topic, and the influence of their scholarly studies reached far beyond the pages of a few academic journals. The topic became especially meaningful as Americans attempted to reconcile Japan's development into a world power with their assumptions about race and progress. Nineteenth-century Western scholars sifted through archaeological and anthropological clues in their efforts to discover the geographic and racial origins of the Japanese people. Romyn Hitchcock, a former curator at the U.S. National Museum who spent three years teaching in Japan, observed that the Japanese differed ethnologically not only from the aboriginal Ainu, but also from continental Asians. Hitchcock was among the majority, including Griffis and Morse, who believed that the solution to this puzzle lay in a theory of separate prehistoric origins. They argued that the ancestors of the Ainu had migrated from Northeast Asia into Japan, where prehistoric remains indicated that they had settled throughout the islands. As additional proof of the Ainu presence, Griffis maintained that Ainu place-names had been appropriated by the Japanese and remained in every corner of the country. These scholars concluded that, over the course of centuries, a migration stream of various races from southern Asia had conquered and absorbed all of the Ainu except those in Hokkaido, who survived as Japan's last pure aborigines. This model explained why the Japanese differed from the Ainu.[25]

Intellectuals in both the United States and Japan were convinced that the Japanese as a "race" differed also from continental Asian "races." Griffis and Morse both pointed out that the Japanese were a composite race, formed from the fusing of the "Ainō, Malay, Nigrito, Corean, and Yamato" races. This racial intermixture made the Japanese "ethnologically, physically, and morally" as distinct from the Chinese as Americans were from Turks, claimed one observer. Japanese scholars presented a similar case. To highlight differences between Japan and Korea, Imperial University's Inoue Tetsujirō emphasized the Malay-Polynesian component in Japan's racial heritage. Much like Fukuzawa's call for Japan to "escape" from Asia, the conviction that the Japanese were a composite race served to differentiate between Japan and its Asian neighbors.[26]

Scholars also noted that Japan's heterogeneous racial background linked it to certain Western powers. Anthropologist W J McGee, head of the Bureau of American Ethnology at the Smithsonian Institution and husband of surgeon Anita

Newcomb McGee, believed that the world's most advanced nations were of mixed blood.[27] The commingling of blood strains in Japan, McGee contended, had made it "the most complex nation of the Orient, just as the Anglo-Saxons, through the waves of successive populations that swept over the continents, were made the most complex nation of the Occident." And in Ōkuma Shigenobu's view, the intermixture of races in Japan resembled England's racial heritage: the best qualities of each race had been fused into a single nation. This discourse on Japanese racial origins not only separated Japan from Asia, but also associated Japan with the West's most prominent powers.[28]

Many Western scholars and travelers further observed that the Ainu also offered a sharp contrast to Japanese civilization. Having identified separate Japanese and Ainu origins, Westerners quickly proceeded to typecast the "hairy Ainu" of Hokkaido as aboriginal savages on Japan's northern frontier. The Ainu were "barbarians pure and simple" who drank too much and washed too little. Indeed, Americans and Britons agreed that the Ainu's "antipathy to water and utter ignorance of soap" made it difficult to determine their skin color. On this point, Ainu practice contrasted sharply with the scrupulous Japanese bathing habits that so many American writers had already described. Thus cleanliness continued to be an identifying characteristic of civilization. Like hogs born to delight in filth, the Ainu were "excluded from progress by an impassable barrier." Writers agreed unanimously that the Ainu had never been and would never be civilized.[29]

Hitchcock, who had met the Ainu firsthand, provided a scientific stamp of approval to this assertion. After traveling throughout Hokkaido in 1888 to collect Ainu artifacts, he reported to the U.S. National Museum that the Ainu remained savage despite centuries of close contact with Japanese civilization. Weak and degraded, they could not assimilate with the superior Japanese and so were doomed to extinction. He and other scholars believed that the Ainu had no written past and would have no future.[30]

Although there was no shortage of American reports on the Ainu, two Britons were most responsible for bringing them to the attention of large American audiences. Both Isabella L. Bird and John Batchelor helped to reinforce the perception of the Ainu as a dying race, but they also found much to admire among this people. In her widely read account, *Unbeaten Tracks in Japan*, Bird recalled that her most interesting experience during seven months in Japan had been the three days she spent living with an Ainu family in their hut. These "uncivilisable and altogether irreclaimable savages," she wrote, were infested with vermin and sunk in ignorance. A thoroughly conquered and unprogressive race, they had nothing to offer the world, nothing to set them apart as a people, and nothing that would endure beyond their impending demise. And yet, she noted, their kindness and hospitality frequently made her forget that they were savages. Beneath their thick hair, their eyes were beautiful, their smiles sweet, and their voices musical. The Ainu were in fact an attractive people whose company Bird enjoyed in those moments when she shed her preconceptions about civilization and savagery.[31]

Bird's sympathy for the Ainu paled in comparison to that of Batchelor, an Anglican missionary who produced the first Ainu translation of the New Testament. After five years of work in Hokkaido, Batchelor began in 1882 to work full time with the Ainu, a mission he continued until World War Two. His books and essays established him as the foremost Western expert on the Ainu and, like Bird's travelogue, were highly regarded in the American religious, secular, and scientific press. In their own reports, American missionaries and scholars regularly recognized his contributions.

While Batchelor portrayed the Ainu as a defeated and disappearing people, he assailed writers who exaggerated Ainu hirsuteness and treated them as Darwin's missing link. Such accounts, Batchelor charged, were completely unreliable. The Ainu were a civilized and good-natured people, not wild savages. He noted that the Ainu were "a nation of drunkards," but pointed out that this was true only because the Japanese often paid Ainu workers with sake. The Ainu man was what other people made of him: "Treat him as a man, and he will show himself to be a man; but treat him as a child, and he will act as a child, and at the same time think how very foolish the one is who treated him so." Yet Batchelor damned the Ainu with faint praise; he recognized the Ainu as human brethren and at the same time considered them a victimized people, unable or unwilling to recapture the upper hand.[32]

Thus even such a sympathetic witness as Batchelor had mixed feelings and contributed to the argument that the Ainu were beyond redemption. Although he found them gentle in character, he agreed that they were filthy in appearance and habits. Believing that God had created the Ainu for some purpose, he objected strongly to the view that their existence was purposeless, yet he concurred that their extinction seemed inevitable. As a missionary, Batchelor continued to work for the Ainu's spiritual deliverance even as he was convinced that they had no hope of ethnological salvation.[33]

To Americans, the image of a conquered and vanishing race was familiar. Many believed that it revealed affinities between two conquered races—the Ainu and Native Americans—and two conquering races—the Japanese and white Americans. Griffis, the first popular writer to make this comparison, recalled that on his transcontinental railroad journey en route to Japan in 1870, a Union Pacific Railway conductor's "scalpless cranium bore witness" that Indians roamed the plains. Once in Japan, he became convinced that the relationship between Ainu and Japanese was like that between Indians and whites. Although he did not visit Hokkaido, Griffis studied the Ainu in Tokyo under the instruction of the Hokkaido Colonization Commission. In his opinion, both the Ainu and the Indians had been treacherous savages whose preferred method of warfare was the ambush: on Japan's ancient frontier, the Ainu had incited a history of confrontation like the continuing conflicts of the United States with its own aborigines. "Like the 'blanket Indians' on the reservations," he concluded, the Ainu were now defeated and disappearing. Leaving nothing more than geographic names, these races were "embalmed" in such words as "Niagara" and "Noto."[34]

Griffis's interpretation gained influence as it was adopted by the American scientists, missionaries, and travel writers who followed in his footsteps. For the National Museum, Hitchcock classified both the Ainu and American Indians as "lower types of human existence" whose lifestyle appeared picturesque at a distance but actually was miserable and savage. Missionary writers explained that Ainu culture was inferior to the higher civilization of the Japanese. Like the Indians, missionaries contended, the Ainu retreated as civilization advanced. Similarly, writers in popular magazines concluded that both the Ainu and the Indians were vanishing because they were not fit enough to survive. According to Edward Greey, who wrote a trilogy of novels on Japan for young readers, the looming extinction of the Ainu was no fault of the Japanese. When one of Greey's characters, an American visitor to Hokkaido, is told that the Japanese treat the Ainu just as Americans treat the Indians, he responds, "Kill them off, eh?" His Japanese host patiently corrects him by explaining that the Japanese, in their work to reclaim the island for agriculture, had no desire to exterminate the harmless Ainu.[35]

In fact, the Ainu and Native Americans did have much in common. Before Japan and the United States began to expand overseas, both nations had gained experience in subjugating and relocating indigenous peoples and had expropriated their hunting lands for farming. In the United States, the Dawes Severalty Act of 1887 permitted the allotment of reservation lands to individual Indians in an effort to weaken tribal ties; in Japan, the Hokkaido Former Natives Protection Act of 1899 allotted land—often of inferior quality—to Ainu families in an effort to turn them into farmers. Moreover, the ideas of Hitchcock and Bird directly influenced Japanese attitudes toward the Ainu. Classifying the Ainu as a primitive, inferior race enabled the Japanese to justify their efforts to eradicate Ainu culture and explained the Ainu's failure to adopt Japanese civilization.[36] Japanese and Americans both believed that, within their national borders, they confronted uncivilized races that were unfit and would not survive.

In their studies of the Ainu, Americans determined also that the two conquering races shared a similar legacy. Like Americans, the Japanese were progressive and expansive. Civilization had faced savage enemies on the Japanese and American frontiers, but it had been ably defended by two peoples, now battle-hardened. Like Japan's victories over China and Russia, Japan's defeat of the Ainu won American esteem. By identifying and highlighting differences between the Ainu and the Japanese, Americans believed they had discovered affinities between the Japanese and themselves. Hence, American discussions of the Ainu elevated the Japanese.[37]

One Ainu trait, however, complicated matters: these "savages" who were failing in the struggle of races appeared to be white. Since their first encounters with the Ainu, Americans had noted with fascination the ruddiness of Ainu skin and the full beards of the men. These physical characteristics indicated to Americans that the Ainu were a Caucasian or an Aryan people who had drifted eastward in prehistoric times before migrating into Japan from the north. In their influential studies of the Ainu, both Bird and Batchelor lent support to this thesis. During her stay with her Ainu hosts, Bird became convinced that their facial features and expressions were more European than Asian. And Batchelor, whose expertise on the Ainu language was unsurpassed by any Westerner, claimed that it was an Aryan language and that the Ainu race itself was of Aryan stock. As the anthropologist McGee put it, the Ainu were an "ethnologic puzzle" because their physical characteristics were more Caucasian than Mongolian. If the Ainu were Caucasian, would not this undermine the hierarchy of race in which so many Americans believed?[38]

By 1904, Americans had at hand a variety of written sources on the Ainu; in the same year, many had the opportunity to study the Ainu firsthand. The Louisiana Purchase Exposition in St. Louis featured ethnological exhibits including more than thirty living groups of racial, ethnic, and cultural "types." As head of the exposition's Anthropology Department, McGee arranged for groups of Ainu, Native Americans, Africans, and Filipinos to live on the fairgrounds as objects of study and sightseeing. They were to illustrate his theory of human progress through "the four culture grades of savagery, barbarism, civilization, and enlightenment." McGee contended that Americans belonged to the higher Caucasian race as well as to the enlightened culture grade. The Ainu, however, continued to pose a mystery.[39]

At McGee's request, University of Chicago anthropology professor Frederick Starr had gone to Hokkaido and, with the assistance of Batchelor, recruited nine Ainu to travel to St. Louis. (During Starr's visit, many Japanese had carefully emphasized to him that neither their race nor their culture had Ainu roots.) Yet at the exposition, the Ainu disappointed those who had hoped to see "dog-eaters or wild men." Visitors instead found these "mysterious little Japanese primitives" to be clean and courteous. Even more surprising, the Ainu group attended a nearby Episcopal church. Of course the Ainu were "semi-civilized savages," but they did seem to be Caucasian.[40]

Using the living exhibits as the centerpiece of a three-week ethnology course, Starr delivered a lecture on the "Physical Characters of Race" before taking his students to visit the Ainu group. In his published account of the Ainu, which was sold as a souvenir at the fair, he offered a solution to the Ainu puzzle by suggesting that they undermined the idea of racial hierarchy. Starr declared that Ainu physical features—white skin, abundant hair, and a prominent nose—"are those of the white race rather than the yellow." Clearly, the Ainu were the racial kin of Caucasians, not the Japanese, he averred, and thus the failure of the Ainu in their struggle against the Japanese struck at the heart of the American belief in white superiority. "We take it for granted that all white men are better than any red ones, or black ones, or yellow ones. Yet here we find a *white race that has struggled and lost!*" In Starr's view, the Ainu proved that Caucasians were not biologically destined to prevail over other races.[41]

But Starr's solution was short-lived; Americans were beginning to find other ways to classify the Ainu and Japanese without sacrificing these hierarchies. For decades, Americans had occasionally identified physical resemblances between the Ainu and Russian peasants. Accompanied by Starr, scholar and editor Paul Carus visited the Ainu in St. Louis and remarked on the striking resemblance between one of the men and Tolstoy. Carus concluded that the Ainu, obviously white, were closest in blood to the Russians. Both were passive peoples, "amenable to authority." If the Ainu truly were an Aryan people, he maintained, they seemed to be from the Slavic branch of the Aryan family.[42]

During and after the Russo-Japanese War, the perceived affinities between the Ainu and Russians proved useful in modifying and preserving the belief in Anglo-Saxon superiority. Americans could acknowledge the Ainu and Russians as members of the Caucasian or Aryan "race," but could still separate them from the Anglo-Saxon "race": though white and Caucasian, the Ainu and Russians were inferior Slavs, not superior Anglo-Saxons. As Griffis noted, if the Ainu were scrubbed clean, anyone could see they were white. Just as importantly, however, they looked "exactly like fresh arrivals at Ellis Island"—in other words, less advanced East Europeans.[43]

While distinguishing between Russians and Anglo-Saxons, American analysts found a variety of means to liken the latter to the Japanese. Americans commonly referred to the Japanese as an Anglo-Saxon proxy in the competition for imperial power in East Asia. In the opinion of Captain Alfred Thayer Mahan, who as a young naval officer had visited Japan in 1867–69, the Japanese were "racially Asiatic" but "adoptively European." Japan, he wrote, was the only Asian nation to embrace Anglo-Saxon principles of government. It had sided with the United States and Great Britain as sea powers in the effort to thwart the expansion of Russia, a land power bent on establishing an exclusive commercial sphere in China. Roosevelt read and concurred with Mahan's analysis.[44]

Many others agreed that the Russo-Japanese War was a contest between Slav and Anglo-Saxon, with Japan representing the latter. They, too, held that Japan had become Occidental by adopting the political and social hallmarks of "Anglo-Saxon civilization." In the estimation of American observers, the Japanese seemed to have all the qualities necessary to succeed in a competitive struggle. As a writer for the *Nation* quipped, surely Secretary of State Hay would arrange a ceremony to adopt the Japanese as a white race.[45]

Some Americans argued that such a rite was unnecessary because the Japanese already were *ethnologically* a white race—a claim that attracted significant attention and support. Arthur

May Knapp, a former Unitarian missionary and the author of a popular 1897 work on Japan, observed that the Japanese complexion was as white as that of southern Europeans. Furthermore, he suggested, in their capacity for progress the Japanese were "Aryans to all intents and purposes," a claim with which *Current Opinion* and the *Outlook*'s Kennan agreed.[46]

While Griffis was discussing the intermixture of races in prehistoric Japan in his 1876 work, he wrote that the primary racial stock of the Japanese was Ainu. He claimed that the prehistoric Ainu, who had lived throughout the archipelago, had been assimilated and had contributed the main component of the modern Japanese racial heritage. (The Ainu remaining in Hokkaido were the descendants of those who had resisted Japanese expansion and had not been assimilated.)[47] He revisited this topic in the aftermath of the Russo-Japanese War, when American concerns about Japanese immigration and military ambitions began to grow. In lectures at churches, universities, and business associations, Griffis contended that the Japanese had descended from the prehistoric Ainu, who were white and spoke an Aryan language. Linguistics, archaeology, and history, he stated, demonstrated that the ancestors of the Japanese and the Europeans were kinsmen, and in temperament, the contemporary Japanese were akin to Anglo-Saxons. Advertising copy for Griffis's 1907 book, *The Japanese Nation in Evolution*, declared that it revealed for the first time the secret of Japan's success: "The White Blood in the Japanese."[48]

According to Griffis, Americans maintained the false orthodoxy that the Japanese were "Mongolian" and different from Anglo-Saxons only because of racial prejudice—"cuticular repulsions," in Griffis's words. In the *North American Review* he declared that "in mind, body, speech, thought, ways, institutions, [and] mental initiative," the Japanese were "the most un-Mongolian people in Asia." Other popular journals recognized Griffis as an authority on Japan and gave favorable attention to his pronouncement that the Japanese were a white race of Aryan descent.[49]

Knapp, Kennan, and Griffis had set two targets. First, by redefining the Japanese as white, they hoped that Japanese immigrants would be considered eligible for American citizenship. (In 1790 Congress had limited the right of naturalization to "any alien, being a free white person," and in 1870 it had extended this to persons of African nativity or descent.)[50] This trio of Japan experts tried to demonstrate that the Japanese were "free white persons" and thus statutorily fit for citizenship. Second, they aimed to undermine the growing movement to prohibit Japanese immigration, a campaign ignited in 1905 by the formation of the Asiatic Exclusion League in San Francisco. As they wrote in 1912–13, the California state legislature was on its way toward passage of a bill prohibiting land ownership by Japanese immigrants. Knapp, Kennan, and Griffis argued publicly that American-Japanese similarities overwhelmed any differences. An examination of Japan's achievements in recent decades proved to them and many other Americans that it had successfully assimilated Anglo-Saxon political institutions. Some further believed that scholarship and common sense revealed the Japanese to be white. They were not aliens but kin, and so deserved to be treated as equals in every sense.

Although this argument swayed few, if any, of those agitating against Japanese immigration, it did offer a new and effective means of preserving the accepted hierarchy of races. It provided an interpretation that reconciled the belief in white, Anglo-Saxon superiority with the seeming contradictions posed by Japan's stunning rise to power. By grouping the contemporary Ainu together with the Russians, Americans were able to explain away the defeat of these "races": though white, the Ainu and Russians were backward Slavs, not conquering and progressive

Anglo-Saxons. In contrast, Griffis and others proclaimed, the Japanese were both white and similar to Anglo-Saxons. They were white because of their assimilation of the prehistoric Ainu. Moreover, American observers agreed that the Japanese were a composite race like the Anglo-Saxons. And finally, these Americans concurred that the Japanese had successfully adopted those institutions and strategic interests that defined Anglo-Saxon nations.

This argument was an integral part of widespread American anxieties about race and religion at the turn of the century. With the 1885 publication of *Our Country*, a revised edition of the American Home Missionary Society handbook, Congregational minister Josiah Strong had emerged as a spokesman for those who feared that immigration posed a peril to Protestant, Anglo-Saxon civilization. Strong, who himself had nearly gone to Japan as a missionary, identified the Anglo-Saxon as the world's "great missionary race" because it espoused civil liberty and Protestant Christianity. Roosevelt, exhorting fellow English-speaking Americans to "work—fight—breed," agonized over the prospect of "race suicide" posed by their diminishing birth rate.[51]

Japan was an important component in American discussions of race, but not only as a looming yellow peril. While those who saw Japan as a rival differentiated the Japanese from themselves, many sought to explain the Japanese anomaly by dissolving differences and stressing similarities between Japan and the United States. When Japan challenged American assumptions about race and religion, American missionaries and scholars responded by redefining the Japanese. Japanese officials and intellectuals offered significant support to such efforts.

These Japanese tried to persuade the American public that Japan represented modern, Western civilization in the East: Japan was "Occidentalizing" the Orient. It was opening doors to civilize and Christianize the backward Asian heathen. Japan, they asserted, had much more in common with the United States than with its Asian neighbors. In presenting their case, the Japanese had notable success in the American press and among American statesmen, missionaries, and other experts on Japan. Missionaries and scholars who lived and worked in Japan often had personal and professional interests in promoting their host country. American missionaries agreed that heathen nations were indeed despotic but claimed that Japan was practically Christian. Scholars maintained that Asiatics were indeed backward but asserted that the Japanese were not Asiatic. Unable to accept Japan as both an equal and an Other, these Americans ranged far and wide to bring Japan within the fold of Anglo-Saxon Christendom. From this perspective, Japan had succeeded not in spite of, but because of its religious and racial traits.

Tokutomi Sohō, a prominent journalist, wrote in 1904 that the world had considered the Sino-Japanese War to be "simply a conflict among fellow heathens." With its victories over Russia, however, Japan was "dispelling the myth of the inferiority of the non-white races."[52] But Tokutomi, once a Christian himself, proved too optimistic. To most Americans, this myth was sacrosanct. Rather than part with it, they manipulated images of Japanese success to confirm their belief that modern civilization was synonymous with whiteness and Christianity.

Although the American faith in Anglo-Saxon and Christian superiority was unbending, race and religion themselves proved to be resilient categories. In order to acknowledge Japanese achievements, many analysts pushed these categories to their limits and resorted to intellectual contortions. They sought to cultivate American respect for Japan, but their efforts verified the ostensible primacy of whiteness and Christianity. Instead of accepting Japan as a modern power that disproved these beliefs, they stretched the terms "Christian," "Anglo-Saxon," and

"white" to co-opt the Japanese. This flexibility helped to legitimate Japanese power in East Asia in the early twentieth century
and enabled many American missionaries, statesmen, and scholars to erase—at least for themselves—the anomaly of a modern
yet heathen Asian nation.

CONCLUSION

[I]deals may well be theoretically divided into good and bad, into superior and inferior, but men—and the actual battle is one of men against men—cannot be thus divided and set off against one another, and each one of them contains within himself in varying degree the true and the false, the high and the low, spirit and matter.

—Benedetto Croce, *History of Europe in the Nineteenth Century*

On the night of 13 September 1912, the funeral procession for Emperor Meiji left the palace grounds. Born in 1852, the year before the Perry Expedition's first visit, the emperor had ascended the throne in 1867 and presided over an era of unprecedented change. As his funeral cortege made its way through the streets of Tokyo, the black lacquer wheels of his ox drawn cart reflected both the glow of torches and the glare of arc lights. Crowds of mourners lined the three-mile route and watched silently as thousands of courtiers, officials, military guards, and Shinto priests accompanied the imperial casket. Cannons thundered and temple bells tolled in salute. To a character in Natsume Sōseki's 1914 novel *Kokoro*, the booming of the cannon "sounded like the last lament for the passing of an age." Sōseki, modern Japan's most beloved writer, had felt Japan shift under his feet. The imperial ox-cart and silk court robes were anachronisms in twentieth-century Japan. Now a power with its own colonies, Japan was better characterized by the frock coats and khaki uniforms of the officials and soldiers in the cortege.[1]

The end of the Meiji era also coincided with the passing of an age in American-Japanese relations. Treaties signed with the United States and Great Britain in 1911 had restored tariff autonomy to Japan. Japan had eliminated the last humiliating vestige of the unequal treaties and claimed its place as a sovereign equal of the Western powers. Veteran observers of Japan now argued that the Japanese had indeed escaped from Asia: Christian at heart if not in name, they were cousins of the Anglo-Saxon. Like their newfound kin, they were establishing and defending outposts of civilization in their East Asian colonies.

Other developments also signalled the passing of an age. In the first years of the twentieth century, when Japanese immigration to the United States began to grow, its American opponents argued that Japanese immigrants were racially and culturally incapable of assimilating into American society. No achievement, immigration opponents argued, could change Japan's Mongolian—hence inferior—racial heritage. The Chinese, not the Anglo-Saxons, were the true cousins of the Japanese. Groups like San Francisco's Asiatic Exclusion League believed that the exclusion of Chinese immigrants two decades earlier had protected the American stronghold of civilization. Rejecting the idea that Anglo-Saxons shared any characteristics with the Japanese, American exclusionists worked to bar the doors to their entry. The exclusion movement assailed Japanese immigrants as a fifth column whose loyalties would lie forever with Japan (an allegation repeated during World War Two to justify the internment of Japanese Americans). Japan's new military strength also stoked the fears of anti-Japanese activists and kindled a series of war scares that punctuated the early twentieth century.

In 1907, the exclusion movement achieved a partial victory when the United States and Japan negotiated the Gentlemen's Agreement, halting the immigration of Japanese laborers; in connection with the 1911 treaty on tariff autonomy, Japan pledged to continue the ban. Finally, the movement succeeded in excluding all Japanese immigrants (and also in sharply reducing the number of East European immigrants) when an overwhelming majority in Congress passed the National Origins Act of 1924. The act did not specifically mention the Japanese, but it prohibited the immigration of aliens ineligible for citizenship. The Japanese were the clear target of this provision: two years earlier, the Supreme Court had ruled that Japanese residents were "clearly of a race which is not Caucasian" and thus not among the "free white persons" entitled to citizenship.[2]

Other nations, facing related questions, responded differently but no less perniciously. In the Netherlands Indies in 1899, after Japan's defeat of China, the Dutch promoted the Japanese within the colony's system of racial classification. No longer "Foreign Orientals," the Japanese were now officially "Europeans." This status granted them a wide range of legal and political rights denied to "Orientals" and native Indonesians. More recently, South Africa's apartheid regime bestowed upon the Japanese— who were important trade partners—the ostensible privilege of being "honorary whites."[3] Consider this: both a judicial decision denying citizenship to Japanese residents because they were not white and government policies granting Japanese visitors special rights because they were white appear to us as willfully absurd. Should not this lead us to question the utility, if not the integrity, of any notion of race?

The Dutch and South African responses to Japanese power parallel the mental contortions of those Americans who tried to adopt the Japanese as Anglo-Saxons but declined to use Japan as an instrument to dismantle the hierarchy of races. As Americans defined and redefined Japan, they were also engaged in other projects of identity construction. At home, they were removing Native Americans from ancestral lands. Abroad, they were annexing Hawaii and imposing colonial government on the Philippines. Missionaries were also active in China, Burma, India, and Africa. Americans pictured themselves as the bearers of civilization to backward and benighted peoples. In their relations with these peoples, Americans were able to quell resistance to U.S. expansion and to strengthen their confidence in white, Christian superiority.

In this environment, Japan was unusual. After suffering the indignity of the unequal treaties, it had remade itself using the Western powers as a model. Many Americans believed that Meiji Japan had done what no other Asian nation seemed able to do: with Western guidance, it had civilized itself. This constituted a challenge to American ideas about race, religion, and civilization. Americans defended these ideas by reconstructing Japanese identity.

Their efforts demonstrate that the histories of American foreign policy and culture not only overlap, but also are interwoven. Assumptions about the nature of modern civilization spurred American diplomats first to restrict Japanese sovereignty and later to support its restoration. Missionaries, in their attempts to sway American policy, highlighted the relationship between religion and progress. Japan became a frequent and salient component of American discussions of race and religion. As Gilded Age scholars indicated, if one was to explain the relationship between racial characteristics and levels of civilization, one had to account for the case of Japan. As missionaries recognized, if one was to compare the roles of religion and science in the advance of knowledge, one had to note Japan's recent history. And, as artists showed, if one was concerned about the corrosive effects of modern progress, one could point to Japan's experience. In this manner, foreign relations influenced several domestic discourses.

The Japanese themselves deliberately sought to influence American opinion by cultivating supporters—men and women such as Griffis and Bacon who became convinced that the Japanese, "to all intents and purposes," were Christian and white. This assessment, though widely disseminated, did not take root. In the twentieth century, American friends of Japan failed to persuade the public at large that the Japanese truly were civilized kin across the Pacific. After the craze for Japanese arts peaked, the image of Japan as a menace prevailed.

The formative era of American-Japanese relations presented an exceptional opportunity to Americans. It was not merely a period of friendship that evaporated in the face of immigration conflicts or imperialist aspirations; it did not simply set the stage for the well-known series of clashes leading to Pearl Harbor. Instead, it introduced a significant challenge to American beliefs.

Many Americans took this opportunity to reexamine and revise their assumptions about race and religion. Few, however, used this occasion to question the hierarchical framework that supported these beliefs. They rearranged the seating chart rather than scrapping the hierarchies. The central question was not whether Mongolians were innately less capable than Caucasians: most Americans answered in the affirmative. The debate focused on whether the Japanese were an exception to this rule or were not Mongolian after all. Although Griffis, Kennan, and their colleagues tried to adopt the Japanese as whites, they did not attack the entire notion of racial hierarchy. Thus, the American faith in Christian, Anglo-Saxon civilization and heathen, Mongolian backwardness remained robust and ready to those who saw the Japanese as unexceptional Mongolians and who saw in Japan a challenge only to American immigration and commercial policy. These cultural components of international relations did not lead the two nations to war but were a continuing irritant—an irritant that persists today. They have fuelled American concerns not only about the Japanese as immigrants, but also about Japan as an imperial power and a postwar economic superpower.

In another sense, too, Meiji Japan was an exception: it became an Asian imperialist. Japan saw its neighbors through its own reversed opera glass. It aimed successfully at joining not only the community of Western powers, but also the circle of imperial powers. During its relatively brief but infamous career as an imperialist, Japan constructed its own elaborate framework of identities. The Japanese elevated themselves as the world's leading race (*shidō minzoku*), collectively pure and uniquely divine. This Yamato race was to preside over Asia as a patriarch, guiding its lesser neighbors.[4] Japan escaped from Asia only to return as a colonizer.

Since World War Two, the Japanese discussion of self-identity has continued. In the large and popular literature of one facet of this discourse, *Nihonjinron* (Japanese-identity theory), the Japanese people appear as a homogeneous race endowed with a unique culture and society superior to others. Like the nineteenth-century project of escaping Asia, these myths of identity emphasize Japan's difference from others in order to elevate the Japanese nation or "race." Nihonjinron theorists wield homogeneity as an instrument to distinguish Japan from heterogeneous societies: homogeneity becomes a strength upon which Japan is said to have drawn in its rise to economic power, while racial and ethnic diversity in the United States becomes a weakness that tears at the American social fabric.[5]

In 1986, these ideas burst into American consciousness when Prime Minister Nakasone Yasuhiro claimed at a Liberal Democratic Party meeting that Japan's intellectual level was higher than that of the United States because of the presence in the latter of "blacks, Puertos Ricans and Mexicans." Under sharp American criticism, Nakasone attempted an apology, claiming that he had referred to literacy rates, not intelligence. He added that there were goals the United States "has not been able to accomplish in education and other areas because it's a multiracial society. It's easier in Japan because we're a homogeneous race." Few if any of his American critics were satisfied.[6]

The Japanese claim of uniqueness is itself hardly unique. It resembles the civilizing and Christianizing missions that Americans constructed for themselves in the nineteenth century. They, too, considered themselves uniquely endowed, superior in all fields of endeavor, and biologically destined for global supremacy. In the post–World War Two era, these Western convictions have assumed a different form: modernization theory, whose advocates have attempted to identify and analyze the economic, political, and social processes by which modern societies develop. As a project of identity construction, modernization theory elevates the West—especially those omnipresent Anglo-Saxons, the Americans and the British—as the model for others to follow. Implicitly, modernization is synonymous with westernization. This twentieth-century notion of a universal path of development is the successor to the nineteenth-century faith in a universal path of progress blazed by the white, Christian powers.[7]

At our turn of the century, we continue to hear echoes of the past. Popular analysts such as Karel van Wolferen commonly address "the Japan Problem" by arguing that the Japanese sociopolitical "System" (Wolferen's capitalization) squelches intellectual curiosity and creative thought. Attempting to explain the Japanese "enigma," a metaphor that Griffis identified as hackneyed more than 120 years ago, they warn their readers that Japan has not become a genuinely modern nation because it suppresses individualism. Why is this so? According to *Japan 2000*, a report based on a closed academic seminar funded by the C.I.A., the Japanese are an amoral race. Japan's large role in the world economy poses a grave threat "because of the absence of any absolutes or moral imperatives in the Japanese paradigm, unlike [in] the Western paradigm, anchored on the Judeo-Christian ethic." The unchanging and irrational Japanese "are creatures of an ageless, amoral, manipulative and controlling culture—not to be emulated—suited only to this race, in this place."[8] It seems that the modern, civilizing glow of Anglo-Saxon morality still has not enlightened Japan, at least in the imaginations of many contemporary observers. Carrying the torch of Spencer and Lowell, their unwitting heirs continue to insist that our differences are rooted in immutable racial and religious characteristics that have prevented the evolution of a "sense of self" in the Japanese. "Why must there always remain the width of a world between us?" Hearn wondered in 1904, discovering his answer in these very characteristics.[9]

How we define others, of course, says much about how we define ourselves. Much of our own identity is invested not only in the qualities we ascribe to our particular people, but also in the allegedly unchanging differences between these qualities and those we ascribe to other peoples. We assume that these attributes are objectively defined and permanent. Despite Japan's evidence to the contrary, Americans at the last turn of the century steadfastly believed that race and religion were determinants of behavior. Their sense of self-identity was closely tied to these convictions. Because the American faith in white, Christian superiority was ultimately unshakable, many American experts on Japan constructed remarkably flexible racial and religious categories.

This study began with a discussion of the history of racial categorization and the debate over the reality and utility of race as an objective biological category. Few Americans in Meiji Japan doubted either its reality or its utility. Their attempts to define Japan by both race and religion highlight the malleability of representations of difference and similarity. If a category can be bent to suit changing circumstances, its objectivity vanishes. The qualities ascribed to races and religions are not innate or immutable: they can be subjectively constructed, just as communities can be "imagined" and traditions "invented."[10] American depictions of Japan underscore the artificial nature of constructed identities.

Meiji Japan offered Americans an important lesson in race, religion, and civilization. Most failed to recognize it. Today, too, the lesson remains lost to many.

NOTES

Notes to the Introduction

1. Alice Mabel Bacon, *A Japanese Interior* (Boston: Houghton, Mifflin, 1893), 228.

2. Minister Robert H. Pruyn to Secretary of State William H. Seward, no. 31, 30 June 1862, Despatches from U.S. Ministers to Japan, 1855–1906 (M133, roll 4), Department of State, Record Group 59, National Archives.

3. Ruth Benedict, *The Chrysanthemum and the Sword* (Boston: Houghton Mifflin, 1946; reprint, New York: New American Library, 1974), 14.

4. For pathbreaking works on the construction of race, see Henry Louis Gates, Jr., ed., *"Race," Writing, and Difference* (Chicago: University of Chicago Press, 1986); Theodore W. Allen, *The Invention of the White Race*, 2 vols. (New York: Verso, 1994–97); Matthew Frye Jacobson, *Whiteness of a Different Color* (Cambridge: Harvard University Press, 1998).

Notes to Chapter 1

1. Matthew C. Perry, *The Japan Expedition*, ed. Roger Pineau (Washington, D.C.: Smithsonian Institution Press, 1968), 168; idem, *Narrative of the Expedition*, comp. Francis L. Hawks (Washington, D.C.: Beverly Tucker, Senate Printer, 1856; reprint, New York: AMS Press, 1967), 1:356–57.

2. Konishi Shirō, *Kaikoku to jōi*, vol. 19 of *Nihon no rekishi* (Tokyo: Chūō Kōronsha, 1974), 53; Perry, *The Japan Expedition*, 177, 194; idem, *Narrative of the Expedition*, 1:357–58, 372.

3. Katō Yūzō, *Kurofune ihen* (Tokyo: Iwanami Shoten, 1993), 136–37; Perry, *The Japan Expedition*, 190–94; idem, *Narrative of the Expedition*, 1:369–72.

4. Perry, *The Japan Expedition*, 194–96; George Henry Preble, *The Opening of Japan*, ed. Boleslaw Szczesniak (Norman: University of Oklahoma Press, 1962), 146, 150; Samuel Wells Williams, "A Journal of the Perry Expedition to Japan, 1853–1854," ed. Frederick Wells Williams, *Transactions of the Asiatic Society of Japan* (Yokohama) 37, part 2 (1910): 148.

5. Jared Diamond, "Race Without Color," *Discover* 15 (November 1994): 83; Jonathan Marks, *Human Biodiversity* (New York: Aldine de Gruyter, 1995), 125–33, 157–80.

6. Carolus Linnaeus quoted in Marks, *Human Biodiversity*, 49–50.

7. Stephen Jay Gould, "The Geometer of Race," *Discover* 15 (November 1994): 65–69. For nineteenth-century depictions of Blumenbach's taxonomy, see Michael H. Hunt, *Ideology and U.S. Foreign Policy* (New Haven: Yale University Press, 1987), 49–50.

8. Samuel George Morton quoted in William Stanton, *The Leopard's Spots* (Chicago: University of Chicago Press, 1960), 33; Gould, *The Mismeasure of Man* (New York: W. W. Norton, 1981), 50–69.

9. Josiah C. Nott and George R. Gliddon, *Types of Mankind* (Philadelphia: Lippincott, Grambo, 1854), 52–53, 458–59.

10. Reginald Horsman, *Race and Manifest Destiny* (Cambridge: Harvard University Press, 1981), 9–10, 32–44; Thomas F. Gossett, *Race: The History of an Idea in America* (Dallas: Southern Methodist University Press, 1963), 88–110.

11. William H. Truettner, ed., *The West as America* (Washington, D.C.: Smithsonian Institution Press, 1991), 130–31, 134–35.

12. Charles Darwin, *The Descent of Man*, 2d ed. (New York: A. L. Burt, 1874), 160–61; idem, *On the Origin of Species* (London: John Murray, 1859).

13. Herbert Spencer, *The Principles of Biology* (New York: D. Appleton, 1866–67; reprint, New York: D. Appleton, 1884), 1:444; Robert C. Bannister, *Social Darwinism* (Philadelphia: Temple University Press, 1979), 59.

14. Spencer, *The Principles of Sociology*, 3d ed. (New York: D. Appleton, 1880–96; reprint, New York: D. Appleton, 1925–29), 1:90–93; idem, "The Comparative Psychology of Man" [1875], in *Essays: Scientific, Political, and Speculative* (New York: D. Appleton, 1891; reprint, Osnabrück, Germany: Otto Zeller, 1966), 1:354–59; idem, *The Principles of Psychology*, 4th ed. (London: Williams and Norgate, 1899; reprint, Osnabrück, Germany: Otto Zeller, 1966), 1:460–71.

15. Spencer, *First Principles*, 5th ed. (New York: A. L. Burt, 1880), 343; idem, *The Principles of Biology*, 1:473–75, 2:377–88; idem, *The Principles of Sociology*, 1:449–53, 2:597–600, 607–8.

16. William James, "Herbert Spencer," *Atlantic Monthly* 94 (July 1904): 99; [Edward L. Youmans, comp.], *Herbert Spencer on the Americans* (New York: D. Appleton, 1883), 22–24.

17. Donald L. Philippi, trans., *Kojiki* (Tokyo: University of Tokyo Press, 1968), 79–85; Noah Brooks, "Awakened Japan," *Scribner's Monthly* 3 (April 1872): 669–71.

18. [Robert Tomes], "Commodore Perry's Expedition to Japan," *Harper's Monthly* 12 (March 1856): 441; "Japan," *Putnam's Monthly* 1 (March 1853): 241; "Japan," *Democratic Review* 30 (April 1852): 332.

19. Duane B. Simmons, "Five Years in Japan," *Galaxy* 5 (May 1868): 606–8; "Japan," *Republic* 1 (May 1873): 123.

20. Edward H. House, "The Present and Future of Japan," *Harper's Monthly* 46 (May 1873): 859–60; Edward Warren Clark, "International Relations with Japan," *International Review* 4 (January–February 1877): 53–57; William Elliot Griffis, *The Mikado's Empire* (New York: Harper and Brothers, 1876), 102, 140–46, 293; Brooks, "A Chapter of Condensed History," *Overland Monthly* 9 (August 1872): 108.

21. Griffis, *The Mikado's Empire*, 293, 304.

22. Griffis, *The Mikado's Empire*, 291–324; House, "The Present and Future of Japan," 859–61; Clark, "International Relations with Japan," 54–57.

23. Brooks, "A Chapter of Condensed History," 114.

24. W. H. Hallock, "Jaunts in Japan," *Scribner's Monthly* 2 (July 1871): 242, 245; W. E. McArthur, "Some Japanese Interiors," *Overland Monthly* 6 (January 1871): 22; J. Bishop Putnam, "A New Yorker in Japan," *Putnam's Magazine* 1 (June 1868): 761–62.

25. Hallock, "Jaunts in Japan," 242–44; Griffis, *The Mikado's Empire*, 331–33, 360–61, 417; McArthur, "Some Japanese Interiors," 15–24.

26. J. Edward Kidder, Jr., "The Earliest Societies in Japan," in *Ancient Japan*, ed. Delmer M. Brown, vol. 1 of *The Cambridge History of Japan*, ed. John Whitney Hall et al. (New York: Cambridge University Press, 1993), 48–49, 97; Edward Howland, "With the Count de Beauvoir in Japan and California," *Lippincott's Magazine* 13 (April 1874): 410.

27. McArthur, "Some Japanese Interiors," 17–18, 20; Howland, "With the Count de Beauvoir," 405, 410.

28. Clark, *Life and Adventure in Japan* (New York: American Tract Society, 1878), 19–21; Henry M. Field, *From Egypt to Japan* (New York: Scribner, Armstrong, 1877): 404–5.

29. Lyman Abbott, "Pictures of the Japanese," *Harper's Monthly* 39 (August 1869): 308–9; "Japan and the Japanese," *Southern Review* 16 (January 1875): 36–37.

30. Percival Lowell, "The Soul of the Far East," part 3, *Atlantic Monthly* 60 (November 1887): 619–20; John La Farge, "An Artist's Letters from Japan," *Century* 40 (August 1890): 572; Griffis, *The Mikado's Empire*, 446; Putnam, "A New Yorker in Japan," 759.

31. Williams, "A Journal of the Perry Expedition to Japan," 183–84; Preble, *The Opening of Japan*, 183; Perry, *Narrative of the Expedition*, 1:405, facing 408.

32. Richard Hildreth, *Japan As It Was and Is* (Boston: Phillips, Sampson, 1855; reprint, Wilmington, Del.: Scholarly Resources, 1973), 487; Laurence Oliphant, *Narrative of the Earl of Elgin's Mission* (New York: Harper and Brothers, 1860; reprint, New York: Praeger Publishers, 1970), 638–39; Stafford Ransome, *Japan in Transition* (New York: Harper and Brothers, 1899), 115; Edward Yorke McCauley, *With Perry in Japan*, ed. Allan B. Cole (Princeton: Princeton University Press, 1942), 108.

33. Griffis, *Hepburn of Japan* (Philadelphia: Westminster Press, 1913), 84; "Letter from Mr. [Orramel H.] Gulick," *Missionary Herald* 67 (July 1871): 208; Reginald Heber, "From Greenland's Icy Moun-

tains," in Protestant Episcopal Church in the United States, *Hymnal*, rev. ed. (New York: Pott, Young, 1875), 261; James C. Hepburn, "Monthly Concert," *Foreign Missionary* 32 (September 1873): 108.

34. Edward S. Morse, *Japanese Homes and Their Surroundings* (Boston: Ticknor, 1886; reprint, Rutland, Vt.: Charles E. Tuttle, 1972), 199–202; idem, *Japan Day by Day* (Boston: Houghton Mifflin, 1917; reprint, Tokyo: Kobunsha Publishing, 1936), 1:97–101; James Jackson Jarves, *A Glimpse at the Art of Japan* (New York: Hurd and Houghton, 1876; reprint, Rutland, Vt.: Charles E. Tuttle, 1984), 64–65.

35. Sidney L. Gulick, *Evolution of the Japanese* (New York: Fleming H. Revell, 1903), 107; Masao Miyoshi, *As We Saw Them* (Berkeley and Los Angeles: University of California Press, 1979), 73, 78.

36. Clifford Geertz, *The Interpretation of Cultures* (New York: Basic Books, 1973), 3–30.

37. Lowell, "The Soul of the Far East," part 1, *Atlantic Monthly* 60 (September 1887): 411. In book form, the essays went through six editions by 1912.

38. Ibid., 408.

39. Ibid., 405–13; idem, "The Soul of the Far East," part 4, *Atlantic Monthly* 60 (December 1887): 846–49.

40. Ibid., 849.

41. Fukuzawa Yukichi, *An Encouragement of Learning*, trans. David A. Dilworth and Umeyo Hirano (Tokyo: Sophia University, 1969), 15–20, 29–33; idem, *An Outline of a Theory of Civilization*, trans. Dilworth and G. Cameron Hurst (Tokyo: Sophia University, 1973), 13–14, 99; Carmen Blacker, *The Japanese Enlightenment* (Cambridge: Cambridge University Press, 1964), 31–40, 52–56.

42. Fukuzawa, *An Encouragement of Learning*, 93–100; idem, *An Outline of a Theory of Civilization*, 171; idem quoted in Watanabe Masao, "Science across the Pacific," in *The Modernizers*, ed. Ardath W. Burks (Boulder: Westview Press, 1985), 370–71.

43. Michel Foucault, *Discipline and Punish*, trans. Alan Sheridan (New York: Vintage Books, 1995), 200–209.

44. Francis Hall, *Japan through American Eyes*, ed. F. G. Notehelfer (Princeton: Princeton University Press, 1992), 132–35.

45. Ann Yonemura, *Yokohama* (Washington, D.C.: Smithsonian Institution, 1990).

46. McArthur, "Some Japanese Interiors," 20; Morse, *Japan Day by*

Day, 1:438–39, 2:67–68; Theodore Wores, "The Wistaria Shrine of Kameido," *Cosmopolitan* 25 (May 1898): 21–22.

47. Isabella L. Bird, *Unbeaten Tracks in Japan* (London: John Murray, 1880; reprint, Boston: Beacon Press, 1987), 49; Jonathan Swift, *Gulliver's Travels* (1726; reprint, New York: W. W. Norton, 1961), 11; Helen P. Curtis, "Japan," *Missionary Review of the World* 11 (November 1888): 850.

48. Simmons, "Five Years in Japan," 613; Jas. Harris, "Japanese Holy Places," *Overland Monthly* 1 (September 1868): 242.

49. Robert F. Berkhofer, Jr., *The White Man's Indian* (New York: Alfred A. Knopf, 1978), 120–21, 138; Mary Louise Pratt, *Imperial Eyes* (New York: Routledge, 1992), 51–52.

50. Because the school underwent several name changes in the early Meiji period, I use "Kaisei Gakkō" for simplicity's sake in subsequent chapters.

51. Clark, *Life and Adventure in Japan,* 136–37. In 1870, Japan's first telegraph line opened between Tokyo and Yokohama; the first railroad line, also between Tokyo and Yokohama, opened in 1872.

52. For differing approaches to hegemony and multiplicities in colonial discourse, see Edward W. Said, *Orientalism* (New York: Vintage Books, 1979); Nicholas Thomas, *Colonialism's Culture* (Princeton: Princeton University Press, 1994); Homi Bhabha, "Of Mimicry and Man," *October,* no. 28 (spring 1984): 125–33.

53. Clark, *Life and Adventure in Japan,* 10–11, 36–37; Clark to Griffis, 24 November 1871, roll 9, Japan Letters, Group 1, William Elliot Griffis Collection, Special Collections and University Archives, Rutgers University Libraries. After returning to the United States in 1875, Clark became an Episcopal minister.

Notes to Chapter 2

1. "Map of the World," *Spirit of Missions* 37 (1872): frontispiece; "Go, Teach All Nations," *Life and Light for Heathen Women* 1 (March 1870): between 172 and 173.

2. Julius H. Seelye, "Heathen Civilizations," *Baptist Missionary Magazine* 54 (April 1874): 107; A. R. R. Crawley, "Christian Missions, or Perpetual Heathenism," *Baptist Missionary Magazine* 53 (September 1873): 337–39.

3. William Elliot Griffis, *Verbeck of Japan* (New York: Fleming H. Revell, 1900), 174.

4. Seelye, "Heathen Civilizations," 107; "Letter from Mr. [Orramel H.] Gulick," *Missionary Herald* 67 (July 1871): 207. Because many Gulick family members served as missionaries in Japan, their full names are given hereafter.

5. "Amity and Commerce," Charles I. Bevans, comp., *Treaties and Other International Agreements* (Washington, D.C.: U.S. Department of State, 1972), 9:362–72.

6. Secretary of State William H. Seward to Minister Robert B. Van Valkenburgh, no. 27, 9 September 1867, U.S. Department of State, *Foreign Relations of the United States* (hereafter *FRUS*), *1867* (Washington, D.C.: Government Printing Office, 1868), 2:59–61; Seward to Van Valkenburgh, no. 32, 7 October 1867, ibid., 2:63.

7. Suzuki Yūko, "Meiji seifu no Kirisutokyō seisaku," *Shigaku zasshi* 86 (February 1977): 177–95; Ebisawa Arimichi and Ōuchi Saburō, *Nihon Kirisutokyō shi* (Tokyo: Nihon Kirisuto Kyōdan Shuppankyoku, 1970), 154–62.

8. Van Valkenburgh to Seward, no. 55, 30 May 1868, *FRUS, 1868*, 1:749–51; Seward to Van Valkenburgh, no. 54, 14 July 1868, ibid., 1:757–58; Van Valkenburgh to Seward, no. 8, 27 January 1869, Despatches from U.S. Ministers to Japan, 1855–1906 (M133, roll 11), Department of State, Record Group 59, National Archives (hereafter Diplomatic Despatches, RG 59).

9. Van Valkenburgh to Seward, no. 44, 23 August 1867, *FRUS, 1867*, 2:56–58; Van Valkenburgh to Seward, no. 63, 12 November 1867, ibid., 2:68–72.

10. Van Valkenburgh to Seward, no. 44, 23 August 1867, *FRUS, 1867*, 2:56–58; Thomas W. Burkman, "The Urakami Incidents and the Struggle for Religious Toleration in Early Meiji Japan," *Japanese Journal of Religious Studies* 1 (June–September 1974): 162–63.

11 Van Valkenburgh to Seward, no. 67, 8 July 1868, *FRUS, 1868*, 1:766–71; Seward to Van Valkenburgh, no. 69, 5 September 1868, ibid., 1:811–12; Minister Charles E. De Long to Secretary of State Hamilton Fish, no. 13, 22 January 1870, *FRUS, 1870*, 460–68.

12. Consul Willie P. Mangum to Minister Charles E. De Long, no. 7, 18 January 1870, Records of the U.S. Legation in Japan, 1855–1912 (T400, roll 51), Department of State, Record Group 84, National

Archives (hereafter Legation Records, RG 84); "Japan," *New York Times*, 18 October 1868, 3; "Japan and China," *New York Times*, 26 February 1870, 2; "The Persecution Now Going On in Japan," *Spirit of Missions* 35 (May 1870): 295–300; Channing M. Williams, "From Bishop Williams," *Spirit of Missions* 35 (May 1870): 301–5.

13. "Appeal from Japan," *Missionary Herald* 67 (October 1871): 292–93.

14. Orramel H. Gulick, "Persecution," *Missionary Herald* 67 (October 1871): 294–96.

15. Vice-Consul Paul Frank to De Long, no. 129, 18 July 1871 (T400, roll 56), Legation Records, RG 84; Daniel Crosby Greene, "Death of Yeinoski," *Missionary Herald* 69 (April 1873): 125–26; idem, "Readiness to Hear," *Missionary Herald* 69 (June 1873): 191–92.

16. Orramel H. Gulick, "Persecution," 296.

17. Jonathan Goble, "The Japanese Embassy," *New York Times*, 20 February 1872, 8; "Annual Meeting of the Board," *Missionary Herald* 68 (November 1872): 337.

18. 16 March, 18 March 1872, Records Relating to the Treaty of Yedo (T119, roll 1), Department of State, Record Group 59, National Archives; M. L. Gordon, *Thirty Eventful Years* (Boston: Congregational House, 1901), 12–13.

19. Marlene J. Mayo, "The Iwakura Embassy and the Unequal Treaties, 1871–1873" (Ph.D. diss., Columbia University, 1961), 220.

20. De Long to Fish, no. 349, 23 February 1873 (M133, roll 22), Diplomatic Despatches, RG 59; Orramel H. Gulick, "Removal of the Edicts against Christianity," *Missionary Herald* 69 (June 1873): 192; Otis Cary, *A History of Christianity in Japan* (New York: Fleming H. Revell, 1909; reprint, Rutland, Vt.: Charles E. Tuttle, 1976), 1:333, 2:83–84.

21. Guido F. Verbeck, "History of Protestant Missions in Japan," in *Proceedings of the General Conference of the Protestant Missionaries of Japan* (Yokohama: R. Meiklejohn, 1883), 56–57.

22. "Letter from Miss Julia Gulick," *Life and Light for Woman* 14 (April 1884): 166; John 4:35; Richard Henry Drummond, *A History of Christianity in Japan* (Grand Rapids, Mich.: William B. Eerdmans Publishing, 1971), 200.

23. F. F. Ellinwood, "Monthly Concert," *Foreign Missionary* 34 (September 1875): 111.

24. Barbara Welter, "She Hath Done What She Could," *American Quarterly* 30 (winter 1978): 626–31; Griffis, *Verbeck of Japan*, 23, 64, 297.

25. "Missionary Work in Japan for the Year 1889," *Missionary Herald* 86 (May 1890): 183; "Statistics of Christian and Missionary Work in Japan for the Year 1899," *Missionary Herald* 96 (June 1900): 236.

26. Mark Twain and Charles Dudley Warner, *The Gilded Age* (1873; reprint, New York: Oxford University Press, 1996): 197.

27. "The Ninth Annual Session of the General Executive Committee," *Heathen Woman's Friend* 9 (June 1878): 266; Frances J. Baker, *The Story of the Woman's Foreign Missionary Society*, rev. ed. (Cincinnati: Curts and Jennings, 1898), 114.

28. Mrs. L. H. Daggett, ed., *Historical Sketches of Woman's Missionary Societies* (Boston: Daggett, 1883), 62, 128, 166; Psalm 72:11; S. A. Wilson, "Uniform Study," *Heathen Woman's Friend* 18 (April 1887): 267.

29. Mary J. Holbrook, "Answers from Japan," *Heathen Woman's Friend* 11 (August 1879): 29.

30. "Care for Your Missionary," *Life and Light for Woman* 5 (November 1875): 329–30; "Extract from Miss [Julia E.] Dudley's Letters," *Life and Light for Woman* 6 (April 1876): 120; "Letter from Miss [Eliza] Talcott," *Life and Light for Woman* 6 (January 1876): 6.

31. Marjorie King, "Exporting Femininity, Not Feminism" in *Women's Work for Women*, ed. Leslie A. Fleming (Boulder: Westview Press, 1989), 117–35.

32. Kathryn Kish Sklar, *Catharine Beecher* (New Haven: Yale University Press, 1973); Mary P. Ryan, *Womanhood in America* (New York: New Viewpoints, 1975), 12–13, 144–47.

33. Patricia R. Hill, *The World Their Household* (Ann Arbor, University of Michigan Press, 1985)

34. Kohiyama Rui, *Amerika fujin senkyōshi* (Tokyo: Tokyo Daigaku Shuppankai, 1992), 141, Shigehisa Tokutaro, *Kyoiku, shūkyō*, vol. 5 of *Oyatoi gaikokujin* (Tokyo: Kajima Shuppankai, 1968), 58–65.

35. Mary Sparkes Wheeler, *First Decade of the Woman's Foreign Missionary Society* (New York: Phillips and Hunt, 1881), 167, 210; "Sixth Annual Report of the Woman's Foreign Missionary Society," *Heathen Woman's Friend* 7 (July 1875): 7; Dora E. Schoonmaker, "Our Work in Tokio: No. I," *Heathen Woman's Friend* 8 (February 1876):

175; idem, "From Japan," *Heathen Woman's Friend* 8 (February 1876): 183; idem, "Japan," *Heathen Woman's Friend* 8 (July 1876): 21.

36. Schoonmaker, "From Japan," *Heathen Woman's Friend* 7 (August 1875): 38; idem, "Our Work in Tokio: No. II," *Heathen Woman's Friend* 7 (March 1876): 194; idem, "A Message Out of the Past," Dora Schoonmaker, Mission Biographical Reference Files, United Methodist Church Archives, Madison, N.J. (hereafter Methodist Archives); "Kwassui Jo Gakko, 1879–1929," pamphlet in Jennie Gheer, Mission Biographical Reference Files, Methodist Archives; M. L. Gordon, *An American Missionary in Japan* (Boston: Houghton, Mifflin, 1892), 27.

37. "Letter from Miss [Martha J.] Barrows," *Life and Light for Woman* 13 (February 1883): 67; Schoonmaker, "Our Work in Tokio: No. II," 194 (Schoonmaker's emphasis); "Notes of the Week," *Japan Weekly Mail* (Yokohama), 30 September 1876, 891.

38. Herbert Spencer, *The Principles of Sociology*, 3d ed. (New York: D. Appleton, 1885; reprint, New York: D. Appleton, 1925), 1:90–93.

39. Mrs. J. F. Willing, "Christian Marriage," *Heathen Woman's Friend* 1 (February 1870): 69; Mrs. M. B. Norton, "Japan: Manners and Customs," *Life and Light for Woman* 6 (May 1876): 132.

40. Mary A. Priest, "About Hakodate," *Heathen Woman's Friend* 11 (April 1880): 223; "Girls in Japan," *Life and Light for Woman* 10 (November 1880): 408–9.

41. Alice Mabel Bacon, *Japanese Girls and Women* (Boston: Houghton, Mifflin, 1891; reprint, New York: Gordon Press, 1975), 36, 76–77, 118; Dora S. Soper [nee Schoonmaker], "Uniform Readings for June," *Heathen Woman's Friend* 12 (April 1881): 230–31.

42. Nakagawa Zennosuke, "A Century of Marriage Law," *Japan Quarterly* 10 (April–June 1963): 185–86; Julia D. Carrothers, *The Sunrise Kingdom* (Philadelphia: Presbyterian Board of Education, 1879), 72.

43. Ross C. Houghton, *Women of the Orient* (Cincinnati: Hitchcock and Walden, 1877), 321–23, 328; Flora Best Harris, "The Daughters of Dai-Nippon," *Potter's American Monthly* 10 (May 1878): 350–52.

44. Fukuzawa Yukichi, *An Encouragement of Learning*, trans. David A. Dilworth and Umeyo Hirano (Tokyo: Sophia University, 1969), 51–53; Mori Arinori, "On Wives and Concubines," in *Meiroku Zasshi*, trans. William Reynolds Braisted (Cambridge: Harvard University Press, 1976), 105, 189–90.

45. Norton, "Japan: Manners and Customs," 129; hymn quoted in a letter from Alice J. Starkweather, *Life and Light for Woman* 9 (July 1879): 264; Jennie K. McCauley, "Why Do We Educate the Japanese?" *Woman's Work for Woman* 3 (September 1888): 235.

46. Elizabeth Russell, "Progress in Nagasaki," *Heathen Woman's Friend* 15 (August 1883): 28–30; Harris, "A Way to Help the Women of Japan," *Heathen Woman's Friend* 18 (March 1887): 232–33.

47. Kohiyama, *Amerika fujin senkyōshi*, 184–85; Masaya Yamamoto, "Image-Makers of Japan" (Ph.D. diss., Ohio State University, 1967), 94.

48. Willing, "Christian Marriage," 69; Soper, "Uniform Readings for June," 231.

Notes to Chapter 3

1. Jon H. Roberts, *Darwinism and the Divine in America* (Madison: University of Wisconsin Press, 1988).

2. Bayard Taylor, "Sights in and around Yedo," *Scribner's Monthly* 3 (December 1871): 142; "Japan," *Republic* 1 (May 1873): 123–27.

3. Taylor, "Sights in and around Yedo," 133; "Japan," 123–27.

4. Robert A. Rosenstone, "Learning from Those 'Imitative' Japanese," *American Historical Review* 85 (June 1980): 572–95; Edward H. House, "The Present and Future of Japan," *Harper's Monthly* 46 (May 1873): 858–64; [D. A. Wells], "The Japanese Experience of Our Civil Service," *Nation* 15 (3 October 1872): 213.

5. J. Bishop Putnam, "Familiar Letters from Japan," *Putnam's Magazine* 1 (May 1868): 634; House, "A Japanese Doctor and His Works," *Atlantic Monthly* 28 (December 1871): 685.

6. Jos. J. Taylor, "A Day's Ramble in Japan," *Overland Monthly*, 2d ser., 2 (November 1883): 534; Edward S. Morse, *Japanese Homes and Their Surroundings* (Boston: Ticknor, 1886; reprint, Rutland, Vt.: Charles E. Tuttle, 1972), 284; Putnam, "Familiar Letters from Japan," 634–35.

7. House, *Japanese Episodes* (Boston: James R. Osgood, 1881), 4.

8. House, "The Present and Future of Japan," 858–64; idem, "A Japanese Doctor," 681–82; idem, "A Japanese Statesman at Home," *Harper's Monthly* 44 (March 1872): 589–90, 595.

9. House, "A Japanese Doctor," 678–89; Guido F. Verbeck to William

Elliot Griffis, 7 September 1871, roll 18, Japan Letters, Group 1, William Elliot Griffis Collection, Special Collections and University Archives, Rutgers University Libraries (hereafter Griffis Collection).

10. Griffis, *The Mikado's Empire* (New York: Harper and Brothers, 1876), 8, 527; Edward R. Beauchamp, *An American Teacher in Early Meiji Japan* (Honolulu: University Press of Hawaii, 1976).

11. Griffis, "A Call on a Bonze," *Lippincott's Magazine* 13 (June 1874): 731.

12. Griffis, *The Mikado's Empire*, 331–33, 360–61, 399–425; idem, *Verbeck of Japan* (New York: Fleming H. Revell, 1900), 230–31; idem, 29 December 1870, Journal 8 (1870–71), Group 1, Griffis Collection.

13. Curio [Griffis], "In the Heart of Japan," *Christian Intelligencer* 42 (27 April 1871): 2; Griffis, *The Mikado's Empire*, 430, 434.

14. Griffis, *The Mikado's Empire*, 429, 434, 517–18, 539.

15. Ibid., 533–35, 540, 549–50.

16. Ibid., 7.

17. Alice Mabel Bacon, *A Japanese Interior* (Boston: Houghton, Mifflin, 1893), 228.

18. Morse, "Health-Matters in Japan," *Popular Science Monthly* 12 (January 1878): 281; Frederick Jackson Turner, "The Significance of the Frontier in American History" [1893], in idem, *The Frontier in American History* (New York: Henry Holt, 1920), 3; Griffis, *The Mikado's Empire*, 7.

19. Griffis, "Inside Japan," *Lippincott's Magazine* 12 (August 1873): 181.

20. Griffis, *The Mikado's Empire*, 477–78, 578; idem, "The Religions of Japan," *Missionary Review of the World* 20 (September 1897): 650–58.

21. Verbeck, "Ten Years in Japan," *Missionary Magazine* 50 (August 1870): 331–32; James C. Hepburn, "Missionary Work in Japan," *Foreign Missionary* 29 (April 1871): 309.

22. "Japan," *Spirit of Missions* 37 (July 1872): 423; Edward Warren Clark, "International Relations with Japan," *International Review* 4 (January–February 1877): 62–63, 66–67.

23. "A Light That Does Not Illumine," *Missionary Herald* 77 (January 1881): 7–9; "The Dying Buddhist," *Life and Light for Woman* 7 (November 1877): 337.

24. Edwin Arnold, *The Light of Asia* (1879; reprint, Garden City,

N.Y.: Dolphin Books, 1961); Oliver Wendell Holmes, "The Light of Asia," review of *The Light of Asia,* by Arnold, *International Review* 7 (October 1879): 347, 370–71; Brooks Wright, *Interpreter of Buddhism to the West* (New York: Bookman Associates, 1957), 73–75. Wright estimates that between one half-million and one million copies were sold.

25. "A Light That Does Not Illumine," 8–9; Elizabeth Russell, "Progress in Nagasaki," *Heathen Woman's Friend* 15 (August 1883): 30.

26. H. F. Barnes, "The Light of the World," *Baptist Missionary Magazine* 60 (September 1880): 324–27.

27. "Buddhism: The Darkness of Asia," *Spirit of Missions* 47 (June 1882): 216–19; Griffis, *The Mikado's Empire,* 578; Barnes, "The Light of the World," 323–27.

28. House, *Yone Santo* (Chicago: Belford, Clarke, 1888), 12, 62. House presented Japanese names with the given name first, surname second.

29. "Review of *Yone Santo,*" *Japan Weekly Mail* (Yokohama), 9 February 1889, 132–34; "Editorial Paragraphs," *Missionary Herald* 85 (June 1889): 224–25; "Editorial Notes," *Independent* 40 (3 May 1888): 11.

30. "The Women of Japan," *Tokio Times,* 22 and 29 November 1879, 283–84, 297–99; House, *Yone Santo,* 76, 111–12, 181; Showa Joshi Daigaku, Kindai Bungaku Kenkyūshitsu, "E. H. Hausu," in *Kindai bungaku kenkyū sōsho* (Tokyo: Showa Joshi Daigaku, 1957), 5:387, 404, 409; Flora Best Harris, "The Daughters of Dai-Nippon," *Potter's American Monthly* 10 (May 1878): 352.

31. Thomas Bailey Aldrich to House, 2 May 1888, 7 May 1888, 13 June 1888, 15 June 1888, Thomas Bailey Aldrich Papers, Manuscript Division, Library of Congress; Houghton, Mifflin and Company to House, 24 May 1888, 5 June 1888, Box 1, Edward Howard House Collection (#10762), Clifton Waller Barrett Library, Special Collections Department, University of Virginia Library (hereafter House Collection); E. L. Burlingame [Charles Scribner's Sons] to House, 27 June 1888, Box 2, House Collection; Harper and Brothers to House, 18 July 1888, Box 2, House Collection.

32. House, *Yone Santo,* 283–84.

33. George William Knox, "Monthly Concert," *Foreign Missionary* 37 (September 1878): 107.

34. "Prospectus," *Our Day* 1 (January 1888): 1; Joseph Cook, "Japan, The Self-Reformed Hermit Nation," *Independent* 35 (29 March 1883): 391; "Dr. Hepburn's Address," *Foreign Missionary* 39 (September 1880): 158–59.

35. James H. Pettee, "A New Peril in Japan," *Missionary Herald* 82 (May 1886): 174; Cook, "Twenty-Four Questions on New Japan," *Independent* 35 (25 October 1883): 1350–51.

36. Carmen Blacker, *The Japanese Enlightenment* (Cambridge: Cambridge University Press, 1964), 150, 159; Michio Nagai, "Herbert Spencer in Early Meiji Japan," *Far Eastern Quarterly* 14 (November 1954): 55; "Letter from a Japanese Student," *Missionary Herald* 74 (February 1878): 36.

37. Henry Thomas Buckle, *History of Civilization in England* (1857–61; reprint, London: Oxford University Press, 1903–4), 1:207, 271; John William Draper, *History of the Conflict between Religion and Science* (1875; reprint, New York: D. Appleton, 1897), vi–vii, 367.

38. Morse, *Japan Day by Day* (Boston: Houghton Mifflin, 1917; reprint, Tokyo: Kobunsha Publishing, 1936), 2:209; "Professor Morse on Japan," *Boston Evening Transcript*, 17 January 1882, 2; David Strauss, "The 'Far East' in the American Mind, 1883–1894," *Journal of American-East Asian Relations* 2 (fall 1993): 225.

39. Ueno Masuzō, *Shizen kagaku*, vol. 3 of *Oyatoi gaikokujin* (Tokyo: Kajima Shuppankai, 1968), 199–206; "Personal Intelligence," *Tokio Times*, 1 February 1879, 68; Masao Watanabe, *The Japanese and Western Science*, trans. Otto Theodor Benfey (Philadelphia: University of Pennsylvania, 1990), 68–69; Isono Naohide, "Contributions of Edward S. Morse to Developing Young Japan," in *Foreign Employees in Nineteenth-Century Japan*, ed. Edward R. Beauchamp and Akira Iriye (Boulder: Westview Press, 1990), 202.

40. "Personal Intelligence," *Tokio Times*, 30 June 1877, 309; Morse quoted in Watanabe, *The Japanese and Western Science*, 65; Dorothy G. Wayman, *Edward Sylvester Morse* (Cambridge: Harvard University Press, 1942), 205, 407.

41. Morse, *Japan Day by Day*, 1:339–40, 2:426–29; idem, "Science Lectures in Japan," *Popular Science Monthly* 14 (January 1879): 388–89; Wayman, *Edward Sylvester Morse*, 250, 390; Robert S. Schwantes, "Christianity versus Science," *Far Eastern Quarterly* 12 (February 1953): 125.

42. "Letter from Miss [Mary J.] Holbrook," *Heathen Woman's Friend* 9 (February 1878): 177.

43. Shigehisa Tokutarō, *Kyōiku, shūkyō*, vol. 5 of *Oyatoi gaikokujin* (Tokyo: Kajima Shuppankai, 1968), 171–76; "Personal Intelligence," *Tokio Times*, 1 February 1879, 67; Henry Faulds, "Evolution," *Japan Gazette* (Yokohama), 11 January 1879, 3; idem, "Evolution," *Japan Gazette*, 18 January 1879, 4.

44. "Tokio Christian Association," *Japan Weekly Mail*, 15 February 1879, 188–89; Helen Ballhatchet, "The Religion of the West versus the Science of the West," in *Japan and Christianity*, ed. John Breen and Mark Williams (New York: St. Martin's Press, 1996), 109, 115–16; Watanabe, *The Japanese and Western Science*, 79; Irwin Scheiner, *Christian Converts and Social Protest in Meiji Japan* (Berkeley and Los Angeles: University of California Press, 1970), 110–11.

45. "Japanese Gossip," *New York Herald*, 11 January 1880, 6; Verbeck quoted in Cook, "Twenty-Four Questions on Japan," 1350; Morse, "Our Manners Are Not Good," *Boston Herald*, 6 May 1894, 17.

46. "Notes," *Japan Weekly Mail*, 19 May 1883, 52–53; Charles S. Eby, *Christianity and Humanity* (Yokohama: R. Meiklejohn, 1883), 2.

47. Eby, *Christianity and Humanity*, 16–17, 22–27, 95–96, 104–10, 293; Herbert Spencer, *First Principles*, 5th ed. (New York: A. L. Burt, 1880), 13–17, 56–57, 110–11, 239–40.

48. Lafcadio Hearn, "Science and Religion," *Japan Weekly Mail*, 20 June 1891, 740; Theodosius S. Tyng, "Mr. Lafcadio Hearn on Herbert Spencer," 3 July 1891, *Japan Weekly Mail*, 43; "Taking Issue with the Japs," *New York Times*, 23 September 1891, 9.

49. Hearn to Basil Hall Chamberlain, [1893], Part 7, Lafcadio Hearn Collection (#6101), Clifton Waller Barrett Library, Special Collections Department, University of Virginia Library; Hearn, "Mediaeval Superstitions in Journalism," 10 November 1894, in *Editorials from the Kobe Chronicle*, ed. Makoto Sangu (Tokyo: Hokuseido Press, 1960), 95–98; idem, *Glimpses of Unfamiliar Japan* (Boston: Houghton, Mifflin, 1894; reprint, Rutland, Vt.: Charles E. Tuttle, 1976), xvi; "Miscellaneous," *Missionary Review of the World* 18 (December 1895): 947.

50. Shigehisa, *Kyōiku, shūkyō*, 100–102; Addison Gulick, *Evolutionist and Missionary* (Chicago: University of Chicago Press, 1932),

251, 391–93; John T. Gulick, "Danger from Imported Skepticism," *Missionary Herald* 74 (June 1878): 196–97; Griffis, "The Religions of Japan," 657–58.

51. Griffis, *The Mikado's Empire*, 7; Morse, *Japanese Homes and Their Surroundings*, xl.

Notes to Chapter 4

1. Henry Adams, *Novels, Mont Saint Michel, The Education*, ed. Ernest Samuels and Jayne N. Samuels (New York: Library of America, 1983), 290; Adams to John Hay, 11 June 1886, *The Letters of Henry Adams*, ed. J. C. Levenson et al. (Cambridge: Harvard University Press, 1982), 3:12 (hereafter *Adams Letters*); John La Farge, "An Artist's Letters from Japan," *Century* 40 (August 1890): 569–70. (La Farge's *Century* essays are hereafter referred to by title and date.)

2. T. J. Jackson Lears analyzes American antimodernism in *No Place of Grace* (New York: Pantheon Books, 1981).

3. Minister Richard B. Hubbard to Secretary of State Thomas F. Bayard, no. 551, 20 February 1889, Despatches from U.S. Ministers to Japan, 1855–1906 (M133, roll 59), Department of State, Record Group 59, National Archives (hereafter Diplomatic Despatches, RG 59); clipping from the *Japan Daily Mail* (Yokohama), 26 March 1887, enclosed with Hubbard to Bayard, no. 310, 5 April 1887 (M133, roll 56), Diplomatic Despatches, RG 59.

4. Clay Lancaster, *The Japanese Influence in America* (New York: Walton H. Rawls, 1963); William Hosley, *The Japan Idea* (Hartford, Conn.: Wadsworth Atheneum, 1990); Julia Meech and Gabriel P. Weisberg, *Japonisme Comes to America* (New York: Harry N. Abrams, 1990).

5. William Dean Howells, *A Hazard of New Fortunes* (1890), vol. 16 of *A Selected Edition of W. D. Howells*, ed. Don L. Cook and David J. Nordloh (Bloomington: Indiana University Press, 1976), 13–14, 118, 122, 388.

6. Michael Kammen, *Mystic Chords of Memory* (New York: Alfred A. Knopf, 1991), 45–47.

7. Edwin Arnold, *The Light of Asia* (1879; reprint, Garden City, N.Y.: Dolphin Books, 1961), 111; Adams, *Novels*, 225.

8. Adams to Hay, 9 July 1886, *Adams Letters*, 3:15–17; Adams to

John White Field, 4 August 1886, ibid., 3:26–27; Royal Cortissoz, *John La Farge* (Boston: Houghton Mifflin, 1911; reprint, New York: Da Capo Press, 1971), 1.

9. La Farge, "An Artist's Letters from Japan" (August 1890): 566; Arnold, "Japonica: Fourth Paper," *Scribner's Magazine* 9 (March 1891): 323; Robert Blum, "An Artist in Japan," *Scribner's Magazine* 13 (April 1893): 409. (Arnold's and Blum's essays in *Scribner's* are hereafter referred to by title and date.)

10. Blum, "An Artist in Japan" (April 1893): 407, 412, 414; Theodore Wores, "An American Artist in Japan," *Century* 38 (September 1889): 675.

11. William Eleroy Curtis, *The Yankees of the East* (New York: Stone and Kimball, 1896), 1:24; "Sir Edwin Arnold in Japan," *New York Times*, 18 September 1892, 3; John Liggins, "Rehabilitating Buddhism," *Spirit of Missions* 55 (September 1890): 352–53; "Sir Edwin Arnold's Farewell," *New York Times*, 16 February 1892, 8; Brooks Wright, *Interpreter of Buddhism to the West* (New York: Bookman Associates, 1957), 142–46; "Sir Edwin Arnold's Readings," *New York Times*, 1 November 1891, 2.

12. Arnold, "Japonica: Third Paper" (February 1891): 165; idem, "Love and Marriage in Japan," *Cosmopolitan* 12 (February 1892): 387–88, 398.

13. Arnold, *Seas and Lands*, new ed. (New York: Longmans, Green, 1897), 243; William Elliot Griffis, illus. Wores, "Nature and People in Japan," *Century* 39 (December 1889): 234; Wores, "Art Notes," *Argonaut* 20 (9 April 1887): 10.

14. "Letter from Mrs. John [Frances A.] Gulick," *Life and Light for Woman* 17 (August 1887): 286–88; "Letter from Miss [Abby M.] Colby," *Life and Light for Woman* 18 (March 1888): 88.

15. "The Dress of Japanese Ladies," *Japan Weekly Mail* (Yokohama), 30 June 1888, 607–8; "The Japanese Dress," *New York Commercial Advertiser*, 8 September 1888, 2.

16. "Notes," *Japan Weekly Mail*, 21 August 1886, 181; "Foreign Dress for Japanese Ladies," *Japan Weekly Mail*, 25 September 1886, 315.

17. "The Dress of Japanese Ladies," 608; E. M. King et al., "How Shall Women Dress?" *North American Review* 140 (June 1885): 557–71.

18. Blum, "An Artist in Japan" (April 1893): 414; La Farge, "An Artist's Letters from Japan" (February 1890): 490–91.

19. Ernest Francisco Fenollosa, *East and West* (New York: Thomas Y. Crowell, 1893), v–vi.

20. Arnold, "Love and Marriage in Japan," 393; Blum, "An Artist in Japan," (June 1893): 747; idem, "An Artist in Japan" (April 1893): 406, 413–14.

21. Adams to Hay, 9 July 1886, *Adams Letters*, 3:16; Adams to Theodore F. Dwight, 30 July 1886, ibid., 3:25; clipping from the *Japan Daily Mail*, 26 March 1887, enclosed with Hubbard to Bayard, no. 310, 5 April 1887 (M133, roll 56), Diplomatic Despatches, RG 59.

22. Percival Lowell, *Occult Japan* (Boston: Houghton, Mifflin, 1894; reprint, Rochester, Vt.: Inner Traditions International, 1990), 288–89.

23. La Farge, "From Tokio to Nikko" (March 1890): 717; Blum, "An Artist in Japan" (April 1893): 411.

24. "Some Japanese Paintings," *New York Daily Tribune*, 23 April 1888, 6; "In the World of Art," *New York Herald*, 23 April 1888, 6; Griffis, *The Mikado's Empire* (New York: Harper and Brothers, 1876), 360–61.

25. Homi Bhabha describes the process of "a flawed colonial mimesis" in "Of Mimicry and Man," *October*, no. 28 (spring 1984): 125–33.

26. Edward S. Morse, *Japanese Homes and Their Surroundings* (Boston: Ticknor, 1886; reprint, Rutland, Vt.: Charles E. Tuttle, 1972), 284.

27. Dorothy G. Wayman, *Edward Sylvester Morse* (Cambridge: Harvard University Press, 1942), 258–63, 292, 355–58; Morse, *Japan Day by Day* (Boston: Houghton Mifflin, 1917; reprint, Tokyo: Kobunsha, 1936), 2:245–47, 264–65.

28. Morse, *Japanese Homes and Their Surroundings*, 117, 309, 348–49; La Farge, "An Artist's Letters from Japan" (June 1890): 203.

29. Lafcadio Hearn, "In a Japanese Garden," *Atlantic Monthly* 70 (July 1892): 16; Wores, "An American Artist in Japan," 681; La Farge, "From Tokio to Nikko" (March 1890): 712.

30. Morse, *Japanese Homes and Their Surroundings*, 274; Wores, "Japanese Flower Arrangement," *Scribner's Magazine* 26 (August 1899): 205–12.

31. La Farge, "An Artist's Letters from Japan" (August 1890): 568–69, 574; Cortissoz, *John La Farge*, 161–66.

32. [Hearn], "Recent Buddhist Literature," *New Orleans Times-Democrat*, 1 March 1885, 4; idem, "In a Japanese Garden," 32–33.

33. Alfred Parsons, "Autumn in Japan," *Harper's Monthly* 90 (April 1895): 768; Hearn, "A Trip to Kyōto," *Atlantic Monthly* 77 (May 1896): 619.

34. Griffis, "A Japanese Marriage in High Life," *Lippincott's Magazine* 15 (February 1875): 176; Basil Hall Chamberlain and W. B. Mason, *A Handbook for Travellers in Japan*, 3d ed. (London: John Murray, 1891), 2, 12; Parsons, "The Time of the Lotus," *Harper's Monthly* 90 (December 1894): 52.

35. James Jackson Jarves, *A Glimpse at the Art of Japan* (New York: Hurd and Houghton, 1876; reprint, Rutland, Vt.: Charles E. Tuttle, 1984), 16, 136–38, 147; Morse, *Japan Day by Day*, 2:185–87.

36. Fukuzawa Yukichi, *An Outline of a Theory of Civilization*, trans. David A. Dilworth and G. Cameron Hurst (Tokyo: Sophia University, 1973); Karl Kiyoshi Kawakami, ed., *Japan and the Japanese as Seen by Foreigners* (Tokyo: Keiseisha, [1904?]), viii–ix; "What Value Has Foreigners' Flattery?" *Kokumin no tomo* (Tokyo), 22 June 1889, quoted in Kenneth B. Pyle, *The New Generation in Meiji Japan* (Stanford: Stanford University Press, 1969), 33–42, 85–86.

37. Pyle, *The New Generation in Meiji Japan*, 64–71; Stefan Tanaka, *Japan's Orient* (Berkeley and Los Angeles: University of California Press, 1993).

38. Okakura Kakuzō, *The Awakening of Japan* (New York: Century, 1904), 97–98, 197; idem, *The Ideals of the East* (New York: E. P. Dutton, 1903; reprint, Rutland, Vt.: Charles E. Tuttle, 1970), 237, 244.

39. Okakura, *The Ideals of the East*, 5, 19–20, 222–23; idem, *The Awakening of Japan*, 190–92, 200.

40. Morse, *The Steam Whistle* (Salem, Mass.: Newcomb and Gauss [printer], 1905), 1–3, 7; idem, *Can City Life Be Made Endurable?* (Worcester, Mass.: Davis [printer], 1900), 4–7; Steven J. Ericson, *The Sound of the Whistle* (Cambridge: Harvard University, 1996), 54–62; Mark Twain, *A Connecticut Yankee in King Arthur's Court* (1889; reprint, Berkeley and Los Angeles: University of California Press, 1983).

41. La Farge, "Bric-à-Brac" (July 1893): 429.

42. Henry James to Sir John Clark, 13 December 1891, *Henry James Letters*, ed. Leon Edel (Cambridge: Harvard University Press, 1980):

3:367; La Farge, "Passages from a Diary in the Pacific," *Scribner's Magazine* 30 (July 1901): 72; Adams to Elizabeth Cameron, 13 September 1891, *Adams Letters*, 3:544.

43. Ernst Scheyer, "The Adams Memorial by Augustus Saint-Gaudens," *Art Quarterly* 19 (summer 1956): 178–97; Adams to Cameron, 19 April 1903, *Adams Letters*, 5:488–89; Adams to Homer Saint-Gaudens, 24 January 1908, ibid., 6:109; Adams, *Novels*, 1020–21.

44. "American Views of Japan," *New York Times*, 27 April 1888, 4; "Paintings of Japan by Theodore Wores," *Boston Evening Transcript*, 2 March 1895, 13.

45. "Artist Wores at Home," *San Francisco Examiner*, 22 October 1891, 8; Jan Newstrom Thompson, "An American Artist in Meiji Japan," in Wores, *Theodore Wores* (Pasadena: Pacific Asia Museum, 1993), 37, 55.

46. Hearn to Chamberlain, 22 May 1891, Part 7, Lafcadio Hearn Collection (#6101), Clifton Waller Barrett Library, Special Collections Department, University of Virginia Library (hereafter Hearn Collection).

47. Hearn, "The Most Ancient Shrine in Japan," *Atlantic Monthly* 68 (December 1891): 795; idem, *Gleanings in Buddha-Fields* (Boston: Houghton, Mifflin, 1897), 152; idem, *Out of the East* (Boston: Houghton, Mifflin, 1895), 192–99.

48. Hearn, *Japan: An Attempt at Interpretation* (New York: Macmillan, 1904), 9–23, 30–36, 89, 309–30, 415–29, 483–98, 501–11; idem to Chamberlain, 9 August 1893, 16 August 1893, Part 7, Hearn Collection.

49. Hearn, *Japan: An Attempt at Interpretation*, 473.

50. John P. Young, "The Question of Japanese Competition," *Overland Monthly*, 2d ser., 28 (July 1896): 84; Lowell, *Occult Japan*, 330–31; Bhabha, "Of Mimicry and Man," 127.

51. Ernest Francisco Fenollosa, "Chinese and Japanese Traits," *Atlantic Monthly* 69 (June 1892): 774.

Notes to Chapter 5

1. "The Fancy Dress Ball," *Japan Weekly Mail* (Yokohama), 30 April 1887, 413; George B. Sansom, *The Western World and Japan* (New York: Alfred A. Knopf, 1950; reprint, New York: Vintage Books, 1973), 370–71.

2. Quoted in Donald H. Shively, "The Japanization of the Middle

Meiji," in *Tradition and Modernization in Japanese Culture,* ed. idem (Princeton: Princeton University Press, 1971), 96.

3. Fukuzawa Yukichi, "Datsu-A ron," *Jiji shimpō* (Tokyo), 16 March 1885, quoted in Kenneth B. Pyle, *The New Generation in Meiji Japan* (Stanford: Stanford University Press, 1969), 149.

4. Minister Richard B. Hubbard, speech to English Law School (Tokyo), enclosed with Hubbard to Secretary of State Thomas F. Bayard, no. 118, 16 February 1886, Despatches from U.S. Ministers to Japan, 1855–1906 (M133, roll 54), Department of State, Record Group 59, National Archives (hereafter Diplomatic Despatches, RG 59).

5. In the 1870s, about twenty-four hundred Europeans and Americans lived in Japan; in the 1890s, about forty-five hundred.

6. "Rights of American Citizens in Japan," in Charles I. Bevans, comp., *Treaties and Other International Agreements* (Washington, D.C.: U.S. Department of State, 1972), 9:360; "Amity and Commerce," in ibid., 9:365; "Peace and Amity," in ibid., 9:353.

7. Minister John A. Bingham to Secretary of State Hamilton Fish, no. 19, 18 November 1873 (M133, roll 26), Diplomatic Despatches, RG 59; Bingham to Fish, no. 106, 29 July 18/4 (M133, roll 28), Diplomatic Despatches, RG 59; Hirose Shizuko, "Meiji shonen no tai O-Bei kankei to gaikokujin naichi ryokō mondai," part 2, *Shigaku zasshi* 83 (December 1974): 1600–1621.

8. Minister Townsend Harris to Secretary of State Lewis Cass, no. 4, 22 January 1861 (M133, roll 3), Diplomatic Despatches, RG 59.

9. "Amity and Commerce," in Bevans, comp., *Treaties,* 9:372; "Establishment of Tariff Duties with Respect to Japan," in ibid., 1:18–28.

10. Oka Yoshitake, "Jōyaku kaisei rongi ni arawareta tōji no taigai ishiki," part 1, *Kokka gakkai zasshi* 67 (August 1953) 7–8; Akira Iriye, *Nihon no gaikō* (Tokyo: Chūō Koronsha, 1966), 14–27.

11. Quoted in Carol Gluck, *Japan's Modern Myths* (Princeton: Princeton University Press, 1985), 115.

12. Ambassador Iwakura Tomomi, 11 March 1872, Records Relating to the Treaty of Yedo (T119, roll 1), Department of State, Record Group 59, National Archives.

13. Inoue Kiyoshi, *Jōyaku kaisei* (Tokyo: Iwanami Shoten, 1955), 80–81; Kajima Morinosuke, *Jōyaku kaisei mondai,* vol. 2 of *Nihon gaikōshi* (Tokyo: Kajima Kenkyūjo Shuppankai, 1970), 9–10, 187.

14. Niwa Kunio, "The Reform of the Land Tax and the Government

Programme for the Encouragement of Industry," *Developing Economies* (Tokyo) 4 (December 1966): 457.

15. Terashima quoted in Iriye, "Japan's Drive to Great-Power Status," in *The Nineteenth Century*, vol. 5 of *The Cambridge History of Japan*, ed. Marius B. Jansen (New York: Cambridge University, 1989), 738.

16. Bingham to Fish, no. 380, 14 April 1876 (M133, roll 32), Diplomatic Despatches, RG 59; Bingham to Fish, no. 356, 9 March 1876 (M133, roll 32), Diplomatic Despatches, RG 59; Bingham to Secretary of State William M. Evarts, no. 763, 2 April 1878 (M133, roll 36), Diplomatic Despatches, RG 59.

17. In 1876, the value of British exports to Japan totalled nearly fifteen million yen; American exports totalled nearly two million. American exports lagged far behind those of Great Britain until the early twentieth century. Oriental Economist, *The Foreign Trade of Japan*, ed. Ishibashi Tanzan (Tokyo: Oriental Economist, 1935), 361, 364.

18. Bingham to Fish, no. 114, 31 August 1874 (M133, roll 28), Diplomatic Despatches, RG 59; Bingham to Fish, no. 328, 19 January 1876 (M133, roll 31), Diplomatic Despatches, RG 59.

19. Fish to Bingham, no. 211, 9 March 1876, Diplomatic Instructions of the Department of State, 1801–1906, Japan (M77, roll 105), Department of State, Record Group 59, National Archives (hereafter Diplomatic Instructions, RG 59); Fish to Minister Yoshida Kiyonari, 10 January 1877, Notes to the Foreign Legations in the U.S. from the Department of State, 1834–1906 (M99, roll 66), Department of State, Record Group 59, National Archives (hereafter Notes to Foreign Legations, RG 59).

20. Evarts to Bingham, no. 299, 21 June 1877 (M77, roll 105), Diplomatic Instructions, RG 59. Evarts was the uncle of Daniel Crosby Greene, a Congregational missionary in Japan from 1869–1913. Evarts's papers at the Library of Congress contain no correspondence between him and his nephew on the topic of treaty revision.

21. Foreign Minister Terashima Munenori to Yoshida, 24 April 1876, Notes from the Japanese Legation in the U.S. to the Department of State, 1858–1906 (M163, roll 1), Department of State, Record Group 59, National Archives; Ōyama Azusa, "Iwakura kaisei sōan to Terashima kaisei sōan," *Kokusai seiji* 3 (autumn 1957): 60; "Revision of Commercial Treaties," in Bevans, comp., *Treaties*, 9:380.

22. Bingham to Evarts, no. 864, 17 September 1878 (M133, roll 38), Diplomatic Despatches, RG 59.

23. "Japan and America," *New York World*, 16 February 1881, enclosure no. 1; "Japan," *Brooklyn Eagle*, 16 January 1881, enclosure no. 2, both with Bingham to Evarts, no. 1272, 25 March 1881 (M133, roll 44), Diplomatic Despatches, RG 59.

24. Edward H. House, "The Martyrdom of an Empire," *Atlantic Monthly* 47 (May 1881): 610–23; idem, "The Thraldom of Japan," *Atlantic Monthly* 60 (December 1887): 721–34; idem, "The Tariff in Japan," *New Princeton Review*, n.s., 5 (January 1888): 66–77; idem, "Foreign Jurisdiction in Japan," *New Princeton Review*, n.s., 5 (March 1888): 207–18.

25. "Missionary Itinerating in Japan," in *Proceedings of the General Conference of the Protestant Missionaries of Japan* (Yokohama: R. Meiklejohn, 1883), 135–51.

26. "'Extra-Territoriality' in Japan," *Missionary Herald* 80 (August 1884): 305–6.

27. Inoue Kiyoshi, *Jōyaku kaisei*, 87–88; Kajima, *Jōyaku kaisei mondai*, 193.

28. Dallas Finn, *Meiji Revisited* (New York: Weatherhill, 1995), 96–98.

29. Stephen Vlastos, "Opposition Movements in Early Meiji," in *The Nineteenth Century*, ed. Jansen, 419–20.

30. Tsuda Takako, "Inoue jōyaku kaisei no saikentō," *Rekishigaku kenkyū*, no. 575 (December 1987): 26; "Draft Treaty of Commerce and Navigation," in Centre for East Asian Cultural Studies, *Meiji Japan through Contemporary Sources* (Tokyo: Centre for East Asian Cultural Studies, 1969–72), 3:133–48; "Draft of the Jurisdictional Convention," in ibid., 3:148–55.

31. "Stenographic Record of the Conversation on the Proposed Treaty Revision between Inoue Kowashi and Gustave Boissonade," ed. Hayasaka Shiro, trans. Masatoshi Konishi, in *Meiji Japan through Contemporary Sources*, 3:155–61.

32. "Memorial of Tani Kanjo against the Proposed Treaty Revision," in *Meiji Japan through Contemporary Sources*, 3:162–72.

33. "Foreign Minister Inoue's Response," in Ian Nish, *Japanese Foreign Policy* (London: Routledge and Kegan Paul, 1977), 269–70.

34. Inoue Kiyoshi, *Jōyaku kaisei*, 119–28; Irokawa Daikichi, *Kindai*

kokka no shuppatsu, vol. 21 of *Nihon no rekishi* (Tokyo: Chūō Kōron-sha, 1974), 395–400; "Notes," *Japan Weekly Mail*, 13 August 1887, 146–47.

35. "Peace Preservation Regulations," in *Meiji Japan through Contemporary Sources*, 3:43–45; Irokawa, *Kindai kokka no shuppatsu*, 401.

36. Joyce C. Lebra, *Ōkuma Shigenobu* (Canberra: Australian National University Press, 1973), 83–85; Inoue Kiyoshi, *Jōyaku kaisei*, 129–30, 139.

37. "Treaty of Amity, Commerce and Navigation," enclosed in Hubbard to Bayard, unnumbered despatch, 7 January 1889 (M133, roll 59), Diplomatic Despatches, RG 59; Payson J. Treat, *Diplomatic Relations between the United States and Japan, 1853–1905* (Stanford: Stanford University Press, 1932–38), 2:289–92; Inoue Kiyoshi, *Jōyaku kaisei*, 140–42.

38. "The Treaty Drama in Japan," *Times* (London), 19 April 1889, 6; James L. Huffman, *Creating a Public* (Honolulu: University of Hawai'i Press, 1997), 155–57; Shively, "The Japanization of the Middle Meiji," 100; Inoue Kiyoshi, *Jōyaku kaisei*, 147–54.

39. Oka, "Jōyaku kaisei rongi," part 1, 1–24; idem, "Jōyaku kaisei rongi," part 2, *Kokka gakkai zasshi* 67 (September 1953): 69–92; Pyle, *The New Generation in Meiji Japan*, 110–16.

40. Lebra, *Ōkuma Shigenobu*, 88; Irokawa, *Kindai kokka no shuppatsu*, 407–8; Inoue Kiyoshi, *Jōyaku kaisei*, 154–56, 160.

41. Acting Secretary of State William F. Wharton to Minister Mutsu Munemitsu, 19 December 1889 (M99, roll 66), Notes to Foreign Legations, RG 59; Minister John F. Swift to Secretary of State James G. Blaine, no. 113, 14 April 1890 (M133, roll 61), Diplomatic Despatches, RG 59; Swift to Blaine, no. 37, 16 August 1889 (M133, roll 60), Diplomatic Despatches, RG 59.

42. Swift to Blaine, no. 56, 21 October 1889 (M133, roll 60), Diplomatic Despatches, RG 59; Swift to Blaine, no. 58, 25 October 1889 (M133, roll 60), Diplomatic Despatches, RG 59.

43. Swift to Blaine, no. 171, 31 October 1890 (M133, roll 62), Diplomatic Despatches, RG 59; Hubbard to Bayard, no. 470, 9 May 1888 (M133, roll 58), Diplomatic Despatches, RG 59.

44. Alice Mabel Bacon, *A Japanese Interior* (Boston: Houghton, Mifflin, 1893), 129–37.

45. One of the Tokyo Ladies [*sic*], "A Day of Days in Japan,"

Woman's Work for Woman 4 (May 1889): 126; "Board of the Interior," *Life and Light for Woman* 25 (September 1895): 429.

46. "The New Constitution of Japan," *Missionary Herald* 85 (May 1889): 185–86; "The Constitution of the Empire of Japan," in *Meiji Japan through Contemporary Sources*, 1:98; Daniel Crosby Greene, "The Preparation for Japan's New Parliament," *Our Day* 4 (July 1889): 32–36; Griffis, "Representative Government in Japan," *Forum* 7 (June 1889): 404; John H. Wigmore, "Parliamentary Days in Japan," *Scribner's Magazine* 10 (August 1891): 243–55.

47. "The New Japan," *New York Weekly Journal of Commerce*, 18 July 1878, 4; "Japanese Progress," *Commercial and Financial Chronicle* 59 (1 September 1894): 355–56; Minister Edwin Dun to Third Assistant Secretary of State William W. Rockhill, unnumbered despatch, 23 October 1894 (M133, roll 67), Diplomatic Despatches, RG 59.

48. Consul General Warren Green to Assistant Secretary of State John D. Porter, no. 84, 13 May 1886, Despatches from U.S. Consuls in Kanagawa, Japan, 1861–1897 (M135, roll 15), Department of State, Record Group 59, National Archives.

49. [Ernest W. Clement], "A Japanese State Legislature," *Nation* 50 (27 February 1890): 174.

50. Inoue Kiyoshi, *Jōyaku kaisei*, 194–96; Kajima, *Jōyaku kaisei mondai*, 203.

51. Mutsu, *Kenkenroku*, ed. and trans. Gordon Mark Berger (Princeton: Princeton University Press, 1982), 70; "Speech of Foreign Minister Mutsu Munemitsu in the House of Representatives," in *Meiji Japan through Contemporary Sources*, 3:185–86.

52. Nish, *Japanese Foreign Policy*, 31–33; Mutsu, *Kenkenroku*, 71.

53. "Treaty of Commerce and Navigation between Great Britain and Japan," in U.K. Foreign Office, *British and Foreign State Papers, 1893 1894* (London: Her Majesty's Stationery Office, 1899), 86:39–47

54. Dun to Secretary of State Walter Q. Gresham, no. 62, 21 February 1894 (M133, roll 66), Diplomatic Despatches, RG 59; Gresham to Dun, no. 66, 11 June 1894 (M77, roll 107), Diplomatic Instructions, RG 59; "Commerce and Navigation," in Bevans, comp., *Treaties*, 9:387–96.

55. "Status of Japan Raised," *New York Times*, 17 July 1899, 10; "To Full Comity," *Boston Globe*, 17 July 1899, 5; "Japan's New Treaty Relations," *Washington Evening Star*, 17 July 1899, 6.

56. "The New Treaties," *Japan Weekly Mail*, 22 July 1899, 88; M. L.

Gordon, "Japan's New Treaties and Their Effect on Mission Work," *Missionary Herald* 95 (September 1899): 363–64.

Notes to Chapter 6

1. George C. Perkins, "The Competition of Japan," *Overland Monthly*, 2d ser., 28 (October 1896): 393–403; Robert P. Porter, "Is Japanese Competition a Myth?" *North American Review* 163 (August 1896): 144–55.

2. John Barrett, "The Plain Truth about Asiatic Labor," *North American Review* 163 (November 1896): 620–32; "No Danger from Japanese Labor," *New York Herald*, 7 September 1896, 7.

3. Hoshi Tōru, "The New Japan," *Harper's Monthly* 95 (November 1897): 890–98; Ōkuma Shigenobu, "The Industrial Revolution in Japan," *North American Review* 171 (November 1900): 677–91; Mutsu Hirokichi, "A Japanese View of Certain Japanese-American Relations," *Overland Monthly*, 2d ser., 32 (November 1898): 406–14.

4. "A Japanese Cartoon," *New York Tribune*, 5 August 1894, 3; Kurino Shin'ichirō, "The Future of Japan," *North American Review* 160 (May 1895): 621–31; idem, "The Oriental War," *North American Review* 159 (November 1894): 529–36.

5. William Elliot Griffis, "China and Japan at War in Corea," *Chautauquan* 20 (October 1894): 70–74; Joseph Cook, "Open Furrows in the Orient," *Our Day* 15 (July 1895): 13–20.

6. Frederic Villiers, "The Truth about Port Arthur," *North American Review* 160 (March 1895): 325–30; James Creelman, "A Japanese Massacre," *New York World*, 12 December 1894, 1; idem, "The Massacre at Port Arthur," *New York World*, 20 December 1894, 1–2.

7. Mutsu Munemitsu, *Kenkenroku*, ed. and trans. Gordon Mark Berger (Princeton: Princeton University Press, 1982), 75–76; Minister Edwin Dun to Secretary of State Walter Q. Gresham, no. 88, 20 December 1894, U.S. Department of State, *Foreign Relations of the United States* (hereafter *FRUS*), *1894*, Appendix 1 (Washington, D.C.: Government Printing Office, 1895), 85–86; "Japan Confesses," *New York World*, 17 December 1894, 1.

8. Dun to Gresham, no. 90, 7 January 1895, *FRUS*, *1894*, Appendix 1, 88–90; Dun to Gresham, no. 88, 20 December 1894, ibid., 86. Stewart Lone has recently concluded that only the scale, not the occurrence, of

the Port Arthur massacre remains in question. Lone, *Japan's First Modern War* (New York: St. Martin's Press, 1994), 154–63.

9. Alice Mabel Bacon, "Credulous Mr. Villiers," *New York Times*, 26 March 1895, 13; Villiers, "Frederic Villiers Defends Himself," *New York Times*, 27 March 1895, 16; idem, "The Truth about Port Arthur," 325; "The Result in China," *New York World*, 18 December 1894, 4.

10. Matsumura Masayoshi, "Kōkaron to Nichi-Ro sensō," *Kokusai seiji* 71 (August 1982): 40.

11. Alonzo H. Stewart, "Baron Kaneko on the Yellow Peril," *New York Times*, 21 February 1904, 27; Takahira Kogorō, "Why Japan Resists Russia," *North American Review* 178 (March 1904): 321–27.

12. Kaneko Kentarō, "The Yellow Peril Is the Golden Opportunity for Japan," *North American Review* 179 (November 1904): 644–48; idem, "The Far East after the War," *World's Work* 9 (February 1905): 5868–71.

13. Matsumura, *Nichi-Ro sensō to Kaneko Kentarō* (Tokyo: Shin'yūdo, 1987), 42–43, 51, 128, 361; Theodore Roosevelt to Kaneko, 23 April 1904, *The Letters of Theodore Roosevelt*, ed. Elting E. Morison et al. (Cambridge: Harvard University Press, 1951), 4:777–78 (hereafter *Roosevelt Letters*); Roosevelt to Kermit Roosevelt, 5 March 1904, ibid., 4:744; Nitobe Inazō, *Bushido*, 10th ed. (New York: G. P. Putnam's Sons, 1905; reprint, Rutland, Vt.: Charles E. Tuttle, 1969).

14. Roosevelt to Cecil Arthur Spring Rice, 18 January 1904, *Roosevelt Letters*, 3:698; Roosevelt to Spring Rice, 13 June 1904, ibid., 4:831–33; Roosevelt to John Hay, 2 September 1904, ibid., 4:917; Roosevelt to George Kennan, 6 May 1905, ibid., 4:1169; Roosevelt to Hay, 26 July 1904, ibid., 4:865.

15. Hugo Erickson, "The Coming Conflict," *Overland Monthly*, 2d ser., 43 (March 1904): 204–5; J. G. D., "Japan at War," *Outlook* 76 (26 March 1904): 733; Paul Carus, "The Yellow Peril," *Open Court* 18 (July 1904): 431.

16. Sidney L. Gulick, *Evolution of the Japanese* (New York: Fleming H. Revell, 1903), 25. Sidney was the nephew of missionaries John, Orramel, and Julia Gulick.

17. J. P. Moore, "The Present Condition of the Work in Japan," *Missionary Review of the World* 18 (August 1895): 583, 585; "The Opportunity in Japan," *Spirit of Missions* 70 (May 1905): 344; Carol Gluck,

Japan's Modern Myths (Princeton: Princeton University Press, 1985), 132–35.

18. Anna Woodruff Jones, "Contrasted Forces at Osaka," *Woman's Work* 20 (September 1905): 214; letter from Elizabeth P. Milliken, *Woman's Work* 20 (September 1905): 215; "Missions in Japan," *The Church at Home and Abroad* 18 (September 1895): 217; George William Knox, "The Year 1895 in Japan," *Missionary Review of the World* 18 (September 1895): 651–52.

19. Anita Newcomb McGee, "The American Nurses in Japan," *Century* 69 (April 1905): 895–906; idem, "How the Japanese Save Lives," *Century* 70 (May 1905): 133–42.

20. Frances Little [Fannie Caldwell Macaulay], *The Lady of the Decoration* (New York: Century, 1906).

21. Homer B. Hulbert, "The Russo-Japanese War and Christian Missions in the East," *Missionary Review of the World* 27 (August 1904): 570–72; H. G. C. Hallock, "The Influence of Japan on China," *Missionary Review of the World* 28 (October 1905): 756–60; Rufus Benton Peery, "The Evolution of Japan," *Missionary Review of the World* 28 (January 1905): 32; Ernest W. Clement, *A Handbook of Modern Japan*, 6th ed. (Chicago: A. C. McClurg, 1905), 157–58.

22. "The Religious Bodies in Japan," *Japan Weekly Mail* (Yokohama), 21 May 1904, 580–81; William M. Imbrie, *The Church of Christ in Japan* (Philadelphia: Westminster Press, 1906), 24–30.

23. Kennan was a cousin of the grandfather of George F. Kennan, the creator of the Cold War policy of containment.

24. Kennan, "Which Is the Civilized Power?" *Outlook* 9 (October 1904): 515–23; Taylor Stults, "Imperial Russia through American Eyes, 1894–1904" (Ph.D. diss., University of Missouri, 1970), 108–29; John H. DeForest, "The Japanese Environment and Christianity," *Missionary Herald* 101 (April 1905): 169–70; Kennan to Roosevelt, 1 April 1905, series 1, Theodore Roosevelt Papers, Manuscript Division, Library of Congress.

25. Romyn Hitchcock, "Prehistoric Peoples of Japan," *American Antiquarian and Oriental Journal* 16 (July 1894): 209; Griffis, *The Mikado's Empire*, 27–30; Edward S. Morse, "Traces of an Early Race in Japan," *Popular Science Monthly* 14 (January 1879): 257–59. Current scholarship has reversed these origins: the ancestors of the Ainu came from Southeast Asia, while the ancestors of the Japanese came from

Northeast Asia. C. L. Brace, M. L. Brace, and W. R. Leonard, "Reflections on the Face of Japan," *American Journal of Physical Anthropology* 78 (January 1989): 93–113; Hanihara Kazurō, "Dual Structure Model for the Population History of the Japanese," *Japan Review* (Kyoto), no. 2 (1991): 1–33.

26. Griffis, *The Mikado's Empire*, 86–87; Morse, "Traces of an Early Race in Japan," 257; Arthur May Knapp, *Feudal and Modern Japan* (Boston: Joseph Knight, 1897), 1:4; Miwa Kimitada, *Nichi-Bei kankei no ishiki to kōzō* (Tokyo: Nansōsha, 1974), 44–45; Stefan Tanaka, *Japan's Orient* (Berkeley and Los Angeles: University of California Press, 1993), 75–77.

27. McGee himself did not insert periods after his initials.

28. W J McGee, "The Trend of Human Progress," *American Anthropologist*, n.s., 1 (July 1899): 419; McGee quoted in M. Carl Hundt, "Five Great World Leaders," *St. Louis Post-Dispatch*, 19 February 1904, 2; Ōkuma, "A Summary of the History of Japan," in *Fifty Years of New Japan*, comp. idem, ed. Marcus B. Huish (London: Smith, Elder, 1910), 1:14–16.

29. Mabel Loomis Todd, "In Aino-Land," *Century* 56 (July 1898): 343, 345, 347; J. K. Goodrich, "A Study of the Ainu of Yezo," *Popular Science Monthly* 33 (June 1888): 205; Arnold Henry Savage Landor, *Alone with the Hairy Ainu* (London: John Murray, 1893; reprint, New York: Johnson Reprint, 1970), 216–17.

30. Hitchcock, "The Ainos of Yezo, Japan," in U.S. National Museum, *Report of the U.S. National Museum* (Washington, D.C.: Government Printing Office, 1891), 433, 443; Basil Hall Chamberlain, *The Language, Mythology, and Geographical Nomenclature of Japan* (Tokyo: Imperial University, 1887), 75.

31. Isabella L. Bird, *Unbeaten Tracks in Japan* (London: John Murray, 1880; reprint, Boston: Beacon Press, 1987), 230, 236, 239, 259 60, 269, 271.

32. John Batchelor, "Something about the Ainu of Japan," *Missionary Review of the World* 20 (September 1897): 659–61; idem, *The Ainu of Japan* (London: Religious Tract Society, 1892), 20, 29–30.

33. Ibid., 18–19, 24, 330; idem, "Something about the Ainu of Japan," 663.

34. Griffis, *The Japanese Nation in Evolution* (New York: Thomas Y. Crowell, 1907), 8, 337; idem, *The Mikado's Empire*, 27–29, 34–35, 65,

68–69; Chamberlain, *Japanese Things* [originally titled *Things Japanese*], 5th ed. (London: John Murray, 1905; reprint, Rutland, Vt.: Charles E. Tuttle, 1971), 22.

35. Hitchcock, "The Ainos of Yezo, Japan," 442–43; "Aino Village in Japan," *Foreign Missionary* 36 (December 1877): 193–94; Todd, "In Aino-Land," 350; Edward Greey, *The Bear-Worshippers of Yezo* (Boston: Lee and Shepard, 1884), 23.

36. Richard Siddle, *Race, Resistance and the Ainu of Japan* (New York: Routledge, 1996), 68–94.

37. Griffis, *The Mikado's Empire*, 65; Todd, "In Aino-Land," 350.

38. Albert S. Bickmore, "The Ainos, or Hairy Men of Yesso," *American Journal of Science and Arts*, 2d ser., 45 (May 1868): 359–61; Bird, *Unbeaten Tracks in Japan*, 288, 310; Batchelor, *The Ainu and Their Folk-Lore* (London: Religious Tract Society, 1901), 11; McGee, "Introduction," in James William Buel, ed., *Louisiana and the Fair* (St. Louis: World's Progress Publishing, 1904), 5:vi.

39. David R. Francis, *The Universal Exposition of 1904* (St. Louis: Louisiana Purchase Exposition, 1913), 1:522–24; McGee, "The Trend of Human Progress," 414, 446.

40. Frederick Starr, *The Ainu Group at the Saint Louis Exposition* (Chicago: Open Court Publishing, 1904), 98; John Wesley Hanson, *The Official History of the Fair* (St. Louis: n.p., 1904), 385, 393–94; Francis, *The Universal Exposition of 1904*, 1:522, 526.

41. "Professor Frederick Starr," *American Anthropologist*, n.s., 6 (July–September 1904): 582; Starr, *The Ainu Group*, 107–8, 110 (Starr's emphasis).

42. Bickmore, "The Ainos," 359–61; Carus, "The Ainus," *Open Court* 19 (March 1905): 163, 166, 168–69.

43. Griffis, *The Japanese Nation in Evolution*, 10.

44. Alfred T. Mahan, *The Problem of Asia* (Boston: Little, Brown, 1900), xix, 41–44, 113–22, 150; Roosevelt to Mahan, 18 March 1901, *Roosevelt Letters*, 3:23. *The Problem of Asia* was serialized in *Harper's Monthly* and *North American Review*.

45. Sidney L. Gulick, *The White Peril in the Far East* (New York: Fleming H. Revell, 1905), 88, 91–92; [C. J. Bullock], "Japan and the Jingoes," *Nation* 79 (29 September 1904): 255.

46. Knapp, "Who Are the Japanese?" *Atlantic Monthly* 110 (September 1912): 339–40; idem, *Feudal and Modern Japan*, 1:5; "Ethno-

logical Basis of the Japanese Claim to be a White Race," *Current Opinion* 55 (July 1913): 38–39; Kennan, "Can We Understand the Japanese?" *Outlook* 101 (10 August 1912): 822.

47. Griffis, *The Mikado's Empire*, 34–35, 86–87.

48. "Japan Past and Present," *Troy (N.Y.) Times*, 15 February 1906, Item 5, Box 1.3, Group 1, William Elliot Griffis Collection, Special Collections and University Archives, Rutgers University Libraries (hereafter Griffis Collection); "Japs to Fight for Social Equality," *Philadelphia Press*, February 1909, Item 24, Box 1.3, Group 1, Griffis Collection; promotional pamphlet, Folder 4, Box 1.2, Group 1, Griffis Collection.

49. Griffis, *The Japanese Nation in Evolution*, 1–5, 25, 398, 400; idem, "Japan and the United States," *North American Review* 197 (June 1913): 721–33; "The Japanese in Evolution," review of *The Japanese Nation in Evolution*, by idem, *Outlook* 88 (29 February 1908): 509–10; "The Question of White versus Brown," *American Review of Reviews* 48 (July 1913): 108.

50. *Stats. at Large of USA* 1 (1845): 103; ibid. 16 (1871): 254, 256.

51. Wendy Jane Deichmann, "Josiah Strong" (Ph.D. diss., Drew University, 1991), 20, 27–28, 32; Josiah Strong, *Our Country*, rev. ed. (New York: Baker and Taylor, 1891; reprint, Cambridge: Harvard University Press, 1963), 200–202; Roosevelt to Bessie Van Vorst, 18 October 1902, *Roosevelt Letters*, 3:355–56; Roosevelt to Helen Kendrick Johnson, 10 January 1899, ibid., 2:905. Strong's cousin Sophia Davis and her husband, Jerome, went to Japan as Congregational missionaries in 1871.

52. Tokutomi Sohō quoted in John D. Pierson, *Tokutomi Sohō, 1863–1957* (Princeton: Princeton University Press, 1980), 279.

Notes to the Conclusion

1. "Dead Ruler Borne from His Capital," *New York Times*, 14 September 1912, 3; "First Photographs of the Funerals of Emperor Mutsuhito and Gen. Nogi," *New York Times*, 13 October 1912, pt. 3, 3; Natsume Sōseki, *Kokoro*, trans. Edwin McClellan (Chicago: Gateway Editions, 1957), 246.

2. *Takao Ozawa v. United States*, 260 U.S. 198 (1922). The McCarran-Walter Act of 1952 overturned the racial restrictions on naturalized citizenship but set limited quotas on East Asian immigration. The Immigration Act of 1965 abolished national-origins quotas.

3. Cornelis Fasseur, "Cornerstone and Stumbling Block," in *The Late Colonial State in Indonesia*, ed. Robert Cribb (Leiden: KITLV Press, 1994), 35–38; James Barber and John Barratt, *South Africa's Foreign Policy* (New York: Cambridge University Press, 1990), 6.

4. John W. Dower, *War without Mercy* (New York: Pantheon Books, 1986).

5. Harumi Befu, "Nationalism and *Nihonjinron*," in *Cultural Nationalism in East Asia*, ed. idem (Berkeley: Institute of East Asian Studies, University of California, 1993), 107–35; Peter N. Dale, *The Myth of Japanese Uniqueness* (London: Routledge, 1988); Kosaku Yoshino, *Cultural Nationalism in Contemporary Japan* (New York: Routledge, 1992).

6. "A Racial Slur Stirs Up a Storm," *Newsweek*, 6 October 1986, 35; "Nakasone's World-Class Blunder," *Time*, 6 October 1986, 66.

7. For statements of modernization theory, see W. W. Rostow, *The Stages of Economic Growth* (Cambridge: Cambridge University Press, 1960); John Whitney Hall, "Changing Conceptions of the Modernization of Japan," in *Changing Japanese Attitudes toward Modernization*, ed. Marius B. Jansen (Princeton: Princeton University Press, 1965), 7–41. For a critique, see Laura E. Hein, "Free-Floating Anxieties on the Pacific," *Diplomatic History* 20 (summer 1996): 411–37.

8. Karel van Wolferen, *The Enigma of Japanese Power* (New York: Alfred A. Knopf, 1989); Andrew Dougherty, *Japan 2000* quoted in Susumu Awanohara, "Paradigm Paranoia," *Far Eastern Economic Review*, 27 June 1991, 15; Bruce Cumings, "C.I.A.'s *Japan 2000* Caper," *Nation* 253 (30 September 1991): 366–68.

9. Percival Lowell, "The Soul of the Far East," part 1, *Atlantic Monthly* 60 (September 1887): 408; Lafcadio Hearn, *Japan: An Attempt at Interpretation* (New York: Macmillan, 1904), 473.

10. Benedict Anderson, *Imagined Communities*, 2d ed. (New York: Verso, 1991); Eric Hobsbawm and Terence Ranger, eds., *The Invention of Tradition* (New York: Cambridge University Press, 1983).

SELECTED BIBLIOGRAPHY

Primary Sources

Archives and Manuscripts

Aldrich, Thomas Bailey. Papers. Manuscript Division. Library of Congress.

Evarts, William Maxwell. Papers. Manuscript Division. Library of Congress.

Fish, Hamilton. Papers. Manuscript Division. Library of Congress.

Griffis, William Elliot Collection. Special Collections and University Archives. Rutgers University Libraries.

Hearn, Lafcadio. Collection (#6101). Clifton Waller Barrett Library. Special Collections Department. University of Virginia Library.

House, Edward Howard. Collection (#10762). Clifton Waller Barrett Library. Special Collections Department. University of Virginia Library.

Kennan, George. Papers. Manuscript Division. Library of Congress.

Mission Biographical Reference Files. United Methodist Church Archives. Madison, N.J.

Roosevelt, Theodore. Papers. Manuscript Division. Library of Congress.

U.S. Department of State. Diplomatic Instructions of the Department of State, 1801–1906, Japan (National Archives Microfilm Publication M77). General Records of the Department of State, Record Group 59. National Archives.

————. Notes to the Foreign Legations in the United States from the Department of State, 1834–1906 (National Archives Microfilm Publication M99). General Records of the Department of State, Record Group 59. National Archives.

————. Despatches from United States Ministers to Japan, 1855–1906 (National Archives Microfilm Publication M133). General Records of the Department of State, Record Group 59. National Archives.

————. Records of the United States Legation in Japan, 1855–1912 (National Archives Microfilm Publication T400). Records of the Foreign Service Posts of the Department of State, Record Group 84. National Archives.

————. Despatches from United States Consuls in Hakodate, Japan, 1856–1878 (National Archives Microfilm Publication M452). General Records of the Department of State, Record Group 59. National Archives.

————. Notes from the Japanese Legation in the United States to the Department of State, 1858–1906 (National Archives Microfilm Publication M163). General Records of the Department of State, Record Group 59. National Archives.

————. Despatches from United States Consuls in Nagasaki, Japan, 1860–1906 (National Archives Microfilm Publication M131). General Records of the Department of State, Record Group 59. National Archives.

————. Despatches from United States Consuls in Kanagawa, Japan, 1861–1897 (National Archives Microfilm Publication M135). General Records of the Department of State, Record Group 59. National Archives.

————. Despatches from United States Consuls in Osaka and Hiogo (Kobe), Japan, 1868–1906 (National Archives Microfilm Publication M460). General Records of the Department of State, Record Group 59. National Archives.

————. Records Relating to the Treaty of Yedo. Minutes of Treaty Conferences between United States and Japanese Representatives, and Treaty Drafts, March 11–July 22, 1872 (National Archives Microfilm Publication T119). General Records of the Department of State, Record Group 59. National Archives.

Religious Magazines (with Variant Titles)

Chrysanthemum (Yokohama)
Foreign Missionary/The Church at Home and Abroad
Heathen Woman's Friend
Illustrated Christian Weekly
Independent
Life and Light for Heathen Women/Life and Light for Woman
Missionary Herald
Missionary Magazine/Baptist Missionary Magazine
Missionary Review/Missionary Review of the World
Our Day
Spirit of Missions
Woman's Work for Woman/Our Mission Field

Secular Magazines

American Monthly Review of Reviews
Appleton's Journal
Arena
Atlantic Monthly
Bradstreet's
Century
Chautauquan
Commercial and Financial Chronicle
Cosmopolitan
Dial
Forum
Galaxy
Harper's Monthly
International Review
Lippincott's Magazine

Nation
North American Review
Open Court
Outlook
Overland Monthly
Popular Science Monthly
Potter's American Monthly
Putnam's Magazine
Republic
Scribner's Magazine
Scribner's Monthly
Southern Review
Transactions of the Asiatic Society of Japan (Yokohama)
World's Work

Newspapers

Boston Evening Transcript
Japan Daily Herald (Yokohama)
Japan Gazette (Yokohama)
Japan Times (Tokyo)
Japan Weekly Mail (Yokohama)
New York Journal of Commerce and Commercial Bulletin
New York Weekly Journal of Commerce
New York World
New York Times
Tokio Times

Government Publications

Bevans, Charles I., comp. *Treaties and Other International Agreements of the United States of America, 1776–1949, Vol. 1.* Washington, D.C.: U.S. Department of State, 1968.

———. *Treaties and Other International Agreements of the United States of America, 1776–1949, Vol. 9.* Washington, D.C.: U.S. Department of State, 1972.

U.K. Foreign Office. *British and Foreign State Papers.* London.

U.S. Department of State. *Foreign Relations of the United States.* Washington, D.C.

————. *Commercial Relations of the United States*. Washington, D.C.

————. *United States Consular Reports*. Washington, D.C.

U.S. National Museum. *Report of the U.S. National Museum, under the Direction of the Smithsonian Institution, for Year Ending June 30, 1890*. Washington, D.C.: Government Printing Office, 1891.

Books

Adams, Henry. *The Letters of Henry Adams*. Edited by J. C. Levenson, Ernest Samuels, Charles Vandersee, and Viola Hopkins Winner. 6 vols. Cambridge: Harvard University Press, 1982–88.

————. *Novels, Mont Saint Michel, The Education*. Edited by Ernest Samuels and Jayne N. Samuels. New York: Library of America, 1983.

Arnold, Sir Edwin. *The Light of Asia; or, The Great Renunciation (Mahâbhinishkramana)*. 1879; reprint, Garden City, N.Y.: Dolphin Books, 1961.

————. *Japonica*. New York: Charles Scribner's Sons, 1891.

————. *Seas and Lands*. New ed. New York: Longmans, Green, 1897.

Asakawa Kan'ichi. *The Russo-Japanese Conflict, Its Causes and Issues*. Boston: Houghton, Mifflin, 1904.

Bacon, Alice Mabel. *Japanese Girls and Women*. Boston: Houghton, Mifflin, 1891; reprint, New York: Gordon Press, 1975.

————. *A Japanese Interior*. Boston: Houghton, Mifflin, 1893.

Ban, N., comp. *What the United States Buys from Japan: Minister Hubbard's Trade Report and the Views of the Japanese Press*. Yokohama: Japan Gazette [printer], 1887.

Batchelor, John. *The Ainu of Japan: The Religion, Superstitions, and General History of the Hairy Aborigines of Japan*. London: Religious Tract Society, 1892.

————. *The Ainu and Their Folk-Lore*. London: Religious Tract Society, 1901.

Beecher, Catharine E. and Harriet Beecher Stowe. *The American Woman's Home: or, Principles of Domestic Science; Being a Guide to the Formation and Maintenance of Economical, Healthful, Beautiful, and Christian Homes*. New York: J. B. Ford, 1869; reprint, New York: Arno Press, 1971.

Bird, Isabella L. *Unbeaten Tracks in Japan*. London: John Murray, 1880; reprint, Boston: Beacon Press, 1987.

Bisland, Elizabeth. *The Life and Letters of Lafcadio Hearn.* 2 vols. Boston: Houghton Mifflin, 1906.

Blum, Robert F. *Robert F. Blum, 1857–1903: A Retrospective Exhibition.* Introduction by Richard J. Boyle. Cincinnati: Cincinnati Art Museum, 1966.

Braisted, William Reynolds, trans. *Meiroku Zasshi: Journal of the Japanese Enlightenment.* Cambridge: Harvard University Press, 1976.

Buckle, Henry Thomas. *History of Civilization in England.* 1857–61; reprint, 3 vols., London: Oxford University Press, 1903–4.

Buel, James William, ed. *Louisiana and the Fair: An Exposition of the World, Its People, and Their Achievements.* 10 vols. St. Louis: World's Progress Publishing, 1904.

Carrothers, Julia D. *The Sunrise Kingdom; or, Life and Scenes in Japan, and Woman's Work for Woman There.* Philadelphia: Presbyterian Board of Education, 1879.

Cary, Otis. *Japan and Its Regeneration.* Rev. ed. New York: Student Volunteer Movement for Foreign Missions, 1904.

Centre for East Asian Cultural Studies. *Meiji Japan through Contemporary Sources.* 3 vols. Tokyo: Centre for East Asian Cultural Studies, 1969–72.

Chamberlain, Basil Hall. *The Language, Mythology, and Geographical Nomenclature of Japan Viewed in the Light of Aino Studies.* Tokyo: Imperial University, 1887.

———. *Japanese Things* [originally titled *Things Japanese*]. 5th ed. London: John Murray, 1905; reprint, Rutland, Vt.: Charles E. Tuttle, 1971.

Chamberlain, Basil Hall and W. B. Mason. *A Handbook for Travellers in Japan.* 3d ed. London: John Murray, 1891.

Clark, Edward Warren. *Life and Adventure in Japan.* New York: American Tract Society, 1878.

Clement, Ernest W. *Christianity in Modern Japan.* Philadelphia: American Baptist Publication Society, 1905.

———. *A Handbook of Modern Japan.* 6th ed. Chicago: A. C. McClurg, 1905.

Cook, Joseph. *Orient, with Preludes on Current Events.* Boston: Houghton, Mifflin, 1886.

Cooper, William B. *A Lecture on the Manners and Customs of the*

Japanese, and the Progress of Christian Missions in Japan. New York: Board of Managers of the Domestic and Foreign Missionary Society of the Protestant Episcopal Church in the U.S.A., 1880.

Darwin, Charles. *On the Origin of Species by Means of Natural Selection, or the Preservation of Favoured Races in the Struggle for Life*. London: John Murray, 1859.

———. *The Descent of Man, and Selection in Relation to Sex*. 2d ed. New York: A. L. Burt, 1874.

DeForest, John H. *Sunrise in the Sunrise Kingdom*. New York: Young People's Missionary Movement, 1904.

Draper, John William. *History of the Conflict between Religion and Science*. 1875; reprint, New York: D. Appleton, 1897.

Eby, Charles S. *Christianity and Humanity: A Course of Lectures Delivered in Meiji Kuaido, Tokio, Japan*. Yokohama: R. Meiklejohn, 1883.

Faulds, Henry. *Nine Years in Nipon: Sketches of Japanese Life and Manners*. London: Alexander Gardner, 1885; reprint, Wilmington, Del.: Scholarly Resources, 1973.

Fenollosa, Ernest Francisco. *East and West, the Discovery of America and Other Poems*. New York: Thomas Y. Crowell, 1893.

Field, Henry M. *From Egypt to Japan*. New York: Scribner, Armstrong, 1877.

Finck, Henry T. *Lotos-Time in Japan*. New York: Charles Scribner's Sons, 1895.

Francis, David R. *The Universal Exposition of 1904*. 2 vols. St. Louis: Louisiana Purchase Exposition, 1913.

Fukuzawa Yukichi. *An Encouragement of Learning* [1872–76]. Translated by David A. Dilworth and Umeyo Hirano. Tokyo: Sophia University, 1969.

———. *An Outline of a Theory of Civilization* [1875]. Translated by David A. Dilworth and G. Cameron Hurst. Tokyo: Sophia University, 1973.

General Conference of Protestant Missionaries in Japan. *Proceedings of the General Conference of Protestant Missionaries in Japan, Held in Tokyo October 24–31, 1900*. Tokyo: Methodist Publishing House, 1901.

General Conference of the Protestant Missionaries of Japan. *Proceedings of the General Conference of the Protestant Missionaries of*

Japan, Held at Osaka, Japan, April, 1883. Yokohama: R. Meiklejohn, 1883.

Gordon, M. L. *An American Missionary in Japan.* Boston: Houghton, Mifflin, 1892.

———. *Thirty Eventful Years: The Story of the American Board's Mission in Japan, 1869–1899.* Boston: Congregational House, 1901.

Greey, Edward. *The Bear-Worshippers of Yezo and the Island of Karafuto (Saghalin), or the Adventures of the Jewett Family and Their Friend Oto Nambo.* Boston: Lee and Shepard, 1884.

Griffis, William Elliot. *The Mikado's Empire.* New York: Harper and Brothers, 1876.

———. *Verbeck of Japan: A Citizen of No Country.* New York: Fleming H. Revell, 1900.

———. *Dux Christus: An Outline Study of Japan.* United Study of Missions Series, vol. 4. New York: Macmillan, 1904.

———. *The Japanese Nation in Evolution: Steps in the Progress of a Great People.* New York: Thomas Y. Crowell, 1907.

———. *Hepburn of Japan and His Wife and Helpmates: A Life Story of Toil for Christ.* Philadelphia: Westminster Press, 1913.

Gulick, Sidney L. *Evolution of the Japanese: Social and Psychic.* New York: Fleming H. Revell, 1903.

———. *The White Peril in the Far East: An Interpretation of the Significance of the Russo-Japanese War.* New York: Fleming H. Revell, 1905.

Hall, Francis. *Japan through American Eyes: The Journal of Francis Hall, Kanagawa and Yokohama, 1859–1866.* Edited and annotated by F. G. Notehelfer. Princeton: Princeton University Press, 1992.

Hanson, John Wesley. *The Official History of the Fair, St. Louis, 1904.* St. Louis: n.p., 1904.

Harris, Merriman C. *Christianity in Japan.* Cincinnati: Jennings and Graham, 1907.

Hartshorne, Anna C. *Japan and Her People.* 2 vols. Philadelphia: Henry T. Coates, 1902.

Hearn, Lafcadio. *Glimpses of Unfamiliar Japan.* Boston: Houghton, Mifflin, 1894; reprint, Rutland, Vt.: Charles E. Tuttle, 1976.

———. *Out of the East: Reveries and Studies in New Japan.* Boston: Houghton, Mifflin, 1895; reprint, Rutland, Vt.: Charles E. Tuttle, 1972.

————. *Gleanings in Buddha-Fields: Studies of Hand and Soul in the Far East*. Boston: Houghton, Mifflin, 1897.

————. *Japan: An Attempt at Interpretation*. New York: Macmillan, 1904.

————. *The Japanese Letters of Lafcadio Hearn*. Edited by Elizabeth Bisland. Boston: Houghton Mifflin, 1910; reprint, Wilmington, Del.: Scholarly Resources, 1973.

————. *Editorials*. Edited by Charles Woodward Hutson. Boston: Houghton Mifflin, 1926.

————. *Editorials from the Kobe Chronicle*. Edited by Makoto Sangu. Tokyo: Hokuseido Press, 1960.

Hildreth, Richard. *Japan As It Was and Is*. Boston: Phillips, Sampson, 1855; reprint, Wilmington, Del.: Scholarly Resources, 1973.

————. *Japan and the Japanese*. Boston: Bradley, Dayton, 1861.

Houghton, Ross C. *Women of the Orient: An Account of the Religious, Intellectual, and Social Condition of Women in Japan, China, India, Egypt, Syria, and Turkey*. Cincinnati: Hitchcock and Walden, 1877.

House, Edward H. *Japanese Episodes*. Boston: James R. Osgood, 1881.

————. *Yone Santo: A Child of Japan*. Chicago: Belford, Clarke, 1888.

Howells, William Dean. *A Hazard of New Fortunes*. Vol. 16 of *A Selected Edition of W. D. Howells*. Edited by Don L. Cook and David J. Nordloh. Bloomington: Indiana University Press, 1976.

Hubbard, Richard B. *The United States in the Far East; or, Modern Japan and the Orient*. Richmond, Va.: B. F. Johnson Publishing, 1899.

Imbrie, William M. *The Church of Christ in Japan: A Course of Lectures*. Philadelphia: Westminster Press, 1906.

James, Henry. *Henry James Letters*. Volume 3. Edited by Leon Edel. Cambridge: Harvard University Press, 1980.

Jarves, James Jackson. *A Glimpse at the Art of Japan*. New York: Hurd and Houghton, 1876; reprint, Rutland, Vt.: Charles E. Tuttle, 1984.

Kawakami, Karl Kiyoshi, ed. *Japan and the Japanese as Seen by Foreigners prior to the Beginning of the Russo-Japanese War*. Tokyo: Keiseisha, [1904?].

Knapp, Arthur May. *Feudal and Modern Japan*. 2 vols. Boston: Joseph Knight, 1897.

Knox, George William. *Japanese Life in Town and Country*. New York: G. P. Putnam's Sons, 1904.

Knox, George William. *The Spirit of the Orient*. New York: Thomas Y. Crowell, 1906.

———. *The Development of Religion in Japan*. New York: G. P. Putnam's Sons, 1907.

La Farge, John. *An Artist's Letters from Japan*. New York: Century, 1897; reprint, New York: Da Capo Press, 1970.

———. *Reminiscences of the South Seas*. Garden City, N.Y.: Doubleday, Page, 1912; reprint, Garden City, N.Y.: Doubleday, Page, 1916.

Landor, Arnold Henry Savage. *Alone with the Hairy Ainu, or, 3,800 Miles on a Pack Saddle in Yezo and a Cruise to the Kurile Islands*. London: John Murray, 1893; reprint, New York: Johnson Reprint Corp., 1970.

Lowell, Percival. *The Soul of the Far East*. Boston: Houghton, Mifflin, 1888.

———. *Noto: An Unexplored Corner of Japan*. Boston: Houghton, Mifflin, 1891.

———. *Occult Japan: Shinto, Shamanism and the Way of the Gods*. Boston: Houghton, Mifflin, 1894; reprint, Rochester, Vt.: Inner Traditions International, 1990.

Mahan, Alfred T. *The Problem of Asia and Its Effect upon International Policies*. Boston: Little, Brown, 1900.

McCauley, Edward Yorke. *With Perry in Japan: The Diary of Edward Yorke McCauley*. Edited by Allan B. Cole. Princeton: Princeton University Press, 1942.

Morrow, James. *A Scientist with Perry in Japan: The Journal of Dr. James Morrow*. Edited by Allan B. Cole. Chapel Hill: University of North Carolina Press, 1947.

Morse, Edward S. *Japanese Homes and Their Surroundings*. Boston: Ticknor, 1886; reprint, Rutland, Vt.: Charles E. Tuttle, 1972.

———. *Can City Life Be Made Endurable?* Worcester, Mass.: Davis [printer], 1900.

———. *The Steam Whistle: A Menace to Public Health*. Salem, Mass.: Newcomb and Gauss [printer], 1905.

———. *Japan Day by Day, 1877, 1878–79, 1882–83*. 2 vols. Boston: Houghton Mifflin, 1917; reprint, Tokyo: Kobunsha Publishing, 1936.

Mutsu Munemitsu. *Kenkenroku: A Diplomatic Record of the Sino-Japanese War, 1894–95*. Edited and translated by Gordon Mark Berger. Princeton: Princeton University Press, 1982.

Nitobe Inazō. *Bushido: The Soul of Japan.* 10th ed. With an introduction by William Elliot Griffis. New York: G. P. Putnam's Sons, 1905; reprint, Rutland, Vt.: Charles E. Tuttle, 1969.

Nott, J. C., and Geo. R. Gliddon. *Types of Mankind: or, Ethnological Researches, Based upon the Ancient Monuments, Paintings, Sculptures, and Crania of Races, and upon Their Natural, Geographical, Philological, and Biblical History.* Philadelphia: Lippincott, Grambo, 1854.

Okakura Kakuzō. *The Ideals of the East, with Special Reference to Japan.* New York: E. P. Dutton, 1903; reprint, Rutland, Vt.: Charles E. Tuttle, 1970.

————. *The Awakening of Japan.* New York: Century, 1904.

Ōkuma Shigenobu, comp. *Fifty Years of New Japan.* Edited by Marcus B. Huish. 2 vols. London: Smith, Elder, 1909.

Oliphant, Laurence. *Narrative of the Earl of Elgin's Mission to China and Japan in the Years 1857, '58, '59.* New York: Harper and Brothers, 1860; reprint, New York: Praeger Publishers, 1970.

Parsons, Alfred. *Notes in Japan.* New York: Harper and Brothers, 1896.

Perry, Matthew C. *Narrative of the Expedition of an American Squadron to the China Seas and Japan, Performed in the Years 1852, 1853, and 1854, under the Command of Commodore M. C. Perry, United States Navy, by Order of the Government of the United States.* Compiled by Francis L. Hawks. 3 vols. Washington, D.C.: Beverly Tucker, Senate Printer, 1856; reprint, New York: AMS Press, 1967.

————. *The Japan Expedition: The Personal Journal of Commodore Matthew C. Perry.* Edited by Roger Pineau. Washington, D.C.: Smithsonian Institution Press, 1968.

Pettee, James H., comp. *A Chapter of Mission History in Modern Japan, Being a Sketch for the Period since 1869 and a Report for the Years since 1893 of the American Board's Mission and the Kumiai Churches in Their Affiliated Work.* Okayama: Seishibunsha, [1895].

Philippi, Donald L., trans. *Kojiki.* Tokyo: University of Tokyo Press, 1968.

Preble, George Henry. *The Opening of Japan: A Diary of Discovery in the Far East, 1853–1856.* Edited by Boleslaw Szczesniak. Norman: University of Oklahoma Press, 1962.

Protestant Episcopal Church in the United States. *Hymnal.* Rev. ed. New York: Pott, Young, 1875.

Ransome, Stafford. *Japan in Transition: A Comparative Study of the Progress, Policy, and Methods of the Japanese since Their War with China.* New York: Harper and Brothers, 1899.

Roosevelt, Theodore. *The Letters of Theodore Roosevelt.* Edited by Elting E. Morison, John M. Blum, John J. Buckley, Alfred D. Chandler, Jr., Sylvia Rice, and Hope W. Wigglesworth. 8 vols. Cambridge: Harvard University Press, 1951–54.

Scherer, James A. B. *Japan To-Day.* Philadelphia: J. B. Lippincott, 1904.

Scidmore, Eliza Ruhamah. *Jinrikisha Days in Japan.* New York: Harper and Brothers, 1891.

Siebold, Philipp Franz von, and others. *Manners and Customs of the Japanese in the Nineteenth Century, from the Accounts of Dutch Residents in Japan and from the German Works of Dr. Philipp Franz von Siebold.* New York: Harper and Brothers, 1841; reprint, Rutland, Vt.: Charles E. Tuttle, 1973.

Spalding, J. W. *The Japan Expedition: Japan and Around the World, an Account of Three Visits to the Japanese Empire, with Sketches of Madeira, St. Helena, Cape of Good Hope, Mauritius, Ceylon, Singapore, China, and Loo-Choo.* New York: Redfield, 1855.

Spencer, Herbert. *Social Statics: or, The Conditions Essential to Human Happiness Specified, and the First of Them Developed.* London: John Chapman, 1851; reprint, New York: Augustus M. Kelley, 1969.

———. *The Principles of Biology.* 2 vols. New York: D. Appleton, 1866–67; reprint, New York: D. Appleton, 1884.

———. *First Principles.* 5th ed. New York: A. L. Burt, 1880.

———. *The Principles of Sociology.* 3d ed. 3 vols. New York: D. Appleton, 1880–96; reprint, New York: D. Appleton, 1925–29.

———. *Essays: Scientific, Political, and Speculative.* Vol. 1. New York: D. Appleton, 1891; reprint, Osnabrück, Germany: Otto Zeller, 1966.

———. *The Principles of Psychology.* 4th ed. 2 vols. London: Williams and Norgate, 1899; reprint, Osnabrück, Germany: Otto Zeller, 1966.

Sproston, John Glendy. *A Private Journal of John Glendy Sproston, U.S.N.* Edited by Shio Sakanishi. Tokyo: Sophia University, 1968.

Starr, Frederick. *The Ainu Group at the Saint Louis Exposition.* Chicago: Open Court Publishing, 1904.

Strong, Josiah. *Our Country: Its Possible Future and Present Crisis.* Rev. ed. New York: Baker and Taylor, 1891; reprint, Cambridge: Harvard University Press, 1963.

Swift, Jonathan. *Gulliver's Travels*. 1726; reprint, New York: W. W. Norton, 1961.

Taylor, Bayard. *A Visit to India, China, and Japan, in the Year 1853*. New York: G. P. Putnam, 1855.

————, comp. *Japan, in Our Day*. New York: Charles Scribner, 1872.

Tomes, Robert. *The Americans in Japan: An Abridgement of the Government Narrative of the U.S. Expedition to Japan under Commodore Perry*. New York: D. Appleton, 1857; reprint, Wilmington, Del.: Scholarly Resources, 1973.

Turner, Frederick Jackson. *The Frontier in American History*. New York: Henry Holt, 1920.

Twain, Mark. *A Connecticut Yankee in King Arthur's Court*. 1889; reprint, Berkeley and Los Angeles: University of California Press, 1983.

Twain, Mark and Charles Dudley Warner. *The Gilded Age, a Tale of Today*. 1873; reprint, New York: Oxford University Press, 1996.

Williams, Frederick Wells. *The Life and Letters of Samuel Wells Williams, LL.D.: Missionary, Diplomatist, Sinologue*. New York: G. P. Putnam's Sons, 1889; reprint, Wilmington, Del.: Scholarly Resources, 1972.

Wores, Theodore. *Seodoa Uoresu ten: Kaette kita Nihon no bi*. Introductions by Takashina Shūji and Sakai Tadayasu. Tokyo: Asahi Shimbunsha, 1986.

————. *Theodore Wores: An American Artist in Meiji Japan*. Introductions by William H. Gerdts and Jan Newstrom Thompson. Pasadena, Calif.: Pacific Asia Museum, 1993.

[Youmans, Edward L., comp.] *Herbert Spencer on the Americans and the Americans on Herbert Spencer*. New York: D. Appleton, 1883.

Secondary Sources

Adams, Henry, Kathleen Foster, Henry A. La Farge, H. Barbara Weinberg, Linnea H. Wren, and James L. Yarnell. *John La Farge*. New York: Abbeville Press, 1987.

Adas, Michael. *Machines as the Measure of Men: Science, Technology, and Ideologies of Western Dominance*. Ithaca: Cornell University Press, 1989.

Allen, Theodore W. *The Invention of the White Race.* 2 vols. New York: Verso, 1994–97.

Anderson, Benedict. *Imagined Communities: Reflections on the Origin and Spread of Nationalism.* 2d ed. New York: Verso, 1991.

Anderson, Stuart. *Race and Rapprochement: Anglo-Saxonism and Anglo-American Relations, 1895–1904.* Rutherford, N.J.: Fairleigh Dickinson University Press, 1981.

Bailey, Thomas A. *Theodore Roosevelt and the Japanese-American Crises.* Stanford: Stanford University Press, 1934.

Baker, Frances J. *The Story of the Woman's Foreign Missionary Society of the Methodist Episcopal Church, 1869–1895.* Rev. ed. Cincinnati: Curts and Jennings, 1898.

Bannister, Robert C. *Social Darwinism: Science and Myth in Anglo-American Social Thought.* Philadelphia: Temple University Press, 1979.

Banno Junji. "Meiji shoki (1873–85) no 'taigaikan'." *Kokusai seiji* 71 (August 1982): 10–20.

———. *Kindai Nihon no gaiko to seiji.* Tokyo: Kenbun Shuppan, 1985.

Barber, James and John Barratt. *South Africa's Foreign Policy: The Search for Status and Security, 1945–1988.* New York: Cambridge University Press, 1990.

Barclay, Wade Crawford. *Widening Horizons, 1845–95.* Vol. 3 of *The Methodist Episcopal Church, 1845–1939.* New York: Board of Missions of the Methodist Church, 1957.

Beauchamp, Edward R. *An American Teacher in Early Meiji Japan.* Asian Studies at Hawaii, no. 17. Honolulu: University Press of Hawaii, 1976.

Beauchamp, Edward R. and Akira Iriye, eds. *Foreign Employees in Nineteenth-Century Japan.* Boulder: Westview Press, 1990.

Beaver, R. Pierce. *All Loves Excelling: American Protestant Women in World Mission.* Grand Rapids, Mich.: William B. Eerdmans Publishing, 1968.

Befu, Harumi, ed. *Cultural Nationalism in East Asia: Representation and Identity.* Research Papers and Policy Studies, no. 39. Berkeley: Institute of East Asian Studies, University of California, 1993.

Beisner, Robert L. *From the Old Diplomacy to the New, 1865–1900.* 2d ed. Arlington Heights, Ill.: Harlan Davidson, 1986.

Benedict, Ruth. *The Chrysanthemum and the Sword: Patterns of*

Japanese Culture. Boston: Houghton Mifflin, 1946; reprint, New York: New American Library, 1974.

Berkhofer, Robert F., Jr. *The White Man's Indian: Images of the American Indian from Columbus to the Present.* New York: Alfred A. Knopf, 1978.

Bhabha, Homi. "Of Mimicry and Man: The Ambivalence of Colonial Discourse." *October,* no. 28 (spring 1984): 125–33.

Blacker, Carmen. *The Japanese Enlightenment: A Study of the Writings of Fukuzawa Yukichi.* Cambridge: Cambridge University Press, 1964.

Brace, C. L., M. L. Brace, and W. R. Leonard. "Reflections on the Face of Japan: A Multivariate Craniofacial and Odontometric Perspective." *American Journal of Physical Anthropology* 78 (January 1989): 93–113.

Breen, John and Mark Williams, eds. *Japan and Christianity: Impacts and Responses.* New York: St. Martin's Press, 1996.

Brown, Arthur Judson. *One Hundred Years: A History of the Foreign Missionary Work of the Presbyterian Church in the U.S.A., with Some Account of Countries, Peoples and the Policies and Problems of Modern Missions.* New York: Fleming H. Revell, 1936.

Brown, Richard D. "Modernization: A Victorian Climax." *American Quarterly* 27 (December 1975): 533–48.

Brumberg, Joan Jacobs. "Zenanas and Girlless Villages: The Ethnology of American Evangelical Women, 1870–1910." *Journal of American History* 69 (September 1982): 347–71.

Burkman, Thomas W. "The Urakami Incidents and the Struggle for Religious Toleration in Early Meiji Japan." *Japanese Journal of Religious Studies* 1 (June–September 1974): 143–216.

Burks, Ardath W. "'Coercion in Japan': A Historical Footnote." *Journal of the Rutgers University Library* 15 (June 1952): 33–52.

———, ed. *The Modernizers: Overseas Students, Foreign Employees, and Meiji Japan.* Boulder. Westview Press, 1985.

Cary, Otis. *A History of Christianity in Japan: Roman Catholic, Greek Othodox, and Protestant Missions.* 2 vols. New York: Fleming H. Revell, 1909; reprint, Rutland, Vt.: Charles E. Tuttle, 1976.

Chatterjee, Partha. *Nationalist Thought and the Colonial World: A Derivative Discourse?* London: Zed Books, 1986; reprint, Minneapolis: University of Minnesota Press, 1993.

Chaudhuri, Nupur and Margaret Strobel, eds. *Western Women and Imperialism: Complicity and Resistance.* Bloomington: Indiana University Press, 1992.

Chisolm, Lawrence W. *Fenollosa: The Far East and American Culture.* New Haven: Yale University Press, 1963.

Cohen, Warren I. *East Asian Art and American Culture: A Study in International Relations.* New York: Columbia University Press, 1992.

Cortissoz, Royal. *John La Farge: A Memoir and a Study.* Boston: Houghton Mifflin, 1911; reprint, New York: Da Capo Press, 1971.

Corwin, Edward Tanjore. *A Manual of the Reformed Church in America (Formerly the Reformed Protestant Dutch Church), 1628–1902.* *4th ed.* New York: Board of Publication of the Reformed Church in America, 1902.

Cott, Jonathan. *Wandering Ghost: The Odyssey of Lafcadio Hearn.* New York: Alfred A. Knopf, 1991.

Cott, Nancy F. *The Bonds of Womanhood: "Woman's Sphere" in New England, 1780–1835.* New Haven: Yale University Press, 1977.

Croce, Benedetto. *History of Europe in the Nineteenth Century.* Translated by Henry Furst. New York: Harcourt, Brace, 1933.

Daggett, Mrs. L. H., ed. *Historical Sketches of Woman's Missionary Societies in America and England.* Boston: Daggett, 1883.

Dale, Peter N. *The Myth of Japanese Uniqueness.* London: Routledge, 1988.

Daniels, Roger. *The Politics of Prejudice: The Anti-Japanese Movement in California and the Struggle for Japanese Exclusion.* 2d ed. Berkeley and Los Angeles: University of California Press, 1977.

Dawson, Carl. *Lafcadio Hearn and the Vision of Japan.* Baltimore: Johns Hopkins University Press, 1992.

Deichmann, Wendy Jane. "Josiah Strong: Practical Theologian and Social Crusader for a Global Kingdom." Ph.D. diss., Drew University, 1991.

Diamond, Jared. "Race Without Color." *Discover* 15 (November 1994): 82–89.

Dorwart, Jeffery M. *The Pigtail War: American Involvement in the Sino-Japanese War of 1894–1895.* Amherst: University of Massachusetts Press, 1975.

Dower, John W. *War without Mercy: Race and Power in the Pacific War.* New York: Pantheon Books, 1986.

Drummond, Richard Henry. *A History of Christianity in Japan*. Grand Rapids, Mich.: William B. Eerdmans Publishing, 1971.

Dyer, Thomas G. *Theodore Roosevelt and the Idea of Race*. Baton Rouge: Louisiana State University Press, 1980.

Ebisawa Arimichi and Ōuchi Saburō. *Nihon Kirisutokyō shi*. Tokyo: Nihon Kirisuto Kyōdan Shuppankyoku, 1970.

Ericson, Steven J. *The Sound of the Whistle: Railroads and the State in Meiji Japan*. Cambridge: Council on East Asian Studies, Harvard University, 1996.

Esthus, Raymond A. *Theodore Roosevelt and Japan*. Seattle: University of Washington Press, 1966.

Fasseur, Cornelis. "Cornerstone and Stumbling Block: Racial Classification and the Late Colonial State in Indonesia." In *The Late Colonial State in Indonesia: Political and Economic Foundations of the Netherlands Indies, 1880–1942*, edited by Robert Cribb. Leiden: KITLV Press, 1994.

Finn, Dallas. *Meiji Revisited: The Sites of Victorian Japan*. New York: Weatherhill, 1995.

Fleming, Leslie A., ed. *Women's Work for Women: Missionaries and Social Change in Asia*. Boulder: Westview Press, 1989.

Foucault, Michel. *Discipline and Punish: The Birth of the Prison*. Translated by Alan Sheridan. New York: Vintage Books, 1995.

Fox, Grace. *Britain and Japan, 1858–1883*. London: Oxford University Press, 1969.

Fujita, Fumiko. *American Pioneers and the Japanese Frontier: American Experts in Nineteenth-Century Japan*. Westport, Conn.: Greenwood Press, 1994.

Gates, Henry Louis, Jr., ed. *"Race," Writing, and Difference*. Chicago: University of Chicago Press, 1986.

Geertz, Clifford. *The Interpretation of Cultures*. New York: Basic Books, 1973.

Gluck, Carol. *Japan's Modern Myths: Ideology in the Late Meiji Period*. Princeton: Princeton University Press, 1985.

Goldstein, Jonathan. "Edward Sylvester Morse (1838–1925) as Expert and Western Observer in Meiji Japan." *Journal of Intercultural Studies* (Osaka), no. 14 (1987): 61–81.

Gossett, Thomas F. *Race: The History of an Idea in America*. Dallas: Southern Methodist University Press, 1963.

Gould, Stephen Jay. *The Mismeasure of Man*. New York: W. W. Norton, 1981.

———. "The Geometer of Race." *Discover* 15 (November 1994): 64–69.

Greene, Evarts Boutell. *A New-Englander in Japan: Daniel Crosby Greene*. Boston: Houghton Mifflin, 1927.

Gulick, Addison. *Evolutionist and Missionary, John Thomas Gulick, Portrayed through Documents and Discussions*. Chicago: University of Chicago Press, 1932.

Hanihara Kazurō. "Dual Structure Model for the Population History of the Japanese." *Japan Review* (Kyoto), no. 2 (1991): 1–33.

Harada Kazufumi. *Kaitaku*. Vol. 13 of *Oyatoi gaikokujin*. Tokyo: Kajima Shuppankai, 1968.

Hastings, Sally A. "The Empress' New Clothes and Japanese Women, 1868–1912." *Historian* 55 (summer 1993): 677–92.

Hein, Laura E. "Free-Floating Anxieties on the Pacific: Japan and the West Revisited." *Diplomatic History* 20 (summer 1996): 411–37.

Hill, Patricia R. *The World Their Household: The American Woman's Foreign Mission Movement and Cultural Transformation, 1870–1920*. Ann Arbor: University of Michigan Press, 1985.

Hirama Yōichi. "Mahan no Nihonkan to Nichi-Bei kankei e no eikyō." *Kokusai seiji* 102 (February 1993): 39–54.

Hirose Shizuko. "Meiji shonen no tai Ō-Bei kankei to gaikokujin naichi ryokō mondai." Parts 1 and 2. *Shigaku zasshi* 83 (November/December 1974): 1437–65, 1600–1621.

Hoare, James E. "Extraterritoriality in Japan, 1858–1899." *Transactions of the Asiatic Society of Japan*, 3d ser., 18 (July 1983): 71–97.

———. *Japan's Treaty Ports and Foreign Settlements: The Uninvited Guests, 1858–1899*. Folkestone, Kent, U.K.: Japan Library, 1994.

Hobsbawm, Eric and Terence Ranger, eds. *The Invention of Tradition*. New York: Cambridge University Press, 1983.

Hodgkins, Louise Manning. *The Roll Call: An Introduction to Our Missionaries, 1869–1896*. Boston: Woman's Foreign Missionary Society of the Methodist Episcopal Church, 1896.

Hofstadter, Richard. *Social Darwinism in American Thought*. Philadelphia: University of Pennsylvania Press, 1944; rev. ed., New York: George Braziller, 1959.

Horsman, Reginald. *Race and Manifest Destiny: The Origins of Amer-*

ican Racial Anglo-Saxonism. Cambridge: Harvard University Press, 1981.

Hosley, William. *The Japan Idea: Art and Life in Victorian America.* Hartford, Conn.: Wadsworth Atheneum, 1990.

Huffman, James L. "Edward Howard House: In the Service of Meiji Japan." *Pacific Historical Review* 56 (May 1987): 231–58.

———. *Creating a Public: People and Press in Meiji Japan.* Honolulu: University of Hawai'i Press, 1997.

Hunt, Michael H. *Ideology and U.S. Foreign Policy.* New Haven: Yale University Press, 1987.

Inoue Kiyoshi. *Jōyaku kaisei: Meiji no minzoku mondai.* Tokyo: Iwanami Shoten, 1955.

Ion, A. Hamish. "Edward Warren Clark and Early Meiji Japan: A Case Study of Cultural Conflict." *Modern Asian Studies* 11 (October 1977): 557–72.

Iriye, Akira. *Nihon no gaikō: Meiji ishin kara gendai made.* Tokyo: Chūō Kōronsha, 1966.

———. *Across the Pacific: An Inner History of American-East Asian Relations.* New York: Harcourt Brace Jovanovich, 1967.

———. "Nichi-bei tekitai ishiki no gensen." *Kokusai seiji* 34 (1967): 1–19.

———. *Pacific Estrangement: Japanese and American Expansion, 1897–1911.* Cambridge: Harvard University Press, 1972.

———, ed. *Mutual Images: Essays in American-Japanese Relations.* Cambridge: Harvard University Press, 1975.

Irokawa Daikichi. *Kindai kokka no shuppatsu.* Vol. 21 of *Nihon no rekishi.* Tokyo: Chūō Kōronsha, 1974.

Ishii Takashi. *Meiji shoki no kokusai kankei.* Tokyo: Yoshikawa Kōbunkan, 1977.

Jacobson, Matthew Frye. *Whiteness of a Different Color: European Immigrants and the Alchemy of Race.* Cambridge: Harvard University Press, 1998.

Jansen, Marius B., ed. *Changing Japanese Attitudes toward Modernization.* Princeton: Princeton University Press, 1965.

———, ed. *The Nineteenth Century.* Vol. 5 of *The Cambridge History of Japan,* edited by John W. Hall, Marius B. Jansen, Madoka Kani, and Denis Twitchett. New York: Cambridge University Press, 1989.

Jones, F. C. *Extraterritoriality in Japan and the Diplomatic Relations*

Resulting in Its Abolition, 1853–1899. New Haven: Yale University Press, 1931; reprint, New York: AMS Press, 1970.

Kajima Morinosuke. *Jōyaku kaisei mondai.* Vol. 2 of *Nihon gaikōshi.* Tokyo: Kajima Kenkyūjo Shuppankai, 1970.

Kamikawa Hikomatsu, ed. *Japan-American Diplomatic Relations in the Meiji-Taisho Era.* Translated by Kimura Michiko. Tokyo: Pan-Pacific Press, 1958.

Kasson, John F. *Civilizing the Machine: Technology and Republican Values in America, 1776–1900.* New York: Grossman Publishers, 1976.

Katō Yūzō. *Kurofune ihen.* Tokyo: Iwanami Shoten, 1993.

Kawakami, Karl Kiyoshi, ed. *Japan and the Japanese as Seen by Foreigners Prior to the Beginning of the Russo-Japanese War.* Tokyo: Keiseisha, [1904?].

Kishimoto Hideo, ed. *Japanese Religion in the Meiji Era.* Translated by John F. Howes. Vol. 2 of *Japanese Culture in the Meiji Era.* Tokyo: Toyo Bunko, 1958.

Kohiyama Rui. *Amerika fujin senkyōshi: Rai-Nichi no haikei to sono eikyō.* Tokyo: Tokyo Daigaku Shuppankai, 1992.

Konishi Shirō. *Kaikoku to jōi.* Vol. 19 of *Nihon no rekishi.* Tokyo: Chūō Kōronsha, 1974.

Kosaka Masaaki, ed. *Japanese Thought in the Meiji Era.* Translated and adapted by David Abosch. Vol. 8 of *Japanese Culture in the Meiji Era.* Tokyo: Toyo Bunko, 1958.

Kumamoto Kenjirō. *Bijutsu.* Vol. 16 of *Oyatoi gaikokujin.* Tokyo: Kajima Shuppankai, 1968.

Kuno, Akiko. *Unexpected Destinations: The Poignant Story of Japan's First Vassar Graduate.* Translated by Kirsten McIvor. New York: Kodansha International, 1993.

LaFeber, Walter. *The American Search for Opportunity, 1865–1913.* Vol. 2 of *The Cambridge History of American Foreign Relations,* edited by Warren I. Cohen. New York: Cambridge University Press, 1995.

———. *The Clash: A History of U.S.-Japan Relations.* New York: W. W. Norton, 1997.

Lancaster, Clay. *The Japanese Influence in America.* New York: Walton H. Rawls, 1963.

Lears, T. J. Jackson. *No Place of Grace: Antimodernism and the Trans-*

formation of American Culture, 1880–1920. New York: Pantheon Books, 1981.

Lebra, Joyce C. *Ōkuma Shigenobu: Statesman of Meiji Japan.* Canberra: Australian National University Press, 1973.

Lehmann, Jean-Pierre. *The Image of Japan: From Feudal Isolation to World Power, 1850–1905.* London: George Allen and Unwin, 1978.

Lockwood, William W., ed. *The State and Economic Enterprise in Japan: Essays in the Political Economy of Growth.* Princeton: Princeton University Press, 1965.

Lone, Stewart. *Japan's First Modern War: Army and Society in the Conflict with China, 1894–95.* New York: St. Martin's Press, 1994.

Lowell, Abbott Lawrence. *Biography of Percival Lowell.* New York: Macmillan, 1935.

Marks, Jonathan. *Human Biodiversity: Genes, Race, and History.* New York: Aldine de Gruyter, 1995.

Marx, Leo. *The Machine in the Garden: Technology and the Pastoral Ideal in America.* New York: Oxford University Press, 1964.

Matsumura Masayoshi. "Kōkaron to Nichi-Ro sensō." *Kokusai seiji* 71 (August 1982): 38–53.

———. *Nichi-Ro sensō to Kaneko Kentarō: Kōhō gaikō no kenkyū.* Tokyo: Shin'yūdo, 1987.

Mayo, Marlene J. "The Iwakura Embassy and the Unequal Treaties, 1871–1873." Ph.D. diss., Columbia University, 1961.

———. "A Catechism of Western Diplomacy: The Japanese and Hamilton Fish, 1872." *Journal of Asian Studies* 26 (May 1967): 389–410.

McDannell, Colleen. *The Christian Home in Victorian America, 1840–1900.* Bloomington: Indiana University Press, 1986.

Meech, Julia and Gabriel P. Weisberg. *Japonisme Comes to America: The Japanese Impact on the Graphic Arts, 1876–1925.* New York: Harry N. Abrams, 1990.

Miwa Kimitada. *Nichi-Bei kankei no ishiki to kōzō.* Tokyo: Nansosha, 1974.

Miyoshi, Masao. *As We Saw Them: The First Japanese Embassy to the United States (1860).* Berkeley and Los Angeles: University of California Press, 1979.

Montgomery, Helen Barrett. *Western Women in Eastern Lands: An Outline Study of Woman's Work in Foreign Missions.* New York: Macmillan, 1910.

Motohashi Tadashi. *Nichi-Bei kankeishi kenkyū.* Tokyo: Gakushūin Daigaku, 1986.

Murray, Paul. *A Fantastic Journey: The Life and Literature of Lafcadio Hearn.* Ann Arbor: University of Michigan Press, 1997.

Nagai, Michio. "Herbert Spencer in Early Meiji Japan." *Far Eastern Quarterly* 14 (November 1954): 55–64.

Nakagawa Zennosuke. "A Century of Marriage Law." *Japan Quarterly* 10 (April–June 1963): 182–92.

Neu, Charles E. *An Uncertain Friendship: Theodore Roosevelt and Japan, 1906–1909.* Cambridge: Harvard University Press, 1967.

———. *The Troubled Encounter: The United States and Japan.* New York: John Wiley and Sons, 1975.

Neumann, William L. "Religion, Morality, and Freedom: The Ideological Background of the Perry Expedition." *Pacific Historical Review* 23 (August 1954): 247–57.

———. *America Encounters Japan: From Perry to MacArthur.* New York: Harper and Row, 1965.

Nish, Ian. *Japanese Foreign Policy, 1869–1942: Kasumigaseki to Miyakezaka.* London: Routledge and Kegan Paul, 1977.

Niwa Kunio. "The Reform of the Land Tax and the Government Programme for the Encouragement of Industry." *Developing Economies* (Tokyo) 4 (December 1966): 447–71.

Oka Yoshitake. "Jōyaku kaisei rongi ni arawareta tōji no taigai ishiki." Parts 1 and 2. *Kokka gakkai zasshi* 67 (August/September 1953): 1–24, 183–206.

Oriental Economist. *The Foreign Trade of Japan: A Statistical Survey.* Edited by Ishibashi Tanzan. Tokyo: Oriental Economist, 1935.

Ota, Yuzo. *Basil Hall Chamberlain: Portrait of a Japanologist.* Richmond, Surrey, U.K.: Japan Library, 1998.

Ōyama Azusa. "Iwakura kaisei sōan to Terashima kaisei sōan." *Kokusai seiji* 3 (autumn 1957): 51–66.

Pierson, John D. *Tokutomi Sohō, 1863–1957: A Journalist for Modern Japan.* Princeton: Princeton University Press, 1980.

Pratt, Mary Louise. *Imperial Eyes: Travel Writing and Transculturation.* New York: Routledge, 1992.

Pyle, Kenneth B. *The New Generation in Meiji Japan: Problems of Cultural Identity, 1885–1895.* Stanford: Stanford University Press, 1969.

Richie, Donald. "Henry Adams in Japan." *Japan Quarterly* 6 (October–December 1959): 434–42.

Ritter, H. *A History of Protestant Missions in Japan*. Translated by George E. Albrecht. Revised by Daniel Crosby Greene. Tokyo: Methodist Publishing House, 1898.

Roberts, Jon H. *Darwinism and the Divine in America: Protestant Intellectuals and Organic Evolution, 1859–1900*. Madison: University of Wisconsin Press, 1988.

Rosenstone, Robert A. "Learning from Those 'Imitative' Japanese: Another Side of the American Experience in the Mikado's Empire." *American Historical Review* 85 (June 1980): 572–95.

———. *Mirror in the Shrine: American Encounters with Meiji Japan*. Cambridge: Harvard University Press, 1988.

Rostow, W. W. *The Stages of Economic Growth: A Non-Communist Manifesto*. Cambridge: Cambridge University Press, 1960.

Ryan, Mary P. *Womanhood in America: From Colonial Times to the Present*. New York: New Viewpoints, 1975.

Rydell, Robert W. *All the World's a Fair: Visions of Empire at American International Expositions, 1876–1916*. Chicago: University of Chicago Press, 1984.

Saeki Shōichi. "Amerikajin to Nihon bunkakan." In *Ishitsu bunka ron shōgeki to hadō*, 257–92. Vol. 1 of *Nihon to Amerika: Hikaku bunka ron*, edited by Saito Makoto, Homma Nagayo, and Kamei Shunsuke. Tokyo: Nan'undō, 1973.

Saeki Shōichi and Haga Tōru, eds. *Gaikokujin ni yoru Nihon ron no meicho: Goncharofu kara Pange made*. Tokyo: Chūō Kōronsha, 1987.

Said, Edward W. *Orientalism*. New York: Vintage Books, 1979.

Sansom, George B. *The Western World and Japan: A Study in the Interaction of European and Asiatic Cultures*. New York: Alfred A. Knopf, 1950; reprint, New York: Vintage Books, 1973.

Sawada, Mitziko. "Culprits and Gentlemen: Meiji Japan's Restrictions of Emigrants to the United States, 1891–1909." *Pacific Historical Review* 60 (August 1991): 339–59.

Scheiner, Irwin. *Christian Converts and Social Protest in Meiji Japan*. Berkeley and Los Angeles: University of California Press, 1970.

Scheyer, Ernst. "The Adams Memorial by Augustus Saint-Gaudens." *Art Quarterly* 19 (summer 1956): 178–97.

Schwantes, Robert S. "Christianity versus Science: A Conflict of Ideas in Meiji Japan." *Far Eastern Quarterly* 12 (February 1953): 123–32.

Shibusawa Keizo, ed. *Japanese Life and Culture in the Meiji Era.* Translated by Charles S. Terry. Vol. 5 of *Japanese Culture in the Meiji Era.* Tokyo: Toyo Bunko, 1958.

Shigehisa Tokutarō. *Kyōiku, shūkyō.* Vol. 5 of *Oyatoi gaikokujin.* Tokyo: Kajima Shuppankai, 1968.

Shively, Donald H., ed. *Tradition and Modernization in Japanese Culture.* Princeton: Princeton University Press, 1971.

Shōwa Joshi Daigaku, Kindai Bungaku Kenkyūshitsu. "G. F. Vābekku." In *Kindai bungaku kenkyū sōsho.* Vol. 3. Tokyo: Shōwa Joshi Daigaku, Kindai Bungaku Kenkyūshitsu, 1956.

———. "E. H. Hausu." In *Kindai bungaku kenkyū sōsho.* Vol. 5. Tokyo: Shōwa Joshi Daigaku, Kindai Bungaku Kenkyūshitsu, 1957.

———. "Koizumi Yakumo." In *Kindai bungaku kenkyū sōsho.* Vol. 7. Tokyo: Shōwa Joshi Daigaku, Kindai Bungaku Kenkyūshitsu, 1957.

———. "Wiriamu Eriotto Gurifisu." In *Kindai bungaku kenkyū soshō.* Vol. 28. Tokyo: Shōwa Joshi Daigaku, Kindai Bungaku Kenkyūshitsu, 1968.

Siddle, Richard. *Race, Resistance and the Ainu of Japan.* New York: Routledge, 1996.

Sklar, Kathryn Kish. *Catharine Beecher: A Study in American Domesticity.* New Haven: Yale University Press, 1973.

Spurr, David. *The Rhetoric of Empire: Colonial Discourse in Journalism, Travel Writing, and Imperial Administration.* Durham: Duke University Press, 1993.

Stanton, William. *The Leopard's Spots: Scientific Attitudes Toward Race in America, 1815–59.* Chicago: University of Chicago Press, 1960.

Strauss, David. "The 'Far East' in the American Mind, 1883–1894: Percival Lowell's Decisive Impact." *Journal of American-East Asian Relations* 2 (fall 1993): 217–41.

Stults, Taylor. "Imperial Russia through American Eyes, 1894–1904: A Study in Public Opinion." Ph.D. diss., University of Missouri, 1970.

Suzuki Yūko. "Meiji seifu no Kirisutokyō seisaku: Kōsatsu tekkyo ni itaru made no seiji katei." *Shigaku zasshi* 86 (February 1977): 177–95.

Tanaka, Stefan. *Japan's Orient: Rendering Pasts into History*. Berkeley and Los Angeles: University of California Press, 1993.

Taylor, Sandra C. "The Sisterhood of Salvation and the Sunrise Kingdom: Congregational Women Missionaries in Meiji Japan." *Pacific Historical Review* 48 (February 1979): 27–45.

——. "Abby M. Colby: The Christian Response to a Sexist Society." *New England Quarterly* 52 (March 1979): 68–79.

——. "The Ineffectual Voice: Japan Missionaries and American Foreign Policy, 1870–1941." *Pacific Historical Review* 53 (1984): 20–38.

——. *Advocate of Understanding: Sidney Gulick and the Search for Peace with Japan*. Kent, Ohio: Kent State University Press, 1984.

Thelle, Notto R. *Buddhism and Christianity in Japan: From Conflict to Dialogue, 1854–1899*. Honolulu: University of Hawaii Press, 1987.

Thomas, Nicholas. *Colonialism's Culture: Anthropology, Travel and Government*. Princeton: Princeton University Press, 1994.

Thomson [now Taylor], Sandra C. "Meiji Japan through Missionary Eyes: The American Protestant Experience." *Journal of Religious History* 7 (1973): 248–59.

Tohda Masahiro. "Vikutoria jidai ni okeru Nihon to Chūgoku no imeiji, 1850–1900: Bummeika no shimei to Higashi Ajia." *Seiyō shigaku*, no. 160 (1990): 218–34.

Trachtenberg, Alan. *The Incorporation of America: Culture and Society in the Gilded Age*. New York: Hill and Wang, 1982.

Travis, Frederick F. *George Kennan and the American-Russian Relationship, 1865–1924*. Athens: Ohio University Press, 1990.

Treat, Payson J. *Diplomatic Relations between the United States and Japan, 1853–1905*. 3 vols. Stanford: Stanford University Press, 1932–38.

Tsuda Takako. "Inoue jōyaku kaisei no saikentō: Jōyaku kaisei yogikai o chūshin ni." *Rekishigaku kenkyū*, no. 575 (December 1987): 12–31.

Tweed, Thomas A. *The American Encounter with Buddhism, 1844–1912: Victorian Culture and the Limits of Dissent*. Bloomington: Indiana University Press, 1992.

Ueno Masuzō. *Shizen kagaku*. Vol. 3 of *Oyatoi gaikokujin*. Tokyo: Kajima Shuppankai, 1968.

Umetani Noboru. *Seiji, hōsei*. Vol. 11 of *Oyatoi gaikokujin*. Tokyo: Kajima Shuppankai, 1968.

Valliant, Robert B. "The Selling of Japan: Japanese Manipulation of Western Opinion, 1900–1905." *Monumenta Nipponica* 29 (1974): 415–38.

Watanabe Masao. "John Thomas Gulick: American Evolutionist and Missionary in Japan." *Japanese Studies in the History of Science* (Tokyo), no. 5 (1966): 140–49.

———. "American Science Teachers in the Early Meiji Period." *Japanese Studies in the History of Science* (Tokyo), no. 15 (1976): 127–44.

———. *The Japanese and Western Science.* Translated by Otto Theodor Benfey. Philadelphia: University of Pennsylvania Press, 1990.

Wayman, Dorothy G. *Edward Sylvester Morse: A Biography.* Cambridge: Harvard University Press, 1942.

Weiner, Michael, ed. *Japan's Minorities: The Illusion of Homogeneity.* New York: Routledge, 1997.

Welter, Barbara. "The Cult of True Womanhood: 1820–1860." *American Quarterly* 18 (summer 1966): 151–74.

———. "She Hath Done What She Could: Protestant Women's Missionary Careers in Nineteenth-Century America." *American Quarterly* 30 (winter 1978): 624–38.

Wheeler, Mary Sparkes. *First Decade of the Woman's Foreign Missionary Society of the Methodist Episcopal Church, with Sketches of Its Missionaries.* New York: Phillips and Hunt, 1881.

Wiley, Peter Booth and Korogi Ichiro. *Yankees in the Land of the Gods: Commodore Perry and the Opening of Japan.* New York: Penguin Books, 1991.

Wolferen, Karel van. *The Enigma of Japanese Power: People and Politics in a Stateless Nation.* New York: Alfred A. Knopf, 1989.

Wright, Brooks. *Interpreter of Buddhism to the West: Sir Edwin Arnold.* New York: Bookman Associates, 1957.

Yamamoto, Masaya. "Image-Makers of Japan: A Case Study in the Impact of the American Protestant Foreign Missionary Movement, 1859–1905." Ph.D. diss., Ohio State University, 1967.

Yamashita Eiichi. *Gurifisu to Nihon: Meiji no seishin o toitsuzuketa Beikokujin Japanorojisuto.* Tokyo: Kindai Bungeisha, 1995.

Yanagida Kunio, ed. *Japanese Manners and Customs in the Meiji Era.* Translated by Charles S. Terry. Vol. 4 of *Japanese Culture in the Meiji Era.* Tokyo: Toyo Bunko, 1957.

Yarnall, James L. "John La Farge and Henry Adams in Japan." *American Art Journal* 21 (October 1989): 40–77.

Yonemura, Ann. *Yokohama: Prints from Nineteenth-Century Japan.* Washington, D.C.: Smithsonian Institution, 1990.

Yoshino, Kosaku. *Cultural Nationalism in Contemporary Japan: A Sociological Enquiry.* New York: Routledge, 1992.

INDEX

ABOUT THE AUTHOR

Joseph M. Henning studied at Colorado College, Waseda University, Columbia University, and American University. As a student, he worked one summer on a Japanese dairy farm and another at Cable News Network's Tokyo bureau, writing for "This Week in Japan."

He served as an assistant to Congressman Richard A. Gephardt for three years and taught at American University. He is now an assistant professor of history at Saint Vincent College.